Butler County Memories

As told by

ELMO LINCOLN MARTIN

DEDICATION

In loving memory of my dear wife Ruth Martin,
you will always be in my heart.

ELMO LINCOLN MARTIN

CONTENTS

PREFACE

The following are short stories about what life was like for a boy growing up in the Kentucky foothills of the Appalachian Mountains, in the years of the Great Depression. A time when the ugly face and the hopeless hands of poverty had a firm grip on most of the families in the region.

Where illegal moonshine whiskey flowed as free as water.

It's been said that the place was so remote that only God and the Internal Revenue Service knew where it was located.

These stories are true life experiences with some humor and words of wisdom thrown in for good measure.

—Linc

1

BUTLER COUNTY ROOTS

Kentucky become a state in the year 1772, and Butler County was established in the year of 1810. Kentucky was divided about the Civil War with some of the population favoring the North and some favoring the South.

The Green River divided the county into two sections. Our homestead happened to be on the north side of the river, which was considered to be the less desirable part of the county. We heard many jokes about the north side, such as, the land of moonshine, the land were the hoot owls hoot in the daylight hours, and where it was so remote that only God and the Internal Revenue Service knew where it was located.

I was the son of James Otis Martin, and Pernie Oller Martin. My dad was the son of Vander Wright Martin and Mary West Martin. I was the second son of four children: James Otis Jr., my brother, and my two sisters, Bonnie and Aleta Irene. My dad was born and raised on the north side of the Green River. The area was, and is still, called Bull Creek. Sometime around the turn of the century in the late 1890s it was also called Martindale. I understand that was because so many Martins lived in the area. There was a post office in a small store or trading post that gave it that name. The post office closed, but I was told that that the store lingered on for some time.

My mother was born and raised in Butler County, in a log house up the

Long Branch School Road near Welch's Creek, approximately three miles from Bull Creek. She was the daughter of George Oller and Lillie Napier Oller. My mother had two sisters Kate and Mattie. My grandpa and grandma Oller owned 150 acres of land, 50 acres where their home was located, and another 100 acres near the Long Branch School. My grandfather George Oller passed away at an early age, and Mattie had died when she was very small, due to her dress catching on fire from their fireplace.

When my mom and Aunt Kate got married, my grandmother divided the 100 acres between the two of them. Sometime after my dad returned from the Army, he had the house built there in the sharp bend of Long Branch School Road. And then after he finished college in Bowling Green, we moved into the house and lived there for many years. That is how I became a native of Butler County. My parents lived there and I thought it was important to be near them.

While my dad was going to college they lived in Bowling Green. At that time, my mother was pregnant with me, and my father took her to the movies. The movie happened to be a Tarzan movie. The star in the movie was named Elmo Lincoln. My mom was so impressed by him that a couple of months later, when I was born, she gave me that name.

When I was young growing up in Butler County, most everyone call me Lincoln or Linc. But that all changed when I went to the Army. In the Army, they use first names only. Today, when I visit old friends in Butler, they still call me Linc or Lincoln.

As you will see in some of these stories, life was quite difficult in those days. Mattresses were made from cornhusk or broom sage grass, wood stoves were used for both heating and cooking, and coal oil lamps for lighting. We knew very little about the outside world. There were no newspapers or radios. We thought that the rest of the world had the same problems that we had. Therefore, everyone was quite happy with their way of life. Of course, that was when we were young. When I grew older, I began to dream of having something better than I had when I was a child.

After the Army, I began polishing my dreams, and what I had to do to accomplish them. I looked around Butler County and the surrounding areas. I must say the prospects of accomplishing my dreams looked very dim. It appeared that there were only two jobs available: making moonshine or digging coal. I decided that there was nothing in Butler County or the surrounding area that would satisfy my dreams or ambitions. It was a difficult decision to go elsewhere, but I felt that it was necessary. Out in the world I have followed my dreams, and worked hard, and those dreams became a reality.

When I was away, I often thought about the old home place and where I had grown up. And being the sentimental person that I am, I was very lonesome at times. However, I would come back and visit as often as possible, and when I opened my own business, I named it The Martindale Company, in memory of the area where my father grew up.

One thing for certain, my roots run deep in Butler County. I go back and water them every time I get a chance.

2

LONG BRANCH COMMUNITY

Once upon a time, there was a community in Butler County called Long Branch. It was located on the north side of the river, approximately four miles from Morgantown. I begin this story with: Once upon a time. In the early days, story tellers, such as Hans Christian Andersen, and the brothers Grimm, would start their fairytales, fables, and folklore stories that way. Since the Long Branch Community does not exist anymore, perhaps *Once upon a time* would be an appropriate way to start this story.

It was called the Long Branch Community because it was located on the Long Branch School Road. This road is approximately two and one half miles long, and like most roads in Butler County in the early part of the twentieth century, it was dusty in the summer months and muddy in the winter months. It has followed the same route for many years, except for the last half mile of the south east end. It was re-routed sometime in the early 1930's in an effort to reduce some of the steep inclines of the hill. The new route angled off more to the east. It made the distance to Morgantown a little further. Other than that, it was a substantial improvement.

It has always been understood that once you descended the hill, there was no way out without climbing a hill. With one exception…there was a foot trail, or path that ran south down Welch's Creek and connected with the Morgantown Road near where it passes over the creek. I will have to admit that I never traveled this trail, but I know that it was useable. A friend of mine rode a horse up this trail to pick up a person that had suffered a gunshot wound as a result of a family feud, which wasn't uncommon in Kentucky at that time in history. Legend has it that it was a trail used by the Shawnee Indians, which was the tribe that inhabited the most of Kentucky.

When one turned off the Morgantown road, and descended the hill, the first house you reached was where Thomas Childers and his wife Laura Bell lived. They lived there for many years. Later, the house was occupied by Harrison and Fannie Decker and their children. The next house was the home of Columbus Johnson and his family. A remnant of this house still remains. His son Arvil, his wife, Fannie, and their children lived just off the road near the school house. Alonzo Burden, his wife Lily, and their children lived on the other side of the road near the school house. Across the road and upon the hill from the Burden place, was a house that was occupied by Nick Phelps and his wife Fannie. Then, there in the sharp curve, was the home of my parents James and Pernie Martin and our family. Just up the road a few hundred yards was the home of Hubert Hudson and his wife Kate, who was my mother's sister, and their family. My dad's Aunt Laura, and her husband, Will Childers, lived just a short distance from the Hudson family. Up the road a short distance, Uncle Sylvester Burden lived alone. A little further up the road, my Grandmother, Lillie Napier Oller, and her second husband, William Corley, lived in a log house that was built sometime in the 1800s. William Amos Cardwell, his wife Prudence, and their family, lived a little further up the road. I'm not sure how these ten families chose to make this location their home. As I recall, most of them were born and raised in the surrounding area as many of them spoke about their ancestors, and in some cases, their families that were still living nearby.

In the early days Kentucky was covered with virgin timber. My mom always said people had followed the timber business into the country. However, at the beginning of the twentieth century, the timber was exhausted, and other means of survival had to be found. Most turned to farming, some worked in the coal mines. I would not be completely truthful if I didn't mention that several families dabbled in the moonshine business. In times of despair, and your children are hungry, most of us will take desperate action in order to survive.

My dad's Aunt Laura, and her husband Will were true farmers. Their farm included many acres of bottom land along Welch's creek. And since Aunt Laura was part Cherokee Indian, corn was a very high priority crop to grow. Each spring Will, would plow up the bottom land and plant corn, and more often than not, when the corn was a foot or so high, a large amount of rain would fall. The Green River would rise, and the back water would flood the bottom land and drown the corn. However, there was no giving up for these people. As soon as the water receded and the land dried up, Will would be back planting the corn again and for the most part, they would wind up with corn in their corn crib. In those days, pocket watches were used to keep up with what time it was, and if you didn't have a watch, Aunt Laura would always ring her diner bell at 11:30 each work day to remind her husband that it was dinner time.

For me to say that the Long Branch Community was a thriving community would hardly be appropriate. The truth being, it was a struggling community, facing many hardships. The people living there were honest hard working people. If they gave you their word, you could depend on it.

At the present time, there are only two building standing to represent the past which are the Columbus Johnson and the Will and Laura Childers homes, but neither are fit for habitation.

When these building are gone, there will be very little to show that there ever was a community there. It would be difficult for me to make a clean break from the past. Growing up in the Long Branch community appears to have left an indelible stamp on my memory that time cannot wash away. When I visit the old home place, or find myself alone in a moment of silence, pictures of the past appear as vivid as if it all happened yesterday. I take great pleasure in pondering the early days of my life.

3

A CONDITION OF THE HEART

On one of my recent visits to Butler County, something whispered to me and said that it was time for me to make a visit to Welch's Creek. It was one of those nostalgic feelings that I am afflicted with. Nostalgia is defined as a longing for familiar or beloved circumstances, or something far away, and long ago. The creek looked the same as it did when I was a child, except the large Sycamore tree that grew at an angle out over the creek was gone. It was about thirty-six inches in diameter, and was in the vicinity of 300 years old. It's difficult to explain how much I miss it, and how sad it makes me feel that I will never be able to see it again. One consolation is that I do have a picture of it that gives me some comfort. I have given considerable thought to this nostalgia definition, and have come to the conclusion, that it's a condition of the heart.

Love is another condition of the heart that we are all familiar with. It is defined in a multitude of ways. There is love of money, love of country, love of children, love of life, to just mention a few. However, most people believe that love between two people is the strongest of all loves. The beginning of love starts with fondness, affection, devotion, and works its way up to unconditional love, which is the strongest of all loves. A way to test your love is to do something nice for the one you love, and if he or she is very happy, but you find yourself much happier than the recipient, it can only mean one thing. A condition of the heart.

Hope and compassion are two other conditions of the heart. Hope is expressed in many different ways. To wish for something with high expectations. To look forward to something with confidence. Regardless of how dark and desperate the situational is, there is always a spark of hope left somewhere in every human heart. It could be said that hope is the mother of positive attitudes. It keeps us from surrendering in the face of adversity. Compassion is as old as the ages. It's a human emotion, promoted by the pain and suffering of others people. It even spills over to include puppies, kittens, and many other friends of mankind. In religious tradition, it is considered to be among the greatest of virtues. America is considered to have the most compassionate people on Earth. We give more to help the poor, the hungry, and the oppressed, than the rest of the world combined. Every person that contributes to these worthy causes is to be commended for their love and kindness toward the lives that God has created.

What causes people to care so much? There is only one answer. Hope, and compassion are both… A Condition of the Heart.

4

A BABY ROBIN

The American Robin is a migratory song bird of the thrush family. Its habitat covers most of North America. It winters in the southern states and Mexico, and returns north early in the spring. It is said that if you are the one that sees the first robin in the spring, good luck will come your way. Their diet is beetles, grubs, earth worms, plus fruit and berries. In some cases they have been known to become intoxicated by eating too many fermented berries, and would fall over when they were walking. Robins are beautiful birds. They are the state bird of Connecticut, Michigan and, Wisconsin.

We remember the poem written by Robert Louis Stevenson: "A birdie with a yellow bill hopped upon my window sill, cocked his shining eyes, and said, aren't you ashamed you sleepy head." Of course, Mr. Stevenson was a Scotsman, and lived most of his life there, and to find a robin in the British Isle is very rare indeed. However, he did travel, and lived for some time in America. In his later years, he purchased a large estate on a Samoan Island in the South Pacific. It's just possible that the bird on his window sill was a Robin. I have always thought that when we would say the poem, while attending the Long Branch School, we would began by saying, a robin with a yellow bill. There was a song I remember about the robin that was very popular, named *When the Red Red Robin Comes Bob Bob Bobbing Along*.

It's typical of robins to run fast and stop abruptly. The shrubbery around my home contains many holly bushes, their foliage is thick and somewhat prickly. It makes an ideal place for our feathered friends to build their nests. And the robins appear to choose those holly bushes quite often.

My encounter with the baby robin was when I was working in the garage this past spring, and heard some noise in the back section. I assumed it was the utility people checking meters. I looked out the back door, there was no one there. There were some cartons along the wall, and this little guy that was too young to fly was trying his best to fly up the wall. He no doubt had come inside when the garage door was open. With some effort on my part I was able to capture him. I'm going to refer to this little bird as a him as he was too young for me to determine whether he was male or female. Whatever he was, he was very unhappy about being restricted, his little heart was pounding, his little body was trembling and pushing in all directions. He certainly wanted his freedom. I let him go under some of the holly bushes, and soon thereafter, I saw his parent feeding him.

The robin's struggle for freedom made me realize again how precious freedom is. America has been the shining light of freedom for the rest of the world to watch for the past two centuries. We Americans should not take it lightly. It has come at a very high price, and must be protected at all cost. The baby robin was willing to exert his last ounce of energy to maintain his freedom.

It is my sincere hope that he has survived, and that he will be among the first to decorate our lawn in the spring. Whether he hops upon our window sill, and peeps in at us sleeping, or sings to us some of his beautiful songs. It is my hope that each of us appreciates the contribution the robin has made in making our world a more enjoyable place to live, and that everyone, including God, will help them in their struggle to survive.

5

A GREAT APPLE TREE

One of a number of apple trees in our orchard when I was growing up on Long Branch School Road was an Arkansas Black apple tree. It is said that this apple probably originated from the Wine Sap apple in Benton County Arkansas around 1870, and was produced in volume for many years, until droughts, pest, and the depression of 1930 destroyed most of the orchards. Today, it's difficult to find them in any food market. Myself, and many other people thought they were the best of all apples. They were extremely beautiful, with a smooth round dark purplish skin, turning almost black at maturity. Crisp, firm, and juicy, they were among the last to mature and were best when harvested late in the fall during October and November.

Our tree was very large, and there were always a few of the largest apples at the very top where our ladder could not reach. To harvest them, my brother and I would use our .22 gauge rifle to shoot off the stem so they would fall. To keep them from becoming bruised, one would do the shooting, and the other would stand under the tree and catch them before they hit the ground. Even though we were good marksmen at that age, sometimes more than one shot was required to clip the stem. I can still remember how delicious they were. Once you had eaten down near the core, there would be a very sweet watery substance. I have heard it called several names: water core, sugar core, and pectin. Whatever it was it sure was tasty.

I have always thought this beautiful tree may have been associated with Johnny Appleseed, the legendary American who planted and supplied apple trees to much of the Ohio River Valley. In the early part of the nineteenth century many people thought Johnny Appleseed was a fictional character, but he was a real person. His real name was Johnny Chapman. Born in Pennsylvania on September 26, 1774, Johnny was a skilled nurseryman. He became a legend while he was still alive, largely because of his generous life style, his leadership in conservation, and the symbolic importance he attributed to apples. It is said that he got the Appleseed nick name when he was seen wading along the Ohio River, carrying a bag of apple seeds.

Most historians believe that the apple originated in the mountains between the Black and Caspian Seas, and probably was not part of the forbidden fruit that Adam and Eve tasted in the Garden of Eden. Folklore has it, that in ancient Turkey, if a man wanted to marry a certain girl, he would toss an apple her way. If she caught the apple it was a symbol of engagement.

We Americans are fortunate that we are blessed with an abundance of this fruit. Apples are considered a very healthy food; high in fiber content, and free of fat, sodium, and cholesterol. As long as I live, I will always have fond memories of that beautiful Arkansas Black apple tree that provided food for a struggling family. And if history is true, and I have no reason to believe it's not, we should give thanks to Johnny Appleseed for making it possible.

6

A KEG OF MOONSHINE

A moral person is considered to be a person of high principals and ethical standards. One who religiously abides by the rules of what is right and wrong. A person who would do the right thing when no one was looking. If he or she made a mistake, and hurt someone, they would immediately apologize, and ask forgiveness. Sometimes people with all these admirable qualities, find themselves facing problems where it's almost impossible to figure out what is the right thing to do.

When I was a teenager living on Long Branch School Road, I found myself in a similar situation. As I have mentioned before it was during the Great Depression, and many of our neighbors were involved in the making of moonshine. The making of this product required lots of hard work. The labor content was very intense. First, it was necessary to find as remote a location as possible, away from any roads or trails. The equipment needed to produce moonshine was very heavy and clumsy. Wooden fifty-five gallon barrels, hundred pound bags of sugar, and other ingredients, along with the copper boiler, and the condensing equipment had to be hand carried to the site, which varied from a few hundred yards to a mile or more. Of course, when too many people learned where it was located, or the revenue agents become more aggressive, it would become necessary to move to a new location. This led some people to coin the phrase "Use to be, I would wish my worst enemies were in hell, now I wish they had a moonshine still to operate."

My problem started when some of the neighbor boys that were in the moonshine business told me that one of their 10 gallon kegs of whiskey was missing, and that they were sure it had been stolen. As I recall, about a week later I ran into another neighbor boy, who I considered to be a friend. He mentioned that he had some whiskey down in the woods, and asked if I would like to go down there and have a drink with him. I said yes so we went down in the woods a ways, and he uncovered a 10 gallon white oak keg full of whiskey. We used a small rubber hose, and a small tin cup to siphon out the amount we needed for a drink. Drinking from the same cup or bottle was a way of life in those days. As I recall, we chatted a while, he covered the keg with some leaves, and we went on our way.

Since he and his family were not in the moonshine business, I was quite sure that it was the keg that the boys said had been stolen. It didn't take me long to realize that I had a difficult decision to cope with. What was the right thing to do? On the one hand, my friend that had taken the keg was wrong. On the other hand, I suppose he thought we were good enough friends that I would forget about what I had seen and keep my mouth shut. As it turned out, it wasn't that easy. I wrestled with the problem a couple of days and couldn't sleeping very well.

I finally made the decision to tell the boys where there keg of whiskey was hidden, which they recovered. Looking back, I believe that my decision was partly based on my knowledge of how much work and sweat was required to produce 10 gallons of moonshine, and at that time it was worth ten dollars. Wages were usually fifty cents a day, which means it would take about a month to work out the value of the whisky.

It's been more years than one would like to remember since this happened, but it still crosses my mind quite often. I wonder did I make the right decision?

7

A MOTHER'S PATIENCE

My dad majored in agriculture when he went to college in Bowling Green in the early part of the 20th century. As best I can remember it was called Kentucky Normal College at that time. It didn't become a University until 1966. Due to the fact that it was a small college, and farming was the largest industry in the state at that time, it was understandable why lots of the students chose to study agriculture. It's where my dad learned to raise chickens using the more modern methods that had been developed, which were much different than the normal back yard chicken coop where the chickens went out and scratched in the earth for food, a method that most people in those days were accustom to.

One thing that he learned was that for chickens to be healthy and grow rapidly, they needed a proper and balanced diet. This food consisted of a mixture of corn meal, wheat bran, bone meal, tankage, and shorts, which I believe is a bi-product of wheat. Since the different ingredients came in 50 to 100 pound bags it was necessary to mix them together so the chickens got the proper amount of each product. In order to accomplish this task my dad decided the floor in our kitchen would be the proper place to do the mixing. He would move the table and chairs aside, and dump several hundred pounds on the floor. This would generate a pile of material several feet high. Then with a scoop shovel, and with the help of my brother and me, we would give it a good mixing, and return it back to the original bags. Some of this material was rather dusty and would contaminate everything in the kitchen.

It would be my mother's job to put the kitchen back in order, which would take her several hours of washing and scrubbing to accomplish this chore. I don't recall hearing her complain. I'm sure that she was aware of the fact that it wouldn't do any good if she did. In the early days, women were considered second class citizens, and suffered much abuse. I don't see the women of today letting anyone do such a thing to their kitchens. Mothers have a reputation of being blessed with the patience of Job. Next to God, mothers with their wisdom, hope, love, and patience, are our best hope for holding humanity and civilization together, and to keep our beautiful world from plunging back into the dark ages. Of course, like everything else, there are some mothers that do not live up to their calling, but they are the exception, rather than the rule.

Most mothers are willing to make great sacrifices to protect their families and loved ones. Given their lot in life, one wonders where they find the strength to survive all of life's problems and still wear a perpetual smile on their faces. I loved and miss my mother very much. If you still have your mother, treat her with respect and unconditional love. Later in life you will be glad that you did. To use an old and much worn phrase, mothers are the salt of the Earth. In today's world, I find it gratifying that women are more independent, and taking the lead in helping solve some of our world problems. That in itself is a huge step forward.

8

A MULE NAMED JIM

At one time in my childhood days, the Martin family owned a mule, and his name was Jim. He was of medium size, and was tan in color. He was a good mule, mild mannered, the type of animal you could identify with. I'm not sure how long he resided with us, or what the reasons were that caused us to sell him. I don't recall anyone in our family riding him to Morgantown or anywhere else. However he was a real asset when we needed help cultivating the large garden that was very necessary to support the family.

Everyone worked in the garden in those days, but the chore was made much easier when we had help from Jim. He could pull the double shovel plow that loosened up the dirt which made it much easier than having to dig it up with a hoe. This task had to be performed often in order to keep the weeds from taking over the garden. Anyone that has experienced growing vegetables, especially when there is a shortage of rain or moisture, knows how essential it is to have a loose fine seed bed free from clots. Clots allow the sun and wind to absorb the moisture.

We overcame that problem by using a rock that was 24 inches wide and four inches thick. We would attach a log chain to the rock and our mule Jim would drag it between the furrows. Even in extremely dry weather, one could see the moisture rising to the surface.

We grew some corn in the bottom land that bordered on the branch. One cold and gloomy spring day, perhaps blackberry winter was the reason it was so cold and miserable, Jim and I were using the double shovel plow to till the corn. The ground was rough, I was small, and we were having problems. I was unable to keep the plow running straight, the handles would whip from side to side, and I would lose control of the plow, then we would have to back up a start over again.

After this happened a few times and we got organized again, I asked Jim to "get up," that's what you say to a mule when you want him to move forward. However, this time Jim didn't move forward. Instead, he turned his head around and looked at me. I have always thought that he was trying to tell me something. Like, what are we doing down here in the cold, we are not accomplishing anything. Would it not be better if we went back to the barn? If that was what he was trying to covey to me, he certainly would have been correct. Leaves me to believe that he may have been trying to display some common sense.

The double shovel plow was a necessary tool for all farmers in the early days of farming. However, it required considerable more effort from the person that was using it. The crooked plow was developed from the bent stick plow, which gave it its name, and was used in ancient Greece, Egypt, and by the Romans, as far back as 480 BC. The double shovel is an advanced prototype of the bent stick plow.

As mentioned, Jim the mule and I got along quite well. One time when I was riding him he bucked me off, maybe not as high as the Strawberry Roan horse threw the cowboy, but high enough to frighten me within an inch of my life. That day I was riding him out of the barn, and when I got outside, my brother and some of the neighbor boys started to throw corncobs at us. Jim didn't like to be hit with corncobs, that's why he bucked me off. Good thing the ground was freshly plowed and soft. Otherwise, I could have been injured, of course, under the circumstances, I forgave him immediately.

Mules, like horses, have played a very important role in the early days of our country. Pioneers traveling to the west used mules to pull their covered wagons. The song Mule Train tells a beautiful story about mules pulling a freight wagon west. A sample of the lyrics: "Mule Train clippetty-clopping over hill and plain. Seems that they'll never stop. Clippetty-clop, clippetty-clop, clippetty-clopping along."

A mule is the offspring of a male donkey and a female horse. History tells us that the mule has been around for centuries. Ancient Greeks and Romans used mules and oxen for their transportation needs, mules for lighter jobs, and oxen for heavier loads. Mules are less temperamental than horses, and are easier to train. A mule's hide is thicker and tougher than horses. They can go longer without water. Also their hooves are harder, and are more sure footed.

To recognize some of the outstanding things that mules have achieved, we need to look no further than the twenty mule team that hauled the Borax Ore from the Furnace Creek Mines in Death Valley California to the railroad location at Mojave, California. This was a distance of 165 miles each way. The road, such as it was, ran through deserts and hostile mountains. It took 20 days for the mule teams to make the round trip. They pull two very large wagons with a thousand gallon water tank attached to the rear. The total length of the caravan was 180 feet. The wagons were specially built, they weighed 7,300 pounds when empty, and 78,000 pounds when loaded with ore. Between 1883 and 1886, the mule train hauled 20 million pounds of ore out of Death Valley. During this time not a single mule was lost, nor did a wagon break down. A considerable tribute to the wagon designer and builder, and a much greater tribute to the mules, they should be rewarded with a badge of honor for their dedicated service.

And to our mule Jim, I am honored to have shared some of my life with you, and from the way the mules performed when they were hauling borax ore from Death Valley, you can be very proud of your ancestors.

9

A PLACE CALLED HOME

For most of us the place we call home won't be a mansion on the hill, built with polished stone, and crystal chandeliers in the hallway. But a more modest building which provided us with the bare necessities of life. However, regardless of how modest they are, if it is where we grew up, it is the place we will always call home. We often hear the old adage, "Home is where the heart is. Our feet may walk away but our heart will remain at home." Truer words have never been spoken.

There is a multitude of reasons why we will always have warm thoughts and sentimental feelings for the old home place. In many instances, it was where we were born. It's the house where we found shelter and security when we were small. It's where we lived through happy times, and also times of heartache and sorrow. It's where we learned to love and respect our parents, and our brothers and sisters.

The land on which our old home sits is very precious. It's where we played, and entertained our friends. It's the land that produced us. Some people have so much love for the land, they try to find a spot as close as possible to the old home place for their final resting place.

Many will say that the old homestead built their character, and made them who they are today. History indicates that people who care about their old homestead are caring in many other ways as well. Those of us who were fortunate enough to grow up in a loving environment have an advantage over those who were denied these very important benefits in their lives. It's believed that our formative years help pave the path that we follow in the future.

I have always expressed my love and sentiment for the house and land where I grew up. It's located there in the sharp curve of the Long Branch School Road, about one half mile north of the Long Branch School. It was a rather small house with just two, twelve by twelve rooms, with a small entrance hall. To call it modest may be an over statement. However, with all its short comings, it was a palace compared to the sod homes used by early settlers on the prairie lands in the western states.

The buildings have been gone for a number of years, but the land remains pretty much as it was when our family lived there, except for the improved road which now provides access to the outside world. And the vegetation with now surrounds the old homestead which makes it impossible for one to see what was at one time open farm land.

Before the vegetation obstructed the view from the front yard, you could see down the road perhaps a half mile. After crossing the branch there was a small hill, and it was visible from our place. Most of the time someone in the family would see, and alert the rest of us, that someone was coming over the hill and heading towards our house. This was always exciting because very few people traveled the road in the early part of the 20th century.

Looking back at that time, it appears that my father was the one that used it the most. When my dad was away from home, and we expected him to arrive back before dark, my mom would ask us kids to watch and when we saw him coming over the hill she would start to get supper on the table.

One other thing about this hill was the unique rock outcropping that ran across the road on the downward slope. For the most part this rock was six to eight inches high and was difficult for wagons to negotiate. Each spring the residents of the neighborhood would take a day to work the road. They would cover this rock with a mound of dirt and the next rain would wash it all away. I'm sure that the rock is still there, however at this point in history the county maintains the road and the rock is covered with gravel that doesn't wash way.

As one can see, this hill was very important to our family. It was especially important to me. I can recall the many times when I reached the top of the hill and I could see that the house was still there. Seeing it gave me a feeling that is difficult to explain. A feeling of happiness, comfort, and the satisfaction that nothing had happened to it while I was away, and in a few minutes I would be inside its protective walls, safe and secure from the dangers of the outside world. A world that I had heard so much about, but actually know very little about what was happening beyond this place that I called home, located there on Long Branch School Road in Butler County, Kentucky.

10

A PROMISE

A promise, a very small word, with large and devastating consequences when broken. Promises come in all sizes, shapes, and colors. Some promises are little white lies that are designed to appease and pacify. However, if one continues to make these little appeasing and unimportant promises, this person will soon be considered unreliable. Many promises are of great magnitude, and they affect our lives not only in the present but deep into the future. That's why we should be careful about the promises that we make. To be on the safe side, we need to understand the promise we are making, and the person that we are making it to needs to understand them as well.

We Americans have a promise from Thomas Jefferson and the Declaration of Independence, that we have certain rights. Among them are "Life, liberty, and the pursuit of happiness." So far that promise has been kept. However, there are times when it looks a little shaky. We all look forward to a promising life and a bright future. Most of us struggle so that our lives are not filled with broken promises. And our plan for life does not remain unfulfilled.

Some people take making a promise serious. They would face death before they would break their promise. Us children that attended Long Branch School took making a promise very serious. When pressured about their promise, they would reply, "Cross my heart and hope to die, before I will tell anyone."

When we make or receive a promise, it might be safe to say that it is dictated by our heart and conscience. At that time we are using our heart and conscience as collateral, and it should be the supreme. If the promise maker does not have a heart of stone or a conscience made of rubber, there should be no reason to break the promise. It should be the best insurance available.

Due to economic conditions, there are times when keeping a promise is next to impossible. I recall a boy that was once promised a new pair of khaki trousers, and a shirt to match. Due to the shortage of money, his parents were unable to keep their promise. Under the circumstances, the boy felt that it would be wise to forgive his parents, which he did. However, that was before credits cards were available, and that sort of thing is not likely to happen today.

In the early days, a promise and a hand shake was all that was needed to seal a contract. We need more of this in the world today. Keeping our promises promotes love and happiness. So I challenge each of you to remember "promises are not like pie crust, made to be broken."

11

AGAINST ALL ODDS

Kentucky became a state in 1772, and Butler County was established in the year of 1810. History tells us that in the past 200 years the county has produced many notable and successful people: governors, senators, educators, doctors, bankers, ministers, and many other residents that are worthy of recognition.

From what history tells us about life in the early days of our country, just being able to survive must have been a full time job. In our country today we hear and read a great deal about disadvantaged children in America. If one travels the country roads in the county, it's obvious that some children are still in need of help, even with government help, and many charitable organizations that lend support. Poverty, which I usually refer to as a disease, is alive and rampant in many places. This makes it difficult for these children to compete in the real world which they will be facing in just a few years.

From someone who grew up in a similar environment. I know firsthand how difficult it is, when one has to work their way up from the very bottom of the success ladder. I don't believe that this condition has changed very much between disadvantaged children of today and the children that I grew up with in Butler County. Today they may be able to ride to school in a heated or air conditioned bus, have television, DVD players, cell phones, and other luxuries that my generation didn't have. However, these are superficial things.

The root damage of poverty goes much deeper, and leaves scars that last a lifetime.

The scars that run the deepest and cause the most damage are likely to be a feeling of inferiority and a lack of self-confidence. Both are very essential to living a happy and successful life. I'll admit, that when I was young, I suffered from these and other similar problems. However since I wanted to have a better life than my parents had, and the one I was accustom to as a child, I developed a burning desire to succeed. I struggled to overcome my inferiority complex, and worked on building up my self-confidence. Most people who grow up in poverty are likely to have these symptoms.

To overcome these problems. I suggest that young people take a close look at the country that they live in, America. Its population is made up of people from every nation in the world. It has always been a beacon of freedom. It has liberated more people from hunger and terrorism than any other country in the world. It provides great opportunities for all those that are willing to work and seek them out. Yes, America is an exceptional country. It appears that my generation is the last link to the pioneer days in America. Our lifestyle was patterned very close to the way our grandparents lived in the 19th century. And things didn't change much until after World War II. Before that, my generation had to walk to school—up to five miles was not unusual. Of course, there was no electricity, newspapers, radios, or telephones. When we did get news, it was usually by word of mouth, was weeks old, and had passed through a number of carriers, and generally was far different from the facts.

It's easy to see that if one was trying to get an education and become successful in life in this type of environment, the odds were stacked against them. However, most people of my generation are considered to be somewhat successful. I'm sure that the young people of Butler County will continue to succeed against all odds, and their achievements will make Butler County proud.

AMERICA'S FREEDOM

America's freedom journey began in 1776, at the end of the Revolutionary War with Great Britain. On July 2, 1776, the Second Continental Congress gathered at what is now known as Independence Hall in Philadelphia, and voted to approve a resolution of Independence. After this was approved, Congress turned its attention to the Declaration of Independence, a document explaining the decisions which had been prepared by a committee of five, Thomas Jefferson being the principal author.

Congress debated and revised the document and approved it on July 4th 1776. John Adams, who later became the second president of our country, was involved in its preparation. Mr. Adams was so pleased and excited about this accomplishment that he wrote a letter to his wife Abigail praising this great achievement, stating that it would be one of the most memorial days in American History, and that it should be celebrated for generations to come. It would appear that Mr. Adams' vision of the future was correct. We Americans continue to celebrate this holiday, which gave birth of our nation, a monumental achievement.

Soon after the signing of the Declaration of Independence, in 1787, the second Continental Congress met in Philadelphia to discuss the Articles of Confederation which had guided the country since 1777. In their review of the current Articles of Confederation, they found the articles to be inadequate for the fast developing country, and set about writing a new US Constitution. The new Constitution became effective on December 15, 1791 after it had been ratified by three quarters of the states. It has been a very effective document, and has guided our country through many crises for more than 200 years.

The Bill of Rights is the collective name for the first 10 Amendments of the United States Constitution, which limits the power of the United States Federal Government. The limiting protects the natural rights of liberty and property, including freedom of religion, speech, free assembly, as well as the right to keep and bear arms. It appears that our founding fathers with their infinite wisdom were trying to do everything possible to keep government from growing too large, and to prevent it from eroding the God given freedom of the people.

It's no secret that many people in America today believe that our government has grown too large; the Constitution and the Bill of Rights are being trampled on in an effort to change our governing system that has served us so well for so long. We hope that this never happens, and America will live up to our founding fathers' expectations, and America will continue to be the home of the free and the brave.

Speaking of founding fathers, did you know that the only two signers of the Declaration of Independence that became Presidents of the United States, Thomas Jefferson, and John Adams, both died on the same day? July 4, 1820, the 50th anniversary of the signing of the Declaration of Independence. Makes one wonder how they would feel to know that some of their fellow Americans are trying very hard destroy their historical work.

13

BEAUTIFUL QUILTS

For hundreds of years people have made quilts to keep themselves warm in the winter months. However, somewhere along the way, quilts became more than just a bed covering, they become a work of art, a cherished heirloom to be passed down from generation to generation.

Quilting can be traced back to Egypt and China, where three layers of fabric—top, batting, and bottom—were stitched together to keep the batting from slipping and crumbling. This was thought to be a few hundred years B.C. The first type of material that resembled a quilt in Europe was around the 12th century. It was first worn as padding by crusaders under their armor, which later led to the development of the doublet, a padded vest like jacket, with or without sleeves, that was worn by men during the renaissance period, from the 14th to the 16th century.

There was very little quilt making in America in the 18th and early 19th century. Most women were busy spinning, weaving, and sewing in order to clothe their family, and commercial blankets were more economical for most people. Only the wealthy had the time to make quilts, and they were not made from previously used clothing and leftover scraps, they were show pieces of fine cloth, and precise needle work.

It is not known if the first settlers from Europe brought quilts with them. However, one thing is for sure, they brought the art of quilt making with them, and as materials became less expensive, in the late 19th and 20th centuries, most households were involved in quilt making. Women organized quilting bees, where a group would get together to have food and work on making quilts. At that time it was customary to make a quilt for the young ladies' hope chest. This may have given rise to the song, "It was from Aunt Danah's quilting party, I was seeing Nellie home."

In the early days, wood frames were used to keep the materials spread out so it would be accessible to those who were stitching. My mother made quilts when I was a child growing up on Long Branch School Road. As I recall, the frames were wooden 1x2's with quarter inch holes drilled down the center, and could be attached together with nails or wooden pegs. This allowed the frame to be made large or small so all areas of the quilt could be reached. There were several ways to stabilize the frame. Some folks attached them to hooks placed in the ceiling, some used sawhorses, my mom used the back of setting chairs to hold up the frame. The benefit of using chairs was that you could sit in them while working.

Much to my sorrow, I don't have any of the quilts that my mom made. However, I do have a beautiful double wedding ring design quilt that was made by Lily Childers. Lily was the wife of James Childers. James was the son of my dad's Aunt Laura, and her husband Will, who was one of our closest neighbors. The family farm of James and Lily was on top of the hill, a short distance off the north end of Long Branch School Road. Sometime in the middle '50s we were visiting with their family, and Lily was showing us a number quilts that she had made. Much to our surprise, she asked if we would like to purchase the double wedding ring one. Naturally, we were pleased to do so. We have never used it for bedding purposes, it has stayed in its wrapping for the past fifty years or more. When I decided to write this story I opened it up to see how it was holding up on its journey through time. I was amazed to find that it was in like new condition. Just looking at it flooded my mind with a thousand memories and thoughts of the time and effort it took for her to produce this very lovely work of art. It must have taken hundreds of hours. The top is made up of about fifteen hundred separate pieces, and it took approximately fifty thousand stitches to hold it together. I consider it a treasure from the past.

If we look back a hundred years or so at the mothers and wives who made quilts, we find it was a time when life was fragile. Husbands were killed in wars, children died of uncontrollable diseases; childbirth was often fatal. Even under these difficult circumstances, it is easy to see their sense of pride and accomplishments in the quilts they made. Today we should all give thanks to the women of that time for their work and sacrifice, which has helped to make our lives more comfortable, and America the greatest land on Earth.

14

BUTLER COUNTY BEAVERS

Beaver Dam, Kentucky, is a quaint little town just over the Butler County line in Ohio County. Most of my life I was of the opinion that it got its name because beavers were always trying to dam up the Green River. However, I learned later that it got its name from Beaver Creek which flows through that vicinity. There have always been beavers that lived and made their homes in and around Welch's Creek. I cannot recall ever seeing one up close, but remember seeing them swimming up and down the creek.

Beavers are very intriguing animals, with flat tails and lustrous fur. They use their flat tails as a rudder when swimming, as a prop when they are cutting down trees, and to slap the water to make noise to let the family know that danger is near. They build dams in small streams which causes the water to flood the low land and become what is known as wetland. Such wetland is the cradle of life for many of our endangered species.

The beavers' ability to change the landscape is second only to humans. The lodges they build are considered to be something of an engineering masterpiece. While other animals are suffering in freezing weather, the beavers are warm and snug in their lodges with a food supply that last for several months. Beavers appear to be properly equipped for their lifestyle. They have two layers of oily fur, the outside consists of longer hair, the second layer is very fine, and is waterproof. They can stay under water for up to fifteen minutes, and while under water, they have valves in their ears and nose that close to keep the water out. They also have a third transparent eye lid that is used like goggles for underwater work.

Beavers mate for life and usually have two or more young each year. The older siblings help with taking care of the young, called kits. Most lodges consist of six or more, including the parents. When the lodge becomes crowed, pressure is put on the older ones, which are about two years old, to leave the lodge and start a life of their own.

There is a story about a young beaver that lived with his parents in a lodge located in Welch's Creek just south of what is known as the Horseshoe Bend. Since we are not sure what his name was, we will call him Leo. One day his parents called him into the lodge and explained to him that the family was getting too large, and that it was time for Leo to go and start a life of his own. They suggested that he go down about a mile where the Long Branch empties into the creek, and see if that would be a suitable location for him to start building a lodge. Leo was happy where he was, and didn't want to leave what had been his home for the past two years. Finally his mother had to raise her voice, and in no uncertain terms said "Leo you go now!" So, broken hearted, Leo went away. Leo wandered up and down the creek for several days, very depressed. Then one day he decided to venture back to the old home place. Perhaps his mother had changed her mind. That was not to be the case. His mother was more forceful than ever, she slapped him with her big flat tail and told him to go.

A few days later, for something to do, Leo was gnawing on a tree when he was approached by another beaver. In Leo's state of mind he hardly looked up, when a very feminine voice said "My name is Lolo. Can I help you gnaw on that tree?" This got Leo's attention as there in front of him was the most beautiful female beaver he had ever seen. She had bright sparkling eyes and a beautiful fur coat. It was love at first sight. Leo explained the problems he was having with his family. Lolo mentioned that she was having the same problems with her family. She reached out with one of her little webbed paws and gently stroked Leo's fur. Together they decided to go down where the Long Branch enters the creek, and build a lodge of their own. Now the only time his old family sees Leo is when he and Lolo bring the grandchildren by, and listen to his mom rave about how beautiful they are.

15

BLACKBERRY COBBLER

I may be partial, but I'm convinced that the wild blackberries that grow in Butler County, Kentucky, especially those that grow in the bottom land in and around the Long Branch School Road, are the most delicious, and make the best blackberry cobbler in the world.

Like any other child that grew up there, we were no stranger to this delicious and healthy fruit that grew in abundance just about everywhere. Their thorny vines grew beside the roads, winding through fence lines and on the banks of the branches. I recall one location where the vegetation was so heavy, it could compete with the jungles of South America. However, inside that thorny, chigger, tick, and snake infested jungle was where the largest and sweetest berries were hiding. It took a considerable amount of courage on the part of the picker to fight his or her way into where the prized berries were. But in tough economic times, uncommon courage becomes a common thing.

Blackberries ripen and are ready for harvest in mid-summer. Mothers and fathers would know they were ripe when their children showed up with purple teeth.

Most everyone in the neighborhood was interested in the blackberry crop. In addition to the blackberry cobbler that was so tasty, they are used to make jams and jellies for winter use. They also provided food for the birds and,

and other small animals.

While I don't remember anyone in the Long Branch vicinity doing so, I understand that they make very good wine. I have tasted it once in my life. At one time our home was in suburban Hendersonville, North Carolina. It was a newer development with a number of vacant lots. A creek ran through it as well, which promoted the growth of blackberry vine. I recall one year the berry crop looked very promising. We had discussed picking some when we returned from our vacation. Our neighbors at the time were Clint and Mary Ann Byrd. When we returned, the berry crop was pretty well depleted. When I asked around the neighborhood, I was told that the birds got them. I was puzzled for a moment until I realized that they were referring to Clint and Mary Ann Byrd. They used them to make blackberry wine. Being the good neighbors that they were, they invited us over to sample their expertise in wine making.

As mentioned, picking blackberries was not one of the most desirable jobs. At that time of the year, the weather was hot and muggy. The thorns from the vines are very sharp, and due to their downward hook they wanted to cling to everything they touched. And for those who thought it was too tough a job, us boys would pick as many gallons as they wanted for ten cents per gallon.

It is believed that blackberries have been around for thousands of years. They are found on most every continent. The Greeks used them as a medicine, and in some instances the roots were boiled to make medical tonic.

If we look close at the blackberry plant, we find it is very interesting. The cane that grows to be three to six feet tall are biannual, while the roots are perennial. The canes will not bear any fruit the first year. They bloom in late spring, usually a white pinkish blossom. It may be the only fruit in existence that is red when it's green, and turns black when it's ripe.

16

THE BRUSH ARBOR

Some of our forefathers were willing to leave their homes and risk their lives to sail across an unknown ocean on the Mayflower, and to establish a home in a wilderness country that they knew even less about. They were willing to make that sacrifice and face the many hardships and dangers that they would encounter on their journey. Their religious faith gave them the strength and courage to face this enormous challenge. It was, and has been this type of faith and courage that has made America great.

When I was a child growing up in Butler County, most everyone lived in poverty. Poverty was a disease that medicine would not cure. However, that didn't appear to dampen the faith of most people living there. If you asked them about their faith, and if they believed the Bible, their response would usually be that they believed every word betwixt and between the front and back pages. I think this was proven to be true when you are able to see the effort they demonstrated to build a place where they could go and worship.

As you can imagine, public buildings were very few and far between. So when a church group needed a place to hold their meetings, and there were no buildings available, they would revert back to their pioneer wisdom: build a brush arbor. You would need to find a spot where the ground was reasonably level, and had some trees as well. First, with a cross cuts saw and ax, remove all the trees in an area approximately 30 feet square, except for the two or three trees in the center. Save the trees that you have removed. They will be needed later. Next, use some of these small trees you have removed and hang them up in the forks, or nail them to the trees around the opening you have made. Then attach some small ones to this outside rail you have made, and secure the other end to some of the trees in the center. Now you have a framework over the cleared area. This work is usually done in the summer months when the trees have leaves on them. Cut the branches from the removed trees and place them on top of the framework the branches and leaves to act as a roof and shelter. Split logs with legs nailed to them were usually use for seating. The altar area was raised about eight inches high and was usually made from a rough sawed timber. There are other methods of building brush arbors. If you wanted to build one on open ground you would need to dig holes in the ground and set posts in them to make the frame work. The above explanation is the Butler County method.

The closest brush arbor to the Martin farm was up on Pea Ridge Road, now known as Highway 1328. It was about three miles from our place. And you can imagine why the church services were held in the summer time when the weather was warm and the days were long, this would eliminate the need for heat and light. I was small when we attended church there. The preacher was Brother Wyle Duke. In those days we referred to them as preachers, and not ministers. Being small, I don't remember everything he spoke about, however I do remember the most important subject was that if you are a mean person, the devil will get you. I can also remember the collection plate, I cannot remember what type of plate it was, but I can still see my mom dropping her dime into it, which was what most people donated. As I recall many people in the area referred to the church goers as holy rollers. However, my grandmother, Lillie Oller, when asked about that, said they were part of the holiness church group. She may have been correct, as I can recall some of the shouting and emotions demonstrated at that time. I have always felt that it was an extraordinary honor to have attended church with these very fine and honest people. We will never know for sure, but it may have had something to do with the type of person I am today.

17

BULLDOG GRAVY

Bulldog Gravy and biscuits have been a part of my life since I was a child growing up in the Kentucky hills. The country was suffering under tough economic times due to the Great Depression. People were struggling to find enough food to feed their families. It might be safe to say that Bulldog was invented there in the Appalachian Mountains.

We have all heard the words of wisdom that "necessity is the mother of inventions." Bulldog gravy was inexpensive and easy to make, and become a major part of most meals, especially the noon meal. In those days it was called dinner, and what we now call dinner, was called supper.

There are many different types and recipes for gravy, Bulldog, Sawmill, and Red-eye, just to name a few. Most have one thing in common, they start with some type of fat as a base. Bacon grease, drippings from beef or pork roast, were often used as these tend to improve the taste of the gravy. Red-eye gravy was totally different from bulldog or sawmill. It is made by adding coffee to hot bacon grease. The coffee doesn't completely mix with the grease, and leaves red and brown streaks in the mixture. I have had it many times in my life, and it tastes very good, especially if one is hungry, and boys are always hungry.

Sawmill is much like bulldog, but is made with sausage grease, then the cooked sausage is added back to the gravy. I don't recall ever having any, must be that it was considered to be the premium quality gravy, and it cost too much.

The art of making good bulldog gravy has been handed down through many generations. My brother-in-law, Wayne Constant, was a master technician at making great bulldog, to the point that when he went to visit friends he was always called on to make the gravy. Before I give you the recipe for making good bulldog, I must warn you that it is not highly recommended as a health food. Matter of fact, when I was a child, it was rumored that eating it was the first step to the grave. However, I am not sure all the negative things said about gravy are true. I have eaten it all my life, and have suffered no ill effects from doing so.

To make good bulldog, start with a ten-inch cast iron skillet, some folks call them fry pans. Add three tablespoons of base, this can be the bacon grease or the drippings mentioned earlier, butter, margarine, or any type of vegetable oil. I have found that olive oil makes a good base, but reduce the amount used. Once the base is heated, add sauce and gravy flour mix. This can be purchased in most grocery stores, it comes in a shaker can. You will have to estimate this, but about two tablespoons would be about the correct amount. Stir the base and flour together and cook on medium for two minutes. Don't overcook. Add milk a small amount at a time, stir continuously until it thickens. More milk or flour can be used to reach the proper consistency, then add a generous amount of black pepper, this should make about four servings. Your dinner guests will applaud your cooking if the gravy is free of lumps, and the viscosity is correct.

I would like to tell you a little story about a farmer who wanted to hire a teenage boy to plow up some land for him, using a turning plow and a team of mules. The farmer asked the young man if he had any experience at plowing. "Yes sir, I can do it, I have had lots of experience plowing gravy with a biscuit."

Goes to show how bright and ambitious those little hillbilly children were.

18

BUSHY TAIL

Bushy Tail. That's what we called the squirrels when I was growing up on the north side of the Green River. Before I tell you about bushy tail, I want to tell you a story about cotton tail, that's what we called rabbits. One gloomy and drizzly Thanksgiving Day our neighbor, Zonie Phelps and my dad decided to go rabbit hunting. It was customary for people to hunt on Thanksgiving Day, because the Indians brought wild game when they came to feast with the pilgrims on the first Thanksgiving. Dad and Zonie went down in the bottom land near where the Long Branch empties into Welch's Creek. This land had been planted in corn the past summer, and harvested in the fall. Of course, there was corn left as it was impossible to harvest it all, and since rabbits love corn, they were abundant in that location. The hunters had not been down there very long when we heard lots of shooting. And it grew in intensity until it sounded like a war. When they returned to the house they had only one rabbit between the two of them. They had fired at least twenty-five shots. At that time .12 gauge shotgun shells were three cents each, that put the cost of the rabbit at seventy five cents. That made it one expensive rabbit as wages at that time were fifty cents a day.

My brother and I were assigned the task of dressing the rabbit, and we were surprised to find that there were no BB shots in the rabbit's body. It's possible that there could have been some in the rabbit's head, we didn't examine that. Everyone came to the conclusion that all the shooting caused the rabbit to die of a heart attack.

That story had legs. It went on for some time, and was soon exaggerated to the point where people were saying that perhaps the rabbits attacked the hunters, and I could visualized my dad and Zonie standing back to back defending themselves while the rabbits circle them the way we see Indians circling the wagons in western movies. Perhaps we should not discount this theory completely as I seem to recall a story some years ago about former president Jimmie Carter being attack by a rabbit while fishing at St. Simons Island in his home state of Georgia.

It took dad and Zonie a long time to live down this incident. It's too bad that dad and Zonie didn't know about the method of harvesting rabbits without a gun. It's called the paint and shake method. I have never used it, and have some reservations about its validity. If you would like to check it out, look around your area, and find someone that is clearing some woodland for future agriculture purposes. There will be piles of tree branches, commonly known as brush piles, and stumps as well. Take some black paint and paint a six inch black spot on the stumps near the brush pile, then shake the brush pile to scare the rabbits out. When they see the black spot, they will think it's a hole, and try to enter. Running at breakneck speed they will knock themselves senseless. All you have to do is pick them up.

It appears that we have gotten carried away with this cotton tail story. Bushy tail will feel neglected if we don't get back to him. As history tells us, times were very difficult in the Great Depression days. Everyone that lived along the Long Branch School Road struggled to survive. Hunting small game, especially squirrels, became a major food supply to the point that some folks considered it a sacred ritual. The squirrels were giving up their lives so we could live. Anyone harvesting more than they needed was looked upon with a degree of contempt. Most of our neighbors used .12 gauge shotguns for hunting. When they were fired they made a loud report that could be heard around the neighborhood. If there was an excess amount of shooting, people would worry that the squirrel population was being destroyed, and there would be none left for them. I don't recall there being any laws that controlled hunting at that time.

Hunting was more likely to produce good results in the fall and late spring.

In the fall, hickory nuts were maturing, and squirrels love hickory nuts. If you visited a large hickory nut tree late in the afternoon, chances were good that there would be as many as a half dozen feeding on the nuts. If you stood under the tree, the nut shell they were peeling off would sound like rain falling, but after the first shot they would scatter to the four winds. You would be lucky if you managed to bag two.

In the mid-summer when the mulberries are ripe was also a good time for hunting. We were fortunate to have several of these trees nearby. Squirrels would journey great distances to feed on them, and at times hunters would come from outside the neighborhood to hunt there. The largest of these trees was across the valley, perhaps a distance of one half mile or so from our place. Some evenings the sound of gunfire was heavy, which led my brother and me to think that all the squirrels in the county were being killed. In order to combat this situation, we developed a plan: We would get up early and go hunting down along Welch's Creek, and see if we could bag a large fox squirrel. Our luck was good, and we got a very large one. We carefully removed the hide and stuffed it full of broom sage straw, and with a little stitching it looked like a real live squirrel. With that part of our plan accomplished, we took it over to the big mulberry tree. My brother climbed up the tree, and with me on the ground we selected a spot that was not too conspicuous, but could be seen by anyone searching the tree. With some small wire we secured the phantom squirrel to one of the tree branches. He looked so natural and realistic, with his head pointed down, and his big bushy tail flowing down his back. He represented a picture that all hunters dream of finding. Later that day when the sun started casting long shadows across the valley, the shooting started. The shots were in rapid succession, about the length of time it would take someone to reload and fire. This went on morning and evening for a couple of days. My brother and I decided that we should go over and see what had happened to our squirrel. We found the branch dangling from the tree, and our squirrel reduced to a bunch of broom sage straw.

The upside of this story is that we saved a good many squirrels. The down side is it wasn't a very nice thing to do. I hope you consider the circumstances at the time and will not judge us too harshly. By remembering that boys of twelve and fourteen are a strange and unpredictable piece of humanity.

19

BUTLER COUNTY FARMERS

We should all pay tribute to the farmers of Butler County. They have been tilling Butler County soil ever since it become a county in the year of 1810, and perhaps many years before, when it was part of Logan County. Many of the farms have been handed down from generation to generation, which is a wonderful thing. The topographical landscape of the county is wide and varied. It ranges from the rich fertile land, commonly referred to as the Green River Bottoms, to smaller bottom land along such creeks as Welch's Creek, Bull Creek, and a multitude of other streams and branches. And let us not forget that there's a considerable amount of hill country in Butler County which is not ideally suited for farming.

However, rough hilly country has not stopped the ambitious and determined farm families from clearing the land, digging up the stumps, and making it into a productive piece of land. There was a parcel of land owned by one of our neighbors, and to say that the hillside was very steep would be an understatement. In the early days before tractors were available, tilling the land was done with a hand held plow and draft animals. One day I was watching the owner plow that piece of land. To the best of my memory, and to get the job done, it was necessary to rig up an offset singletree so the horse and the person holding the plow could walk in the previously plowed furrow below, which was the only level spot available on the entire hillside. It may have been difficult, but as I remember, it usually produced a nice corn crop.

Farming is a risky business, considering what farmers must put up front, items such as seed and equipment. Not to mention the many hours spent preparing the land for planting. The weather is always a factor, some years are too dry, while an excessive amount of rain in the spring can delay the planting. The most devastating factor of all is after the crops are planted, a large amount of rain would cause the Green River to overflow its banks and flood all the bottom land, destroying the crops in their early stages of life. However, in most every case where the crops were lost, as soon as the water receded and the ground dried up, you would see the farmers back in the fields preparing the land for replanting.

I have always thought how disappointing it must be to have your crop destroyed. Considering the loss that that they had suffered, it must take a considerable amount of courage and determination to start all over again. Back when I was a boy, I recall listening to a conversation my father was having with one of the larger corn farmers in the county. He was explaining that he had been farming for the past 25 years, and was unable to understand that when he had a poor yield the price of corn was high, and when he had a bumper crop the price was low. He went on to explain that the past year things had improved. It was the only time in his farming career that his yield was high and the selling price was high, as well.

Farming is a great occupation, but it has never been easy. In the early days it was a common practice for the wife and mother of the family to have breakfast ready around 4:00 a.m. every morning, so the men folk could get an early start on all the things that had to be accomplished that day.

Chances are good that the work ethic of farmers hasn't changed a great deal over the years. On behalf of all Americans I would like to say thank you to all farmers, for your hard work and sacrifice. We will be forever grateful.

20

CHRISTMAS MEMORIES

It would be safe to say that our family was like all the other families that lived on Long Branch School Road, and the balance of Butler County for that matter. We all struggled to improve our living standards in a very hostile economic time. Life could have been better for the Martin Family had the John M. Carson Banking Company not failed, causing its depositors to lose their savings. I always felt that my dad never quite recovered from that loss.

However, Christmas comes around once a year, regardless of how scarce money is. It is not easy for children 10-years old or younger to understand financial problems. What does money have to do with it anyway? Santa has a sleigh full of toys, and if you have been a good little boy or girl, Santa will fill your stocking with everything you have wished for.

Our family consisted of six: mom and dad, my brother Otis, myself, and my two sisters, Bonnie and Irene. We were spaced about two years apart. When Otis was ten, my youngest sister Irene was six. Being close together we were able to communicate with each other. We were taught at an early age the meaning of Christmas, and its importance of being the birthday of the Baby Jesus, Son of God, and we children should always remember that.

Like all children, we were very excited about Christmas. I don't believe that we ever had a tree in our house, we would always pretend that the one in the school house was partly ours. Actually our house was very small with just two rooms with a hallway in between, and that didn't leave much room for a tree. However, Mom and Dad always managed to see that Santa found our place. Since our place had no fireplace, we would hang our stockings on a bed post, door knob, or drive a nail in the wall.

There were times when it looked as if Santa might not be able to navigate through the bad weather. I recall one Christmas Eve, it was pouring down rain, and by late afternoon, it showed no signs of stopping. We were all worried, which prompted my sisters to compose a little song. The lyrics were: *Rain rain, stop your raining, or we won't get nothing for Christmas. Santa we know that your sled won't float, maybe someone will lend you a boat.* The rain didn't let up but the inclement weather wasn't able to stop Santa.

On Christmas morning, our stockings contained apples and oranges, a stick of peppermint candy and some kind of a toy. My sisters would receive a doll or other things little girls appreciate. My brother and I would get a cap pistol, or some other toy to share.

There is still a mystery about Christmas at our house. As I mentioned, the house was small, there were no closets, or other places to hide the presents. We kids were never able to figure out how our parents were able to manage keeping the gifts out of sight, and they never did tell us. It's enough to make one believe that Santa is real, even after you grow up.

Christmas is a very special time for children. I can recall how we kids would want to stay up a while longer on Christmas Eve, but that was impossible. The coal oil lamp was running out of oil, and the barrel stove that we used for heating had burned up all the chestnut logs with only ashes remaining. So here was nothing else to do but run off to bed, and sleep tight on the corn husk mattress.

There is no greater pleasure in life, than spending Christmas with the ones you love

21

COLT .45 PISTOL

The M-1911 is a single action semi-automatic, magazine fed, and recoil operated hand gun, chambered for the .45 ACP cartridge. It was a John Browning design. It was the side arm for the United States Armed Forces from 1911 to 1985, and is still carried by some U.S. forces. It has been widely used in all wars since World War I. The United States purchased approximately 2.7 million during its service life.

The reason I'm giving you this little history lesson about this particular pistol is because I was very closely associated with it while growing up in Butler County. My dad was the owner of one of those very fine guns for many years. At this time, I had no idea where he got it, or how much it cost, not more than a few dollars I'm sure.

In the early days in Butler County, it was customary to keep your hand gun under your pillow. However, my dad didn't do that. He tucked it away where the children would be unable to get their hands on it. Our house, like most other houses without a fireplace, had a two foot square opening in the ceiling where the stove pipe went through to carry out the smoke from our wood burning barrel stove. Since the ceiling was low, about seven feet I would guess, Dad could stand on the floor and place the gun in the attic on the ledge of the opening.

When I was about 12 and my brother was 14, one of the neighbor boys came home from the army. He had brought with him one of these guns, exactly like Dad's. He was showing it to us, and asked my brother if he would be interested in buying it from him. My brother said yes, if the price wasn't too high. The young man said he would take two dollars for it. It was in the fall of the year, and my brother had been helping Mr. Eberman gather corn over in the Green River bottoms, and had saved a few dollars. My brother looked at me for approval, and when I gave a slight nod the deal was closed. Even though my brother was older when he made big decisions, like spending two dollars, he seemed to think that my opinion was important.

Since my brother had a gun, and several other boys we knew had guns, I felt sort of inferior, and left out. Peer pressure we call it today. In order to relieve that pressure, I decided to borrow my dad's gun. He didn't check on it very often, and wouldn't miss it if I put it back when I got home. So when my brother and I wanted to go somewhere, he would get his gun from its hiding place, and by standing on a chair, I could reach up in the attic and get my dad's pistol and slip it inside my belt under my shirt. It made me feel as big as the older boys, and the secure feeling it provided when walking alone in the dark was great. One problem was that it weighed over two pounds. The gun was almost as big as the boy who was carrying it around.

Now, don't jump to the conclusion that all boys that carried guns in the early days were bad boys. Guns were a way of life in the early part of the 20th century. The Second Amendment, which provides us the right to bear arms, was still fresh in the minds of most people. The stories of Daniel Boone and his rifle, and the winning of the West, at that time was only 60 years old.

Some folks believe that guns promote murder and violent crime. Let's take a look at what has happened in the last 100 years. In the year of 1910, our population was about one hundred million, and almost everyone had a gun. There were 230 murders in the United States that year. In 2008, we had three hundred million people, and 16,300 murders. This presents a real problem for America today.

22

COUNTRY ICE CREAM

Early Butler County children were no different than children in Aberdeen, Mississippi, or Morgantown, West Virginia. They all loved ice cream. It has become a major food item here in America and generates billions in sales each year. History indicates that the first mixture of anything that resembled ice cream happened in the 4th century BC. The Emperor of Rome had some ice brought down from the mountains, and combined it with some fruit toppings. Later, Marco Polo learned about the Chinese method of mixing milk and ice together and brought the recipe back to Europe. In the early days of our country, it was a very fashionable treat, and was served at parties by George Washington, Thomas Jefferson, Dolly Madison, and many of our other founding fathers.

The discovery of salt to control the temperature, and the wooden freezer bucket with the wooden paddles were the major advancements in the making of ice cream. Of course the ice cream the Martin Family made there on Long Branch School Road in the hot months of July and August was a major undertaking, and happened only on rare occasions.

It wasn't so different from ice cream that was sold at the drug store in Morgantown. The basic ingredients we used were the same: milk, eggs, sugar, and vanilla extract. Our choice of flavors was very broad – you could have any flavor you liked as long as it was vanilla. However, the process we had to go through from the time we decided to produce this cool tasty treat was monumental. First it was necessary to get a 25-pound block of ice from the Morgantown Ice Plant to our place, which was a distance of four country miles. As I recall, a 25-pound block of ice would measure twelve by twelve by six inches thick. If there is a more clumsy thing to carry, it would be nitroglycerin. Ice was usually transported in a burlap bag. Burlap is made from jute or hemp fibers and, was supposed to slow down the melting process of the ice.

Our equipment to make ice cream consisted of a three gallon galvanized pail, and a one gallon pail with a handle, which contained the ice cream mixture. The one gallon pail was placed inside the three gallon pail and chipped ice and salt were added to surround the one gallon pail. Agitation was supplied by holding the handle, also known as the bail, and turning the pail back and forth. It took about 45 minutes to freeze. It was necessary to remove the lid and scrape the frozen ice cream from the sides every ten minutes or so. Once it was finished, everyone bragged about how good it was, and that it was well worth the effort that it took to make it.

In the winter when it snowed, us kids made snow ice cream by putting some snow in a glass and adding some milk and sugar. It was very tasty but the weather was cold, and the winter ice cream didn't create as much excitement as our summer projects. Reminds me of the old adage, "There is enough ice in the world for everyone. The wealthy gets theirs in the summer, the poor get theirs in the winter."

23

COWBOYS

As far as I know, Butler County never had any cowboys. However, we are all intertwined in the cowboy legend. It would be safe to say that no other occupation in America has had a greater impact on our lives than the western cowboy.

After the Civil War, the cowboy became a figure of special significance and a legend in their time. History indicates that the passion to become a cowboy ran high. More than 50,000 men from all parts of our country, some from eastern colleges and even from Europe, traveled west to become cowboys. These men found life on the plains to be very harsh. It's been said that the plains provided only two kinds of weather: rain, sleet, and snow, or hot, dry, and dusty. In addition to the extreme weather, life threatening danger was always near. Indians on the war path, rattlesnakes, storms, stampedes, range wars, and that ever threatening spiny cactus plant that thrived in the arid southwest.

Back in the east men usually settled their disputes with their fists. In the old west they were settled with the roar of a colt .45. It was called the peace maker. It's been said that Abe Lincoln freed all men, but Sam Colt made them all equal. Some were more equal than others, some become professional gun fighters, and some become cattle rustlers. History indicates that the average American cowboy lived a lonely life under very harsh conditions, but always kept his sense of humor, made very little money, didn't talk much, was reserved around strangers, and did not tolerate meanness, cowardliness, dishonesty, or whining. They would fight anyone mistreating the ladies or a horse and were tough as nails, but at the same time was generous and hospitable. Thus, the character of the American cowboy.

They also had a hand in opening up the west with their great cattle drives. Many settlers used these trails on their way westward. South America and Australia are the two other countries that have cowboys that do work similar to our western cowboys. Like our western states, these two regions have a dry climate as well. Where grass was sparse, a large amount of land was necessary in order to feed large herds, and cowboys on horses were needed to control and look after the cattle.

Cowboy movies become very popular in the middle of the 20th century, especially after most homes had television. There were many great characters in shows such as Gunsmoke, Bonanza, and Big Valley and then there were so many great western movie, many that starred John Wayne. I became addicted to western movies when I was in my teens. It happened because I would try very hard to find a way to watch Gene Autry in our little theater there in Morgantown. It would be safe to say that I have seen almost all the western series and movies several times over. Now days it's difficult to find re-runs on the television, or western pictures at the movies, which makes me sad.

Some of my friends accuse me of having been a cowboy in one of my other lives. As cowboys they are known for their love of the land, and loyalty to their beliefs, this may very well be true.

24

CRACKLING BREAD

Have you ever had the pleasure of tasting crackling bread, or crackling hoecakes? If not, you should try to do so at the earliest possible date. I can testify as to how tasty this cuisine is. As a child growing up on Long Branch School Road, it was a dish that our family looked forward to with great anticipation. At that time in history, crackling was made from pork skins and other less desirable pork parts. These parts were usually put in a large pot or kettle and cooked until all the fat was extracted. This process resembled the modern day deep fry systems, and it would produce nice brown crunchy cracklings. To produce this cracking bread it is necessary to mix the crackling with a corn meal bread mix. Adding the cracklings gives corn bread or corn bread hoecakes a completely different flavor.

Cornbread and all the other names associated with corn is a relatively new food. The recipe did not come from Europe with the early settlers, but is a native food. The American Indians introduced corn to the European settlers when they arrived, they had been using corn to make bread for centuries. Some of the early settlers, especially the British and the Dutch were not too fond of cornbread, but were forced to eat it when the ground wheat supply was used up. At that time, cornbread was called Indian bread, or Indian pudding, because it contained corn. I feel certain that if those settlers would have combined some pinto beans and sorghum molasses with that Indian bread, it would have tasted great. Even now cornbread is a very common bread, particular in the south, with the ingredients to make it basically the same. Cornbread is called many different names: Corn pone, hoecakes, Jonny cakes, and hushpuppies to name a few.

At our home on Long Branch School Road, my mom cooked hoecakes in a frying pan. For the corn pone, she always used a special iron skillet as they are considered the ideal pan for baking corn pone. Iron skillets were supposed to improve the quality of the bread if they were never washed. Washing would remove the grease and prevent it from baking into the skillet, which is considered necessary to make good bread.

Our northern neighbors consume a moderate amount of cornbread, and a small amount of crackling bread, but not to the extent that us southerners do. They are more inclined to dress it up with wheat flower, sugar, and other additives to the point where it's difficult to know if you are eating cornbread or cake. Even though cornbread is a southern food, I have no objection to people outside the south enjoying cornbread, I just don't want anyone treading on our culture roots. Cornbread is part of our southern heritage and I believe we should defend it, and show support for our southern culture.

25

CROWN OF THORNS

Near our home place on Long Branch School Road were many thorn trees. The one I remember the best was the one that stood on the bank of the branch that flows down from Possum Hollow. It was basically in our backyard, about 100 feet from our back door. It was quite large, perhaps 24 inches at the trunk, and 30 feet tall. It was rather intimidating, with its large thorns protruding from its body as well as most of the branches. Some of the thorn spines were six to eight inches long, with spikes two or three inches in length. These thorns looked like something used in a medieval torture chamber. They could puncture an automobile tire, or penetrate your shoe with ease. I have heard that in some instances they have been used as nails.

There are many legendary stories about why certain trees have thorns. Perhaps the one that has the greatest possibility is that in the beginning of time large animals roamed the Earth, animals like Mammoths, Mastodons, and Dinosaurs, that were tall enough to reach up and pick the pods from the trees. These pods contained the seeds that would eventually sprout and produce more trees. Of course, these seeds had to be fully mature in the pods and fall to the ground before they were able to produce a new tree. If the animals devoured them in their green state, there would be no replacement seeds. So as a matter of survival, these trees grew thorns to protect their seed pods. The flat green pod is three to five inches long, and the pulp inside is edible.

On occasion we kids would very carefully pick some of the pods to eat at the sweet the pulp inside. The pods were a beneficial diet for Native Americans, and due to the sweetness of the pulp, they called it the honey locust tree. I'm not sure what happened to that tree. One possibility is that the land it stood on belonged to our Aunt Kate, and when she sold it the new owners may have cut it down. Or it may have died from old age as the honey locust has a short life span of an average of 70 years, with a maximum of 150 years.

When we see thorns, most of us Christians think about the crown of thorns that was placed on the head of Jesus at the time of His crucifixion. The crown of thorns is mentioned in the Bible three times: Matthew 27:20; Mark 15:17; and John 19:2-5 and is alluded to by early Christian fathers. However, very few writers in the first 600 years mentioned it as being in existence and venerated by the faithful. There are many stories and much speculation about what has happened to the original crown of thorns. It appears that the thorns were sometimes separated, and pieces sent to kings, queens, and rulers. One story indicates that the ruler of Constantinople, anxious to obtain support for his tottering empire, offered the crown to Louis, King of France. After the French Revolution, it was deposited in the Cathedral of Notre-Dame. It is described as a twisted cornet of rushes. Leaves us to wonder about the historical authenticity of these thorns as 2000 years is a considerable amount of time for a thorn to last.

The origin of the thorns is not known, but it is believed that they come from the jujube tree that grows in abundance around Jerusalem. However, these things are not important, what is important is that these thorns represent a symbol of sacrifice and suffering, imposed on the Son of God, sent here to lead His children out of darkness.

26

DIAMONDS IN THE ROUGH

A diamond in the rough is a person who appears to be just average, but later in life turns out to be above average. They possess hidden abilities and undiscovered talents that are not clear to others due to their rough exterior, much like a diamond stone in its rough state, which has no beauty until it is cleaned up and polished.

Sometimes it's difficult to determine if every person that has hidden talents has a chance to display their true qualities. We don't know for sure, but ambition and opportunity may be the key factors that help them accomplish their dreams in life. These diamonds are usually found among disadvantaged people growing up in poverty. Society leaves them very short on resources and opportunity.

Like the real diamond stone that needs to be polished to bring out its brilliance, so do these human diamonds need help and encouragement to develop their full potential. If we take a look back in history, we will find many of our early leaders rose to the top from very humble beginnings. For example Abraham Lincoln, the 16th president of the United States, was severely criticized by his opponents for his rough and unpolished appearance. Despite these criticisms Lincoln rose from poverty, and overcame setbacks to become one of America's greatest leaders.

Since I go back a ways in time, I can remember some of the Butler County people that were diamonds in the rough, two of which were Girlie Smith and Essie Cardwell.

Girlie Smith began life on the bottom rail, however, after some polishing, he displayed the talent of an extraordinary business man. Girlie owned several businesses in Butler County including a hotel and restaurant. He will always be remembered for the help and kindness he provided to the people of Morgantown and Butler County.

My boyhood friend Essie Cardwell, was a veteran of World War II and was a member of the 82nd Airborne Division which took part in the D-Day invasion at Normandy. While in the service of his country, Essie received many accolades for his marksmanship. He was awarded the Purple Heart with one oak leaf cluster, and several other metals of valor.

Butler County history shows that there were many more respected citizens that fit into this diamond in the rough category. Since I have firsthand knowledge of what the living conditions were like in the early 20th century, it must have taken a tremendous amount of work and determination for each to reach their dreams. Most of us have heard the old platitude about determination: "If the job is difficult, we do it right away. If it's impossible it takes a little longer."

We should not let this story end without a few words of praise for Sam Walton. Sam was born in 1923 on a farm near Kingfisher, Oklahoma. Sam's father was unable to make a living on the farm, and went back to his old job. After moving several more times, he finally settled on a farm in Columbia, Missouri. Sam worked hard to help maintain the family in the days of Great Depression by milking cows, then bottling the milk, and selling it in town. He also delivered papers and magazines. To help himself get through college he waited tables. After his military service, he worked a short time for J.C. Penney. At age 26, he borrowed $20,000 dollars from his father-in-law, and with the $5,000 dollars he had saved from his time in the army, bought his first Ben Franklin store in Newport, Arkansas. With this purchase Sam Walton was on his way to becoming one of the world's richest men. Last time I heard, there were 8400 Wal-Mart stores, and they are building more every day.

Quite an achievement for a boy who started out milking cows.

27

ECHOES FROM THE PAST

The word echo appears to have originated in ancient Greece. Greek mythology tells the story of a beautiful nymph named Echo. She was a great talker whose ability to speak was taken away. Zeus, King of Olympia, was known for his many love affairs with young beautiful nymphs. Echo was accused of distracting his wife with long and entertaining stories, while the king took advantage of the moment to ravish another beautiful nymph. When the king's wife discovered the trickery, she punished the talkative Echo by taking away her voice. She could only repeat what others had said.

Most of us are familiar with audible echoes that are produced when sound waves bounce off other objects. Hills, mountains, and valleys are a great place to listen to echoes. Recently I spent some time at the Fannie Rone Cemetery. It's a very quiet and secluded place, tucked away in the rolling timber covered hills of Butler County, Kentucky. The cemetery is located in the area known as Bull Creek, named for the creek that flows through the valley, and empties into the Green River that passes nearby. This is the area where my dad grew up, and where many of my ancestors called home. Markers in the cemetery date back to the first pioneer families that braved the wilderness and settled the land. Most were patriotic, hardworking, and frugal due to necessity, as well as by principal, and above all very independent. They left behind a great heritage that's still part of the today's culture.

As I viewed the surrounding, I found myself pondering the past of long ago, when the people buried there once tilled the soil and populated the land. They have my sympathy. I know firsthand the many problems they faced. The struggle to survive, the heartbreaks and tragedies they suffered. I feel certain that they would recognize the land today, as it has stood the test of time, and remains about the same as when God made it. Only the manmade objects show signs of deterioration. This is a place where the echoes of the past play softly across the hills and valleys of this sacred land. Echoes of the past are much different than the audible ones we have heard in our lifetime. To hear them, we must first become conscious of the fact they are real in a divine way, and there is no limit to the number that are floating around in places like Bull Creek, and the Fannie Rone Cemetery, just waiting to be heard.

I'm confident that they are watched over by angels with snow white wings, and are riding on the mystic winds of time. And of course, with angels, everything is possible. To capture them, we must open up our hearts, and minds, and listen to what that small inner voice is telling us, because these echoes of the past can only be heard through the heart. Most of us have lost friends and loved ones in the past, listening to echoes of the past will keep their memories alive.

28

ESSIE CARDWELL REMEMBERED

Up the Long Branch Road about a mile from the Martin farm near Welch's Creek was the Cardwell Farm. Like most farms in this area, it was located at the mouth of a hollow, where the land become more flat and level. This land is known as creek bottom land and was ideal for farming. The Cardwell family, like most everyone else in this section of the country, farmed the land. They raised chickens, hogs and cattle, hunted squirrels and rabbits to help feed the family.

Essie was the son of William Amos and Prudence Elams Cardwell. As I recall, Essie had four brothers and three sisters. Essie was born September 5, 1917, which made him one year and five days older than my brother Otis. Dennis, the youngest of the family, was about the same age as me. Since we were all about the same age, we went to the Long Branch School together, and since we were neighbors, we played, hunted and fished together. We would also go over to the Belmont Church and associate with the beautiful girls in that area.

Essie's family owned a few fox hounds and at night we would go out in the woods, build a bonfire, and listen to the hounds chase the fox. Our favorite spot for this was on top of the bluffs on our farm where the huckleberry bushes grew. The reason I mention the huckleberry bushes because it was very unusual to find them growing in Kentucky. They are found primarily in the high country of the Northwest. The fox would lead the dogs on a wide circle. We always said that the fox would make a circle around the Temple View Church, which is about five miles away, before he would start back.

While the dogs could not be heard, we would tell stories. Essie was a great story teller, since he had older brothers that passed along many stories about the birds and the bees. I must say that my brother and I learned a lot about the facts of life from him.

Essie had many talents of which being an expert marksman was one of them. In those days, most boys used a single shot .22 caliber rifle for hunting and target practice. I can recall a group of us boys sitting under the big Sycamore tree doing some target practice with our .22 rifles. We would take some country matches and break off most of the wood and stick the match in a bullet hole with the match head pointing forward. If someone were able to place a perfect shot and actually hit the match head, it would light up. Essie could hit the match head most every time.

Another talent that Essie was believed to have was that he could throw a stone straighter and farther than anyone else in Butler County. There is a place upon Pea Ridge Road, known as the Buzzard Bluff. It is very high above the Green River, perhaps three or four hundred feet, and overlooks the river and the land on the other side. It was a beautiful spot, which made it a perfect Sunday gathering place for young people. Being boys we all loved to throw rocks. Essie, with his great throwing arm, could throw a stone all the way over the river to the land on the other side. I have always believed that he could have been a great baseball pitcher had he had the opportunity. It's always been my thought that he could have made our star pitchers look like a bunch of neophytes.

Essie was a veteran of World War II and was a member of the 82nd Airborne Division which took part in the D-Day invasion at Normandy. While in the service of his country, Essie received many accolades for his marksmanship. He was awarded the Purple Heart with one oak leaf cluster, and several other metals of valor. As a boy growing up together, I was always proud to call him my friend. I'm sure that Butler County is proud to have him as a native son. However, this should not come as a big surprise, Butler County has always stood for freedom and love for America.

29

THE FACTORY OF DREAMS

If you are like me, you must wonder where all those dreams come from. Both nighttime and daytime dreaming, if we put them both together, there are so many of them. There is no end to the hypothesis of sleep dreaming, they go on forever. It appears that researchers have not been able to reach a conclusion about the mysterious world of dreams. Some researchers believe that dreams are a rehash of what one has been thinking about recently.

My experience with dreams appears to be quite the opposite. For instance, I have had many dreams where I have lost my car. Sometimes it is lost in the parking lot, and I think I have located it a few rows over, so I struggle to get over there, and it turns out not to be mine. More recently I dreamed that my car was lost, and the location was in an area where the land was rolling and hilly, similar to Butler County. I could see my car sitting on a hilltop faraway and I struggled to get over there. It was one of those slow motion dreams. By the time I reached the hill I was exhausted. There I found it was my car, down to the last detail, however, it was a toy sized being about 12 inches long.

I have had many cars in my lifetime, but never ever lost one. I have been told that my dreams about losing my cars is associated with insecurity. That could come from my childhood experiences growing up on Long Branch School Road, in the days of the Great Depression. Maybe the logic for this is that, although I may not be able to detect it, my subconscious mind still remembers the stress and problems associated with those days.

Another one of my dreams, one that got me in trouble, was a war dream. In the dream I had been captured by the enemy, and they were stripping me of my belongings. They were having trouble getting my rings off my fingers so one of them said, "Get me a knife. I will cut his fingers off." Somehow, I managed to break free and run, and they were chasing me. I ran into a small building, turned around, and grabbed the top frame of the door, and kicked out at them with both feet. I must have kicked very hard, because I kicked my wife Ruth out of the bed. That incident came close to destroying a very beautiful and solid relationship.

People who know me know I don't like to fly. In fact, I avoid it like the plague. In another dream, I was not just in a plane, but flying it as well. It was pitch dark so I was unable to see anything. Despite these circumstances, I am assured by someone that it would be light when we reached our destination, and I would have no trouble landing the plane. Great comfort for a person who had never been in the cockpit of a plane before.

I have been more successful with daydreams as I feel that they are more important to our lives. We have always heard that necessity is the mother of inventions. However, dreams have played a very important role in that field. They are our everyday thoughts and present a picture of our hopes and aspirations. There are two types of daydreams, the rusty ones, and the bright shiny ones. The bright ones are the ones to pursue. They are bright and polished because we keep thinking about them, and if we follow them, we hope they will be our pathway to success and happiness.

There is no question about how important daydreams are. Americans who have worked diligently to make their dreams come true have not only helped themselves, but have made America great. We who have lived here in America are fortunate indeed. We have been able to think and dream for ourselves. At this point in history, America's traditional values are changing. I hope we don't reach the point where someone else does our thinking and dreaming for us.

30

FALLING OF THE DEW

One of the most interesting and instructive phenomenon in nature is the falling of the dew. This miracle begins with the setting of the sun and goes on mysteriously, collecting and distributing its water jewels all through the stillness of the night, only to be dispelled again by the rising of the sun.

The process of the falling of the dew is easy to explain. It is really one of the most important factors in the laws of nature. Dew is actually a deposit of water from the atmosphere on to the face of the Earth and is formed when the Earth is sufficiently cooled down during the night. On a warm sunny day, lots of vapor and mist is suspended in the air, and if the temperature at sunset falls below the dew point, that vapor can no longer be retained in suspension and falls back to the Earth. Only warm air can suspend mist and vapor, and it is known as humidity. This is why we sometimes complain more on hot summer days about the humidity than about the heat.

Growing up in the Long Branch community of Butler County, I have been subjected to a monumental amount of dew in my life. Having lived in six states, and at least a dozen locations, it appears to me that our old home place was the largest producer of dew. I'm not sure, but altitude may have some effect on the amount of moisture in the air, which of course would affect the amount of dew. The elevation in and around the Long Branch area is approximately 400 feet above sea level, which is rather low.

Besides the amazing miracle in which dew is formed, there are other interesting aspects that we should consider. One is the sparkling display of beauty we can find in the early morning hours when the sun shines through the millions of beads, bubbles, and drops of dew. Every particle of plant life and vegetation, sparkles and twinkles in the morning sunshine. The smallest blade of grass has not been overlooked by the Dew Fairy, and even the dew-covered spider web is worthy of consideration. It is possible that there is nothing more beautiful than a red rose with sparkling beads of dew clinging to its petals.

If we take time to study the dew drop, we will find that each tiny drop of dew is itself a miniature mirror, for upon each clear and crystal surface it portrays some nearby object. Of course the picture is naturally inverted, but you will it find in it a bit of blue sky, and scraps of fleecy clouds, and many other things caught and mirrored in the dew drop.

Some things that happen in life linger in your memory unchanged. I can still recall the fragrance of the dew at twilight time, while running up and down the Long Branch School Road. This was necessary at times to bring the stock back to the barn, or to meet my dad and help him carry the things he had purchased in Morgantown. The fragrant smell was very pleasant and unique. I always believed that it came from two things: the added moisture the dew was dropping on the earth, and the refreshment it provided for the grass, wild flowers, and other vegetation that grew in the area. It must be a very pleasant fragrance as I have noticed that many of the cosmetic companies have tried to imitate it in their perfume products.

Dew is distilled without means to prevent it. No one can cancel it - not kings, presidents, or ruthless dictators. Nature in all her moods, and they are many, is interesting, and instructive, perhaps one of its greatest marvels that takes place in the silence of the night, is the falling of the dew.

31

FLOOD WATERS OF 1937

"Into each life some rain must fall", these are words written by Henry Wadsworth Longfellow in his poem titled, "Some Days Are Dark and Dreary". Yes, Henry, we understand that rain is an essential product of life. What we don't understand is why on certain occasions we receive a three month supply in just three or four days.

This is what happened in the first weeks of January 1937. In and around the Ohio River Valley, it was a torrential downpour that produced flooding conditions from Pittsburgh, Penn., to Cairo, Illinois. The Ohio River crested at an all-time high of 85.44 feet at Louisville. I understand that the next highest water mark was set in 1945 when the Ohio River crested at 74.40 feet at Louisville. All other rivers in and around Louisville, the Salt River, Rolling Fork, and the Rough River, all set record high water marks. Seventy percent of Louisville was submerged, 175,000 residents had to be evacuated. Estimated cost was set at $250,000,000 (3.3 billion in current dollars).

However, the Ohio River and its tributaries were far from finished with their ravishing and destructive forces. South Western Kentucky was in the path of this raging water. The Kentucky River flooded Frankfort, and the Barren River flooded parts of Bowling Green. As far as I can tell, the Green River at Morgantown was at an all-time high. I say this because it was the first and only time our little house, there in the sharp curve on Long Branch

School Road, ever become flooded. Backwaters in this area were a very common thing and we would have two or three each season. But before this one came along, the largest ones would stop before they got to our front yard.

As I recall, it was mid-morning, the backwater was under the house and needed to rise a couple more inches before it got inside. The water had been at this level for a day or so. Everyone was of the opinion that it had stopped rising and would start receding soon. However, those hopes were dashed when it started to rain. It was everything but a nice gentle rain. It was such a deluge of water, I feel certain Noah would have been impressed. With all the streams overflowing their banks, and adding a monumental amount of water to what was already there, water soon started coming into the house. After piling as many of our belonging as possible above what we thought was safe from the water, we departed out the back door, and waded to the high ground. We went around the hill to the home of Aunt Laura and Uncle Will Childers, who took us in and gave us shelter for a few days until the water receded. When we returned, the water marks indicated that water had been three to four inches deep inside the house, and resulted in a small amount of damage to the furniture. In time, the water receded, and my brother and I went up on the hill and found some dry wood and built a fire in the big barrel stove. In a few days ever-thing was dry, and life was back to normal.

I checked the water marks along our road. The recent 2010 flood appeared to be two or three feet below the 1937 high water mark. I found being forced from your home to be a very overwhelming experience that I was never able to forget about. When I got older, I purchased a used car that had been in the flood, which I didn't know about until sand and dust started sifting out from the side panels and other parts of the interior. A constant reminder of the devastating 1937 flood waters.

32

FOLKLORE OF THE APPALACHIAN MOUNTAINS

Folklore consist of legends, music, old stories, proverbs, beliefs, and customs. Tradition, and culture play a large role in the folklore society. Since the Appalachian Mountains are considered to be the birth place of American folklore, it's only natural that Butler County people would have a strong culture of folklore.

One common folklore centers around the way to forecast and predict the weather. At the end of September with shorter days, the falling of the leaves and long shadows, we know that winter isn't far away. Of course, we all become concerned as to how severe the coming winter will be. To find the answer, some folks check the thickness on onion skins and corn husks. Others read the Farmer's Almanac, an annual periodical that has been in continuous publication since 1818 and is still very popular with farmers and gardeners. The company continues to sell four million copies per year.

However, it would appear that the most famous weather predictor of them all is the woolly worm (sometimes spelled wooly worm). This worm is so famous and respected that the town of Banner Elk, North Carolina, has a woolly worm festival each year in mid-October that draws thousands of people from all over the country.

To determine what the coming winter has in store for us, we must look at the colors on the back of the woolly worm. These colors are orange and black. If the orange bands are large, and the black bands are small, that indicates that the coming winter will be mild. If the black bands are large, and the orange bands are small, that indicates that the winter will be harsh.

Are the woolly worm bands really an accurate way to predict the weather? Dr. C. H. Curran, former curator of insects at the American Museum of Natural History in New York City, tested the wooly worm accuracy in the 1950s. He found an 80 percent accuracy rate for the woolly worm.

I'm not surprised at Dr. Curran's findings. The woolly worm is very sophisticated. They are actually a caterpillar, or the larva of the Isabella Moth, which appears in the spring, and displays many beautiful colors. These woolly creatures may look small, but their body contains thirteen segments, with three sets of legs. They survive the winter months by finding shelter under leaves, rocks, and logs, and generate their own antifreeze to keep from freezing.

When I was growing up on Long Branch School Road, there was no shortage of woolly worms. They were something us children would play with. I recall how they would curl up in a ball if they were handled a little too roughly. This is a method they use to defend themselves.

This year as the days become shorter and the shadows become longer, I would like to suggest that you look around your place and find a woolly worm. Take a look at the orange and black colors on his back, and let me know if this coming winter will be harsh or mild.

33

FOOTPRINTS IN THE SAND

The Long Branch School Road had the reputation of being either muddy or dusty at all times. However, there was one spot just after reaching the top of the hill, and just before it connects with the Leonard Oak Road, a stretch of about 200 yards long, that was filled with beautiful white sand. And as everyone knows, in the early days, all children in Butler County went barefoot in the summer months. My brother, Otis, and I were able to recognize each other's footprints and could tell where the other one was by the direction in which the prints were going. Sort of a forerunner of today's GPS system.

As we journey through life, each of us leaves our footprints. One is when we visit the ocean and walk barefoot in the sand. Our feet leave beautiful impressions in the wet sand that will remain for a short time before the waves wash them away. The other is our footprints in the sands of life, which will last much longer. Whether they be large or small, they are a blueprint of our lives, what our accomplishments were, the impact that our lives made on other people and the world. Sort of a posthumous award by our peers after our life here on Earth is over, but they are still subject to be review by the Heavenly Father.

These prints vary in size, some will be large, but the majority of us regular people will leave small prints. Just because they are small doesn't mean that the person did not lead a positive and beneficial life. That someone loved, was loved, and had a kind heart and soul that made the world a better place by the many kind and chartable deeds that they accomplished, is more than enough.

Many people leave large prints. It appears that in some instances, God has seen fit to bestow upon certain people a special gift, an extra talent of some kind. For someone that fits that category, we need to look no farther than the state of Tennessee, our neighbor to the south, and consider the accomplishments of Dolly Parton, a child that was no stranger to poverty, but today is recognized around the world. She will certainly leave a large footprint in the sands of life.

Mother Teresa is another example. She earned the Nobel Peace prize in 1976 for her selfless ministering to the poor, sick, orphaned, and the dying, for over 45 years. Although she was sharply criticized by some, the footprints she left behind are monumental.

There are many other gifted people in the fields of engineering, medicine, and science, just to name a few, that have contributed greatly to our present way of life. Chances are good that they will continue to do so in the future, and leave large footprints in the sands of life. These people have, and will continue to be an asset to humanity as long as they are able to control their celebrity.

It's a forgoing conclusion that most human beings are ambitious, and would like to be remembered by leaving as big a footprint as possible. There is nothing wrong with that, in fact, it is considered to be an asset when people do honest work and show a desire to attain wealth and respect. Those ethics are what made America a great nation. What makes it so distasteful is the method some people use to reach fame and fortune. We see them every day peddling their lies and deception, in order to promote themselves. It would be wise not to follow their advice. They leave behind a carnage of broken dreams and destroyed lives. It's reasonable to believe that when they stand before their maker, their large footprints will be reduced in size to that of a new born baby.

34

GASOLINE PUMPS

The first pump that resembled a gas pump was invented and sold by Mr. Sylvanus Bowser in 1885. The pump was not used to fill up automobiles as they were not invented at that time. Instead, it was used to fill up kerosene lamps and stoves. Later when the automobile was invented, he improved the pump by adding a hose, and gravity would let gas flow directly into the gas tank.

Gas dispensers and gas stations, as they are called today, have gone through many changes in last 90 years. In the 1920s the visible pump was created. It was very tall with a transparent glass tank on the top. The tank was graduated with numbers from one to 10 gallons. So the customer could see how many gallons were being dispensed. The gas was also colored so you could tell what grade it was. To the best of my memory, there was only two grades, regular, and ethyl.

By 1930, the visible tanks were gone, but in many instances the glass bowls on top of the pumps remained for advertising purposes, slogans, such as, "super" "deluxe" "superior" and many others. It was also a time when the measuring system changed to the clock system. This method dispensed gallons by weight. In the '50s there was the rolling ball that indicated the amount of gas that was dispensed. This system was later replaced with digital display number system, which is in use today.

When I was small, I recall seeing my dad put gas in his little overland car from one of those pumps with the transparent tank on the top. I remember watching someone work the pump handle to pump the gas into the glass tank. The gas had a light orange color, and to the best of my memory, three gallons were dispensed into the car by the gravity flow hose. I believe this happened at the Ally Childers grocery store, which was about four miles from Morgantown. This was before the bridge was built, and the ferry boat was in operation. It was called the Morgantown Road at that time, now it is known as Highway 1328.

Gas prices are so high these days they causes us to think that we may have to take out a second mortgage on the home place. It's hard to believe but back in the 1960s, while traveling for work, I recall many times having my tank filled for just 19 cents per gallon. With each fill-up I received S&H green stamps as a bonus. We don't see S&H green stamps any more, but I have a soft spot in my heart for them. My first set of golf clubs were a gift from the green stamp people. Under the present circumstances, it's difficult to visualize gas prices declining any time soon.

Did you know that in the early days when kerosene was widely used in our country, and gasoline was a by-product of the kerosene refining process, gasoline was considered absolutely useless and was disposed of by burning? In addition to gas being overpriced, we have to stand out in the heat, rain and snow and pump our own. There are only two states that have a law against pumping your own gas: New Jersey and Oregon. I might consider moving to Oregon, but never New Jersey.

35

THE GIRLIE SMITH I KNEW

I can recall very vividly the first time I met Girlie Smith. I was about 14 years old, and Girlie, I would estimate, was 35 or 36. He was in the process of building the new Girlie Smith Hotel, there on the corner of what was known at that time as Dog Walk Street in Morgantown. That Saturday, the street was partially closed with workmen mixing cement with shovels and transporting it in wheelbarrows to where it was needed. My brother Otis was manning one of the wheelbarrows. Girlie was supervising the project, and also helping with the work.

While this was all going on, a well-dressed gentleman arrived and asked to have a conversation with Mr. Smith. The visitor appeared to be a salesman that was interested in selling a product for the new hotel. They had their conversation near where I was standing. I paid close attention to what was happening between them. It was a business deal, and at that early age, I was already interested in becoming a business man. I paid particular attention to the way he treated the sales person. He was very polite to him and listened intently to what he had to say. If we hope to be successful in business, we must learn to respect the other person's opinion. It appeared that Girlie was aware of that. I can recall thinking what a nice man he was.

Sometime later, I got to know him better when he ask me if I would like to come and work for him. He had purchased a farm down the river near

Eden. His mother Vianna was living there. She was getting along in years, and needed some help with the farm animals and other chores associated with the farm. Of course, I was grateful, and started working immediately.

Miss Vianna was a very nice lady, and we got along very well. However, transportation in those days was very limited. Getting back and forth to the farm on weekends presented a problem. I don't see it anymore, but there must have been some type of a road running northwest out of Morgantown down the Green River, because Girlie would drive me down that way a few miles, drop me off, then I would walk across some farm land to the river and use a small boat to cross over to the farm.

I remember one time when Girlie was busy, and we didn't get started until it was dark. He was concerned about my safety, but I assured him that it was no problem, that I could handle the situation. It was a fact, that a few days earlier, a farmer had been gored to death by a large bull in or near that location. It was reasonably dark, but I was able to follow the tree lines as a guide. All of a sudden, the loud bellowing of a bull erupted, it appeared to be in front of me, and very close. I was sure that it was the killer bull. So I turned left and ran as fast as possible. That is, until I bumped into a fence. In my frightened condition, I was sure that I could feel the hot breath of that big, sharp, horned animal just a few feet in back of me. Without hesitation, I scaled that fence and came down on the other side. The amazing thing about this is, that the next time I passed through that area and looked at the fence, it looked impossible that anyone would be able to climb over it. Leads one to believe that nothing is impossible with the right motivation. It was an experience that I will never forget.

During his lifetime Girlie Smith did so many things to improve the lives of people in Morgantown and Butler County, and will always be remembered for his generosity. But his life had not been easy and like the rest of us growing up in poverty, he had few advantages. His father passed away when he was only 10 and his mother and her family provided food and shelter only until he was old enough to care for himself. To make ends meet he worked at several jobs, farming, mining coal, and making railroad ties.

Regardless of his beginnings, Girlie was not going to let that stop him. With his strong will and determination, he is living proof that success is attainable if we pursue it with vigor. In additional to the owning the Girlie

Smith Hotel, at one time in the early '30s, with the help of his mother and wife, he operated a restaurant in Morgantown on Dog Walk Street.

I understand that he was a very independent person, and when things became difficult, and help was needed, his first thought was to look on the end of his arms. It was a philosophy he followed throughout his life: I will help you, but first you must be willing to help yourself.

Of course being a business man he was always having to make decisions. However, I believe that the best decision that he ever made was when he decided to marry Dewey Mae Ingram, a very beautiful, kind and caring lady. I feel certain that she contributed greatly to Girlie's success. It's a fact, no question about it, woman is God's gift to man.

36

GOLFERS' LAMENT

The game of golf has been around for many years. History indicates that some type of golf was played as far back as the 12th century. However, golf as we know it today, played over an 18 hole course, clearly originated in Scotland in the middle ages, but didn't become popular until the late 19th century.

There are those who are addicted, and those who think that chasing a little white ball over 50 acres is absolutely ridiculous. I have always loved the game. When I'm on that green fairway, and hit a long drive right down the middle, the accomplishment and the beautiful surroundings make me think I have found a touch of heaven here on Earth.

In my lifetime, Ruth and I had two homes that were situated on a golf course. In Pawley's Island, South Carolina we overlooked the 11th tee. When we lived in Venice, Florida, our condo overlooked the 3rd green which was surrounded on three sides with sand traps. Watching the players struggle to get the ball in the cup prompted me to write this poem.

> At twilight time we see you there
> So silent, peaceful, and serene.
> Your flag so limp, your grass so green

Just hours ago this was not then seen.
In shorts and hats and color schemes
They tried their best to reach the green.

The sand so white, its beacon call
Come rest with me you wayward ball.

As sand would fly toward the sky
Aloud! We hear them wonder why
For in the sand the ball will lie.

For this time they have all gone away
Their shadows fading with the day.
They seek someone so they can tell
Of shots they made, and putts that failed.

So slumber softly through the night
They'll all be back at dawn's first light
To walk your fairways and test your might.

But you need not fear my mystic friend
They missed the green, you've won again.

Winston Churchill was a man of courage, fortitude, and strong convictions. He was also known for his quick wit. He played some golf when he was a teenager but felt that golf required too much precision for him. Polo suited him better as it had a larger ball and a big mallet to smack it with. He once said about golf. "Golf is a game the aim of which is to hit a small ball into even a smaller hole with weapons singularly ill-designed for the purpose." We must remember that Winston never used an oversized driver. His wit showed through when he was having a conservation with the very famous and talented Lady Astor of Great Britain. She said to Winston, "If you were my husband I would put poison in your tea." Winston replied, "Madam, if you were my wife I would drink it."

37

GRANDPA MARTIN REMEMBERED

My grandfather, Vander Wright Martin, was a native of Butler County and lived there all his life. He was born October 14th, 1870, died August 26th, 1954. He was the son of John Marion Martin, born February 22nd, 1848, died June 11th, 1911, and Malissa Renfrow, born January 15th, 1845, died April 19th, 1896.

In October, 1889, Grandpa married Mary Ellen West. Mary Ellen was born January 26th, 1869, and died March 10th, 1910 at the young age of 41 years. Of course, I never knew my grandmother, as she died 10 years before I was born. From what I was told, she appeared to be a very remarkable woman. She and grandpa had five children: Leora, James, Eva, Odell, and Clifford.

In the beginning, when the children were small, and grandmother was still alive, the family lived in a log house that was located on the upper reaches of Bull Creek in the village of Martindale. It was located across the creek from a small country store. I have no information as to who the previous store owners were, most likely it was someone from the Martin family as they were the major part of the population at that time. When I was small it was owned and operated by Charlie Shepherd and his family. I believe it was the same building that housed the Martindale Post Office in the early days before it was closed.

Several years after grandmother passed away and the children were older, grandpa built a houseboat on Green River, and the family lived on the boat for several years. After the children were grown, grandpa returned to the log house in Martindale. It was during this part of his life that us children got to know him. His physical features were great. He was something over six feet tall, with broad shoulders and a slim waist. He had a monumental appetite but never had an ounce of fat on his body. One of his biggest complaints was that he was not getting enough food. I recall visiting him in the nursing home, and the first thing he said, "Can you get me out of here? They are starving me to death." He thought that breakfast should consist of two big slices of country ham, two or three eggs, three or four biscuits, and a generous helping of bulldog gravy.

Due to the fact that he was alone, he lived at our place part of the time. Us kids liked him, we found him amiable and entertaining. He would play the violin for us, he could play all types off musical instruments, and would tell us stories of some of his life experiences. One story was about how he had a confrontation with some fellow, and the guy pulled a revolver from his pocket and pointed it at him. Grandpa explained how frightened he was, said he could see the lead bullets and the cylinder turning. At the last moment the man changed his mind and put the gun away.

It was rumored that he was a little wild in his younger days and would nip the bottle a little too much. However, later in life he put all that behind him and become a Christian. I can still see him at the dinner table blessing the food. He would always say the Lord's Prayer. Now days, when my family gets together around the dinner table, we will say the Lord's Prayer in memory of Grandpa Martin.

38

GREAT FISHING EXPERIENCE

Everyone is familiar with fish stories. The more they are told the bigger they get, especially the ones that got away. In my boyhood years, fishing was a way of life. It was a very important way to supplement the food supply for struggling families in the early days of Butler County, especially us folks that lived on the north side. Without fish, chances are good that we would not have survived.

The beautiful and historic Green River was just about a mile and a half from our place. There were several methods used for fishing its waters. Trotlines were the most popular, everyone used them at one time or another. I recall one story about a fellow that was running his trotline. To do this you use a boat and propel yourself across the river by the trotline itself. As you go, the line rises to the top of the water, and you take the fish off that have hooked themselves to the line. The story is, that when this fellow got out near the middle of the river, the line got heavy, and he was having trouble pulling it up. When he did this large catfish floated up alongside his boat. Now most fishing boats were small in those days, about 10 or 12 feet long, and the fisherman swore that the fish was as long as his boat. While he was contemplating what to do, the big fish must have decided that it had enough and made a dash up the river taking the boat along, and destroying the trotline in the process. I must admit that I never had an opportunity to speak to him personally or knew anyone that did. The story was always second hand, which may have something to do with the size of that fish.

When I was growing up there on Long Branch School Road, it was perceived by everyone I knew, and perhaps everyone in the county, that fish would only bite when the weather was warm, starting in the month of April. Makes one wonder how fish could live all winter without eating. I don't believe that we ever heard about northern people fishing through the ice. If we had, we would not have believed it.

To prove my point, I'll tell you a true story about catching fish. It began about the first day of March. The weather was reasonably warm. On the 2nd, I asked my dad about going to Welch's Creek fishing. I was turned down, his answer was it was much too early for fish to bite. On the 3rd, I begged him again and he finally agreed to go. We took the kerosene lantern, and the rest of the family, and arrived at the Horseshoe Bend, one of our favorite fishing spots. Mom and Dad got their lines in the water first as my brother and I were still working on our fishing poles. Mom and Dad's lines had barely hit the water when they both pull out a couple of nice yellow bellied catfish. My brother and I were standing in back of them so they ask if we would remove the fish and re-bait their hooks. Within moments of their lines entering the water they hook more fish. Amazingly this went on for about an hour until my dad looked at the amount of fish piled on the bank. He then decided that we had better quit, as we already had more fish than we could handle. Everyone that was big enough to carry fish was detailed to carry some. We counted them when we got back to the house, and the total catch was 69. My brother and I didn't get to catch any of them, but the job of dressing them was assigned to us. We ate fish every day for a week. From that point forward, March wasn't too early to go fishing.

It was an experience I never forgot. Over the many years I was away I would always write my parents a letter that would arrive as close to March 3rd as possible to remind them of that great fishing experience.

39

GUARDIAN ANGEL

Almost every day, I think about my early life growing up on Long Branch School Road. As I look back and ponder the memories of those trying times, I'm surprised that I was able to survive. My teenage life from age 10 to 20 years was pretty well taken up by the Great Depression. Hard economic times have a tendency to generate a hostile environment. I sometimes felt that living there at that particular time in history presented some degree of danger. Perhaps this was due in part to the moonshine that was being produced in the area. Since it was readily available, some people would over indulge, which caused them to become depressed, and at times they would do things that they normally wouldn't do.

However, it's safe to say that this danger paled in the face of what teenage boys will do when their parents are not looking. Most boys love to swim, and once my brother and I learned to do so, we thought it was the most pleasant thing in life. In the summer months we made great use of the deep water holes in the Long Branch and the many other branches that were available. Of course, in the hot summer months of July and August, the small streams dry up and the deep holes were the only places where water remained. After a period of time the deep holes would become stagnated, and turn into a breeding ground for mosquitoes. Due to our lack of knowledge, my brother and I would continue to swim in this polluted water and consequently, we both developed typhoid fever. In the early days with limited medical resources, this sickness took many lives. It was touch and go for several weeks, however, by some miracle we both survived.

As we grew a little older, the Green River become a favorite swimming place. Anyone who has lived in the area knows this beautiful river, and is familiar with its moods. In its normal state it is inviting, gentle and placid. However, with the proper amount of rain it can overflow its banks and become a wild and raging river, flowing at great speed, and carrying with it a large amount of debris as it races toward its final destination, the Ohio River. For some reason, which will never be explained, my brother and I, along with some of our friends, would challenge this wild water by swimming out toward the center, and let the fast current carry us down stream for a mile or so. At that time I can recall how exciting it was. Looking back it's hard to believe that anyone would put their life at risk by doing such a dangerous thing.

Other dangers that were always prevalent were avoiding being bit by a poisonous snake, falling from the top of a tree, and wandering around in the middle of the night without any light. I'm grateful that I was able to survive all those dangerous possibilities. Some people would call it luck. I'm inclined to believe that it was a higher power that was looking after us boys.

Over my adult years, whether it be in peace or war, I'm very certain that my guardian angel has always been there to protect me. If you were born on Sunday like me, our guardian angel is Saint Michael. His latest help came when I bumped into a car in Walmart parking lot. My insurance company was very unhappy and increased my insurance $520 per year. I checked with several other companies, with no success. I was about to write the check to my old company when the phone rang. The caller said, "My name is Amy. I'm with State Farm Insurance. Can I help you with your insurance?" She did help. Provided the same coverage, less than $520.

Thank you, Saint Michael.

40

HANDS OF LOVE

Our hands are nothing short of a miracle. They make us independent, and sustain us in our lives by giving us the ability to perform thousands of everyday tasks. How difficult it must be for those people who have to go through life without them. All hands are not the same. In fact no one else has a hand exactly like yours. This is a proven fact, since identical twins have different finger prints.

In most cases, what our hands do is dictated by our heart. Recently I read a short story about a granddaughter that went to visit her aging grandmother who had just recently been placed in a nursing home. "Nice you've come," her grandmother whispered weakly from her bed. The granddaughter noticed that her complexion looked pasty in the morning light, and her colorless hair looked wispy against her pillow, and how her hands lay limp on the white sheets. Hands that had spent a lifetime helping others. After a small conversation, and feeling awkward and helpless, not knowing what to do or say, the granddaughter put her hands in her coat pocket and said, "See you soon, Grandma."

A few days later, the granddaughter had to go to the doctor for a routine treatment, and had taken her three-year old son with her. While they were waiting, her son stood wide-mouthed with fear and concern. Then he took her hand and held it quietly in his two small ones. This caused her heart to be flooded with warmth and thankfulness. And with her little boy still holding her hand, she knew exactly what she was going to do the very next time she visited her grandmother.

It is said that mothers' and grandmothers' hands harbor and display the greatest love on Earth. Every mother's hands tell a story. They are the hands that cradled us when we were small, they comfort us when we fall and skin our knees, and most of all, they soothe the inside hurts that no one else can see. Over the years mothers' hands become weak and frail. We must remember that they are the same hands that peeled the potatoes, baked the bread, gathered the eggs, and churned the butter. They deserve our respect. At this time in their lives, they need you to hold their hands.

Two people in love, mothers and fathers holding the hands of their children, are the ones we see most often. There is something about holding hands that is difficult to explain. It would appear that it generates some kind of an electromagnetic field that stimulates the heart and makes it warm and cuddly. The struggles in life are many, and most of us are aware of someone, either friend or family, that is in need of some additional courage and inspiration. Holding their hand will help them through this difficult time, your rewards will be many, and God will bless you for your kindness.

41

HORSE AND SADDLE

If we look backward, it hasn't been long since the horse and saddle was the primary mode of transportation for most Americans. Horses haven't changed much in the last 400 years. The Spanish explorer Hernando De Soto, is credited with bringing horses to America in the year of 1540, while he was searching for the golden city. History indicates that there were 750 people, and 237 horses, and other livestock in his party.

It's been said that dog is man's best friend. Where this may be true, most people agree that America was built on the back of a horse. If you have a horse you will need a saddle. The earliest saddle like equipment dates back as early as 700 BC and was made from fringed cloth and padding. From the earliest times, saddles become a status symbol to show off individual wealth by adding elaborate stitching, fine leather, gold and silver metal work. This is much like the way we show off expensive automobiles today.

I wanted to give you this tad of history before I told you about my grandmother Lillie Napier Oller. My grandfather, George Oller, passed away early in life, leaving my grandmother to raise her two daughters alone. They lived in the two bedroom log house on the north end of Long Branch School Road, near Welch's Creek. Grandma was of pioneer stock—fearlessly independent, with an iron will. She felt that she could accomplish just about anything on her own. Like everyone else with the means to do so, she had a horse and saddle, which she used for transportation. In the early days when roads were mostly muddy trails, a horse and saddle was very much a necessity. I can remember seeing her horse which was a large gray mare, perhaps 15 or 16 hands tall. I'm not sure what her name was, although something makes me think Grandmother called her Penny.

Times were hard in the early 1920s, and due to cost, not everyone that had a horse necessarily had a saddle. At times, it wasn't unusual to borrow a saddle from one of your neighbors. As I remember the story, my parents borrowed Grandmother's saddle and for some reason failed to return it. When all of Grandmother's efforts failed to get it returned, she asked the sheriff to stop by our house and instruct my dad and mom to return it. Over the years I have thought about this story often. It's difficult to understand why my parents would do such a thing, to deprive a widow lady, and family member, of her only means of transportation. My mom and dad were both generous and caring people. They ever explained their reasoning for what happened, perhaps they felt too embarrassed to discuss it.

The mystery of the saddle still lingers to this day. My dad and grandmother never warmed up to each as long as they lived. At this late date, the mystery of how and why it happened will never be resolved.

Some years later my grandmother's horse become frightened by a snake in the road, and she received a serious back injury when she was thrown from her horse. Due to the lack of proper medical attention, my grandmother walked with a stoop for the rest of her life.

42

IN MEMORY

As Christmas approached in the year of 1944, the war in Europe had progressed to the point where the American forces were about to enter German soil. In a few places they had already done so, such as on the border of Germany and Belgium just in front of the Siegfried line. There was a pause in the ground war at that time, however, bombing raids over Germany had been accelerated. Almost everyone believed that Germany was defeated, and it was just a matter of time until it would surrender. However, Adolf Hitler had a much different plan. He was secretly assembling 21 divisions, an army of one million men. His plan was to make a surprise attack through the Ardennes Forest in Belgium and destroy the American forces. It was certainly a surprise to the Allied forces. Most military men thought that attacking through the Ardennes was impossible, especially in the winter months.

On December 16th, 1944 at approximately 5:30 a.m. following a heavy artillery barrage, the German Panzer and infantry division started pouring through that thinly defended American line on a 90-mile front. The Battle of the Bulge was underway. It was the greatest land battle American troops ever fought. The American forces were greatly out numbered. Many American troops were soon surrounded and captured. Atrocities were high as captured American soldiers were brutally murdered.

Much to the surprise of the German army, bravery was the standard, not the exception with the American soldiers. Some holding their position to the last man, the Americans inflicted heavy causalities on the enemy and slowed their advance for two days. American causalities were 76,890 killed and wounded. The German army lost 81,834, killed and wounded.

As in any war, there are many heart breaking stories associated with battle. The following is a true story told by his nephew, Tim Bartholomew, about his uncle, Private First Class John Edwards Gibbons. John was a member of the 99th Infantry Division. He had survived the Battle of the Bulge, only to lose his life to a land mine shortly after crossing the Rhine River in Germany. The war was almost over when he died on April 16, 1945 as it had ended on May 8th, 1945. Tim was born in 1958, so he never knew his uncle. Tim's mother would tell him stories about the early days of his uncle's childhood, but he would never have the opportunity to know his Uncle John on a personal basis. When his mother would talk about her brother, tears would flow before she finished what she was saying, and she would on occasions mention that the memories of him were stored in the attic.

Attics have always been the place where we keep sentimental things, such as babies' first shoes, wedding dresses, and many other keepsake items. When Tim was about 10 years old, he decided to explore the attic and see what he could find out about his Uncle John. To Tim, the attic was a mysterious, almost magical place; unfinished, with one dim light bulb, and a streaked old window, the glass slightly wavy from age. The window and the lightbulb provided barely enough light to navigate through the wood and cardboard boxes. The boxes seemed to have been there since the dawn of time. In these the boxes, Tim found many personal items that had belonged to his uncle, such as a toy trains that he had played with when he was about Tim's age, his high school letter sweater from the class of '44, and his baseball glove, which still smelled from neatsfoot oil. In another box he found the V-mail letters that he had sent to his family and the neatly folded American flag that had accompanied his casket on the way home.

Regardless of the environment, where danger and death are always near, soldiers usually pretend that there is nothing to worry about. That they are doing fine, and that they will be home in a very short time. This is to try and keep their family from worrying about them. Tim's mother would often mention that his uncle was an outstanding baseball player in high school, and he helped his team win the championship when playing baseball in the Army. Matter of fact, a scout for a major baseball team had asked Private Gibbons to contact him when his military service was over.

It was difficult for Tim's mother to talk about her brother. Because of her grief, the depth of which after 50 years still surprised him, she could say only a few words before the tears would flow. The remark she made most often about her brother was, "He was a wonderful person," or "I hope you never have to know what it feels like to lose someone so close to you."

One Memorial Day, Tim was alone when he visited his uncle's grave, roughly 50 years after his death. A solitary visitor had arrived before him. He was not a family member, or anyone he knew. As he approached the grave, Tim asked, "Did you know Private Gibbons?" and motioned to his uncle's headstone. "I knew him very well," answered the visitor. "He died in my arms." The visitor told him many things about his uncle that he did not know. "A wonderful kid, the kind of a person that people gravitate to." Tim closed his eyes and could visualize a man, a boy really, just 19 years old, far from home, afraid for sure, trying to survive in the midst of trauma, chaos, and tragedy of war. But Tim nor anyone else will never know what his Uncle John might have accomplished had he lived. Would he have made it in to the Cooperstown Baseball Hall of Fame? Would they have had a great uncle-nephew relationship? These thoughts will never be answered.

War has touched every town and community in America. Many of our young people have died, the loss is staggering. Not to mention the grief inflicted on their families and loved ones. Words are inadequate to describe the pain and sorrow they feel. Let's not forget the men like Private Gibbons, and many others with visible wounds, and those who live with invisible wounds, that have paid for America's freedom for over 200 years. Each Veteran's Day, we should all renew our appreciation for the brave men and women that have, and are still, defending our country.

43

INDIAN HERITAGE

"By the shores of Gitche Gumee, By the Shining Big Sea Waters, Stood the wigwam of Nokomas, Daughter of the Moon Nokomas." This is from a poem written by Henry Wadsworth Longfellow in 1855. Based on the legend of the Ojibwa Indian chief, Hiawatha, and his love, Minnehaha. (Laughing Water). This poem was in our textbooks when I attended Long Branch School, and is sometimes referred to as *The Song of Hiawatha.* The setting for this group of poems is in the state of Minnesota, and the Shining Big Sea Waters is Lake Superior, which borders the state on the northeast section. It could have included Canada, which has a long Lake Superior frontage. However, Minnesota appears to lay claim to this legendary story, with its many rivers, parks, waterfalls, and monuments named from the Hiawatha story.

There is also a city named Pipestone in Minnesota. It got its name from the quarry that produces red granite stone. Indians traveled long distances to get this stone. It is used to craft peace pipes. They are considered to be a religious symbol. Since smoke from these pipes traveled upward it carried a message to the great spirits in heaven. Pipestone is filled with Native American history.

My family has always been proud of our Native American ancestry. I have always been told that my Indian heritage comes from my grandmother,

Mary West Martin, who was married to my grandfather Vander Wright Martin. It was said that she was one-quarter Cherokee Indian. The West family moved to Butler County from Grandville County, North Carolina around 1870.

History also tells many stories about Native American activity in the state of Kentucky. The Cherokee tribes were in the east, the Shawnee occupied most of the central part, and the Chickasaw tribes were found in the west. Most historians believe that the Indian population only hunted on Kentucky land, and never established any permanent residence. This may be true, however, there are 22 Indian mounds and grave sites in Kentucky and several in Butler County. Taking into consideration the amount of sites and the Yahoo massacre, there may have been more Indian activity in the state than most people believe.

The Yahoo massacre took place on August the 10, 1810, at Yahoo Falls near Whitney City, Kentucky, in the Big South Fork National Recreation area. History indicates that 110 or more Cherokee women and children gathered there under the shelter of the rock, in back of the water fall. They were on their way to Sequatchie, Tennessee, down near Chattanooga, where the Reverend Blackburn, minister of the Presbyterian Church, had established a school for Indian children. They were also waiting for another group of women and children to join them at the falls, so they could all travel together. The second group was led by Cornblossom, who was the daughter of Chief Doublehead. The chief was well respected, and had recently negotiated a peace treaty with the governor of Kentucky that would settle disputes between the settlers and the Cherokee. Unfortunately, before the second group of women and children arrived, a group of Indian fighters were informed that the women and children were at the falls. This group called themselves the Franklinites and were led by Herman Gregory, an Indian hater. They arrived in the dark morning hours, before daybreak, and savagely murdered and mutilated every woman and child. It is said that Yahoo Creek ran red with blood.

The Franklinite group, and many more like them, had developed a policy to destroy all Indians in America. They thought the best way to accomplish this was to eradicate the women and children. The children before they grew up, and the women, so they could not produce anymore. A similar tactic was used by Adolph Hitler in his plan to destroy the Jewish people.

In 2010 we acknowledged the 200th anniversary of this inhuman massacre. I understand that a few small markers have been placed there to keep history alive and perhaps, to give us pause, so we can try and understand why one group of people would harbor such hatred and malice, as to impose such inhuman torture on another group of God's people.

America has come a long way in the past 200 years as the world leader of freedom. I'm sure that most Americans today would strongly and morally condemn what happened at Yahoo Falls. However, at this time in history, about all we can do is express our sorrow and disappointment, and hope and pray that this type of behavior never happens again. It's impossible to bring them back, help them, or see their faces. However, it's possible that their spirits are being carried around the Earth by the mystic winds of time. And if we listen closely, we might be able to hear their pleading cries for help.

44

INVEST IN LOVE

Many of us spend considerable time in our lives trying to decide what to invest in for the most profitable returns. Some favor the stock market, some believe that houses and land are the best and safest methods. These types of investments are all based on financial growth and dividends. We all know how very important it is for families to have enough resources to live a happy and comfortable life. However, it appears that it is the nature of the human race to be unhappy with the modest achievement in life. They are possessed with a burning desire to become rich and famous. People figure out many methods of achieving these goals. Some have inherited great wealth, some are gifted, some are lucky, and others use lies and deception. With our instant news systems you have probably noticed that a great number of the rich and famous have destroyed their lives. Many of them have passed away at a very young age, usually due to the consumption of drugs and alcohol, causing what was once a happy family life to fall apart.

Since there is so much grief and heartache attached to investing in financial matters, perhaps we should consider investing in love. Being able to love is a gift from God. If we love God, we will find that investing in love comes easy. Love that binds families and friends together is strong enough to overcome all of life's adversities. It could be the principal ingredient that keeps the human race from falling back into the dark ages. Love provides hope and strength in our darkest hour.

Love is the road that's paved with kindness. A collection of thoughts and memories builds a bridge between the living, and our friends and love ones who have passed on. Love is free, we don't have to engage a broker for advice on how to reap the harvest from this very important segment of our lives. If we weigh the advantages of investing in love, to the problems we face in the financial world, we will find in the long run that investing in love will pay far more dividends than any other types of investments.

My sympathy goes out to all those souls who have not been able to find love in their lives. It's been said that people who invest in love lead a happier life than those who fail to recognize love's value. This happens because they tend not to be vindictive, and love causes them to forgive those who trespass against them. I am not going to try and define passionate love. It's far too complicated for most of us to understand. The type of love that has stood the test of time is the one to embrace. It's built on low key emotions, with love and understanding for family and friends with deep concern for the welfare of others. Perhaps, we should call it a warm Sunday kind of love.

As we travel down the road of life, there will come a time when the cold winds blow, and we will have to walk that lonesome valley all by ourselves. That's when our investment in love will pay the greatest dividends. We don't have to look very far to see that there is evil in our world, but we should not let evil diminish our love for humanity.

45

IRENE MARTIN CONSTANT'S LONG BRANCH

The following is an article written by my sister Irene Martin Constant for The Butler County Schools. I wanted to reprint it in memory of her.

When God made our world he made everything for a reason, everything had its place. On the north side of Green River in Butler County, Kentucky, there used to be a thriving community called Long Branch. It was named this because of a large stream of water that headed up at what we called Graf Forsythe Hollow. This branch runs on past great towering bluffs where people used to go to pick huckleberries and visit again the places where there were still signs of where the Indians had lived.

The Long Branch passes on by the Possum Hollow and empties into Welch's Creek. Near the creek on a high bluff are the much talked about imprints of baby tracks in the larger rocks under the bluff. They used to be easy to see but rain and time have faded most of the tracks away.

Near the creek is an old cemetery called the Robin Cardwell Cemetery. This cemetery is one of the oldest in the county as some of the tombstones date back to the 1700s. Some of the first people buried there were Adam and Barbary Rone, the Cardwells, Shephards and other names that have been forgotten through the passing of time.

The first Long Branch school was built of logs. The children attending came from families by these names: William Amos Cardwell, George Oller, Thomas N. Childers, William E. Childers, William (Will) Coleman, Lum Johnson, Rufus West, Lemuel Garrison, and William Wingfield. In 1907, the log school was replaced by the school building that stood until the county consolidated the school system. Families with children going to the last school building were Allie Childers, James O. Martin, Columbus Johnson, Will Colman, Arvil Johnson, James Childers, Zona Phelps, Euk Elms, Alonzo Burden, Estill Coleman, Harrison Decker, Eck Wingfield, Eldrige Smith, Dwight West, Eln Coleman, Homer House, Getty West, and Joe Clark.

Long Branch did not have a church, but most people went to Leonard Oak and the old Brush Arbor at Red Hill, where they held some great revivals. One of the most remembered ministers to this writer and many other people was Brother Robert Burden. I am sure he helped save many souls during his ministry. Let us also remember the Childers family, Beatrice, Rollie, Cleo, and Thrulo. Most of this family moved to Arizona but stood firm in the Christian faith in the Church of the Latter Day Saints.

We have been very fortunate during the past 50 years. We could work and have what we desired, but let us not forget "Our Heritage," where we came from and where we are going. The Long Branch community where 12 families once lived has only two houses remaining. Some moved away because they could live better elsewhere and others preferred the city.

46

IT'S ALMOST TOMORROW

Most of us are familiar with the old saying that "tomorrow never comes." However, there are many reasons that make tomorrow, and the day after tomorrow, two of the most important days in our lives. To begin with, it's these two days, after today, which provide us with the shortest method of looking into the future. It's true, there is hardly a day that goes by that most of us don't say, "I'll put that off until tomorrow." If there is no one to share the decision with, we store it in our mind, and in most cases take care of it on the tomorrow.

Our lives are blessed with many tomorrows. Each of these tomorrows are designed to build stepping stones to the future of our lives. In some instances these stones of tomorrow appear far away in our future, and in many cases they are dimly lit, and at times we struggle to develop a clear mental picture of where this path is leading us. This path is very personal. No other person or individual, whether they be powerful, rich or poor—though many may try—can walk your path for you. It's where we store our dreams for tomorrow.

Rather than building dreams for tomorrow, many of us like to live by the old platitude "Live for today, for tomorrow you may die." God's teaching does not indicate that we should live that type of life. History has shown us that those who follow that path are likely to live a failed life.

We are each allowed a certain amount of tomorrows and God makes that decision for us. If we don't use them properly, and we let them fracture and fall apart "all the Kings horses and all the Kings men cannot put them together again." When our tomorrows are all used up, it will be time for us to stand before God on judgment day, to answer for the type of life we lived back here on Earth. We know that God is the fairest of all judges, and He will probably say, "Welcome, my child. I'm holding in my hand your book of life. It indicates that you believed in me, and always followed in my footsteps, and lived a life of love and kindness for everyone you knew, and when you needed help you asked for it with your prayers, which is my favorite methods of communication. I give considerable weight to the fact that you have not interfered with my work by sending me lots of text messages from your smart phone." Then He might add, "However, there is one question mark. It indicates that in your life on Earth you failed to take advantage of all the tomorrows that I provided for you." Then He will hold your hand and say, "Don't fret. I have a place for you here in my heavenly home. It's not the upscale penthouse. The clouds you rest on may not be quite as soft as some, and at times the view of heaven may be slightly restricted. However, I feel you will be very happy there. It's where your family and friends, and many others who have committed minor infractions back on Earth, are spending their eternal lives."

This is just a reminder of how important it is that we take control of our tomorrows. It's the best way to take control of our lives.

47

KENTUCKY LAND

People who came to Kentucky and Butler County in the early days can give thanks to our American hero and pioneer, Daniel Boone, and a judge by the name of Richard Henderson from North Carolina. Daniel Boone was born in Pennsylvania. He is fondly remembered for his adventures and accomplishments in crossing the mountains. Sometime around 1752, he turned south down through the Shenandoah Valley, and with his father and the rest of the family settled in North Carolina's Yadkin River Valley. In fact, it was close to Sugar Creek that Boone met and married Rebecca Brian.

In the years that followed, Daniel Boone developed a close relationship with Judge Richard Henderson, who was widely known as an adventurous pioneer. They shared a strong desire to open new land and settlement, even though the British had forbid any further western development. Judge Henderson had formed the Transylvania Company, and that company had paid 10,000 pounds in goods to the Cherokee Indians for 20 million acres of land located between the Kentucky and Cumberland Rivers. Of course, all the Indians were not in favor of the sale, and that caused many problems for the pioneers. Judge Henderson hired Daniel Boone to cut a path for the new settlers that would occupy his new land.

On March 10, 1775 (that was exactly 121 years before my dad was born), Daniel Boone assembled 30 mounted axmen at Long Island on the Holston

River in Tennessee. That, by the way, is a stretch of land that lies in the midst of Kingsport, Tennessee today. Boone and his men set off along what would become known as the Boone Trace, and later on as the Wilderness Road, that continued on through the Cumberland Gap. On March 24 1775, Boone and his exhausted men made camp just south of what is now Richmond, Kentucky. They were attacked by Indians, but continued to follow Otter Creek until they reached the Kentucky River. There they stopped and made a station, and named it Boonesboro. Judge Henderson was following close behind and upon his arrival they formed a new government and named it the government of Transylvania. At the time it would have been the largest land sale in our young nation's history as it covered more than half the land in Kentucky and some of North Carolina.

The reason that I'm giving you this bit of history is because Butler County would have been included in this historic land sale. However, the sale never materialized as the authorities in Virginia and North Carolina ruled that it was illegal. There were mixed feeling about Judge Henderson. Some people felt that he was a great hero, others felt that he was a land grabber. At any rate, he helped make it possible for our ancestors to reach Butler County.

It was a difficult life for the pioneers. To make the trip, Boone recommended some essentials: a good gun, a good horse, a good wife, a strong body and a sharp ax, but most of all, some good luck. Another essential was salt. Before 1776, salt had to be shipped to the colonies from the West Indies. It was the only preservative for meat available for people on the move. Reaching Kentucky solved that problem, with its large salt brine lakes located near Richmond and Fort Boones-borough State Park.

The earliest settlers found the chestnut tree to be another great asset. Its logs could be used for building homes, schools, and rail fences. It could be easily split to make shingles for roofs, the bark was used to make medicine and tannic acid for tanning, and its rich nuts were used to fatten the hogs. The chestnut tree is now threatened with extinction from blight because very few are producing nuts. There are organizations working to save this great tree to ensure that future generations can enjoy their beauty and bounty.

So to our ancestors, a word of thanks for your courage and sacrifice in opening up this great land, and for making it the greatest country on Earth.

48

LASTING IMPRESSIONS

The word impression has two distinct meanings. One relates to physical properties, such as the impression of a notary seal, bare footprints in the sand, imprints in metal, and automobile tire tracks in a soft surface. The other meaning that the word impression has relates to our life experiences. This type of impression is defined as something that has an effect on our mind, senses, and our feelings. Some of these effects are so profound that they leave us with a lasting impression. They are so indelibly printed in our minds that we never forget them regardless of where life takes us or if we are fortunate enough to live to a ripe old age. Economic conditions, wars, and adversity in life are the most common conditions that leave us with lasting impressions.

I believe that it is safe to say that growing up on Long Branch School Road in Butler County Kentucky left the greatest impression on my life. Sometime ago I heard Mr. Ted Turner speaking about his childhood. He was born in 1938 and indicated that sometime in his young life he was hungry. Today, Mr. Turner is a very wealthy man. He was the founder of the first twenty-four hour cable news channel CNN. He owns more land in the United States than any other person, and is also known for his billion dollar gift to the United Nations. However, he indicates that being wealthy has not erased the fact from his mind that he was hungry at one time, and every time he donates or spends a large amount of money, the thought of being hungry creeps into his mind, and he still worries that something might happen and he would find himself hungry again.

For many of our military people the circumstances and conditions that they experienced being involved in a war, especially those who found themselves in mortal combat and in close proximity with the enemy, are so overwhelming, that their mind and senses are so saturated that it is impossible for many of them to cleanse their memory and lead a normal and happy life. It's certainly one negative about lasting impressions.

In our world today, we are also impressed by what we see on our televisions screens. On July 20, 1969, we watched Neil Armstrong become the first man to set foot on the moon. It was something that impressed everyone on Earth, and being able to watch it happen from one's living room was no small feat in itself. And how can anyone ever forget the September 11, 2001 terrorist attaches in New York City, Washington D.C., and Pennsylvania killing 2,996 people? It's my hope that this cowardly act will leave a lasting impression on every American.

And of course, we are impressed by people we associate with on a daily basis. Some by their sterling personality, some by how beautiful they are, some by their above average intelligence, or by how kind and considerate they are.

To say to someone that you have an impression that we have met somewhere before, is a clever way to try and make new friends. One thing we all should remember, we get only one chance to make a good first impression.

49

LIGHT THE WORLD

In the beginning the moon and stars were the only source available to light up the darkness. Later, the torch become a method of illuminating the night. Torches were made by soaking cloth in pitch, or some other flammable material, and attaching the saturated cloth to the end of a stick of wood. This method was used to light up castles, crypts, and other ancient buildings. Torches are still used in today's world, such as the Olympic torch, whose journey is followed by millions of people around the world. Torches are considered to be a symbol of hope and enlightenment.

Candles have been around for more than two thousand years. It is believed that they were first made of whale fat or beeswax. Most candles today are made from paraffin. The flame from a burning candle is very beautiful and relaxing and appears to be a very simple process. However, the flame of the candle is actually quite complicated. The blue at the bottom of the wick is hydrogen being separated from the fuel and burned to form water vapor. The brighter yellow part of the flame is the remaining carbon being oxidized. Just a few of the many technical reactions necessary to make it operate efficiently. Candles are still very much in use today, to use when a storm interrupts the electrical power, celebrate our birthdays, and provide a sweet fragrance to fill our homes. They are also used in as a symbol of faith and hope.

At one time, candles were the main source of light for most homes. However, they were replaced in 1845 when George Wilson accidentally discovered that kerosene could be made from crude oil. Coal oil was around before Mr. Wilson discovered kerosene, and is made from shale oil. The two product are very similar, and they both work equally well in all types of wick lamps. However, kerosene was more economical to produce than coal oil, and therefore become the leading fuel for lighting homes.

The only source of lighting in our family was the coal oil lamp. The lamp had a small tank for fuel, a fuel burner attached to the top of the tank, a cotton wick extending from the fuel tank into the fuel burner, and a wick adjustment knob to adjust the size of the flame. The fuel burner provided the metal hood that contained the flame, it was vented to allow the proper amount of air. It had four metal post that supported the globe, also known as the chimney. Coal oil lamps required considerable maintenance to keep them operating. The oil tank required refilling every two days or so, the globe was always getting smoked up and required cleaning. There was always someone in the family that thought that they needed more light and would turn up the flame, which contributed to the globe becoming smoked up, and the wick required trimming every few days to remove the charred material. The coal oil had to be transported from Morgantown or some other retail service. I believe that since this product was so essential to every family in the neighborhood, most of the small country groceries made it available.

I suppose every family had their favorite container in which to transport and keep their fuel supply. I recall vividly that ours resembled a large tea kettle and would hold about two gallon. It had a two inch opening in the top to access filling, and a three inch tapered spout to accommodate filling up the lamp, and whatever other emergency that might develop. If you were trying to build a fire in the wood cook stove, and the wood was wet, a dash of coal oil would perform magic. At one time I am sure that the pouring spout had a cap, or a cork stopper to contain the fuel, and to keep the oil fumes from escaping into the house, since ours was missing, we would always cap it by pushing a small Irish potato into the spout.

Lighting in the early days was very primitive, but it did not keep our ancestors from great accomplishments and building a great nation.

50

THE LAND BEYOND THE RIVER

There's a land beyond the river, they call the great forever. This is the first lines of a beautiful inspirational song titled, "When They Ring Those Golden Bells for You and Me." In my stories I often speak of the land beyond the river, talking about that half of beautiful Butler County that lies across the Green River north of Morgantown, generally referred to as the north side. It appears that this would be the ideal and appropriate time to discuss some of the features that make the north side so unique.

People who worship nature find themselves at home in the rugged hills and valleys of this land. Perhaps it's the majestic Green River that protects its southern border that helps keep its landscape and vegetation much the way God created it. In spite of rising tide of what is known as advanced civilization outside its borders, and where the lifestyle of our country is rapidly changing, the north side remains in many ways the same: Rugged, rebellious, beautiful, and harbors a deep feeling of loneliness.

In the early 18th century, when our ancestors were moving west, for some reason they chose the north side location. Perhaps, for the same reason as mentioned above, its loneliness and rugged beauty. When aroused from winter sleep, and a spring shower washes the land clean, leaving the air soft and sweet, it would be difficult to find a location that displays nature more beautiful than the land across the river. The sun kissed hills and hollows are covered with forest: Great oaks, poplars, maples Sycamores, and many others. It's one of the places on Earth where you can find an abundance of lichen type moss growing on the north side of tree trunks and on the sandstone rocks that surround them.

In the spring it's a land where wild flowers and the May apple plants grow in abundance. It's the land of the cardinal and so many other song birds. It's been said that on occasion when birds are on a bough that overhang a creek or pool of water, they sing louder and longer because they see their reflections in the water which makes them think that they are singing to a very large group.

It's a place where if you listen closely to the speech of the native population, you can still recognize traces of the Appalachia dialect, once used by our ancestors. It's a land where history can still be found carved in the smooth bark of beach trees. Stephen Foster certainly was correct when he wrote, "The Sun Shines Bright in My Old Kentucky Home." It's been said that he got the inspiration to write this song while visiting his relatives in Bardstown, Kentucky. However, I understand that this theory has been rejected. It appears that no one is sure where he was at that time he wrote the song. It's possible that Mr. Foster lost his way and accidentally found himself on Long Branch School Road. The wording of the song fits that area perfectly.

In addition to the sun, the moon has played a major role in adding beauty to the land. It's majestic and a wonder to behold. Due to the clean air, it shines brightly on this land beyond the river. It guided our ancestors through the night, before artificial lighting was available.

After life, many of them are at rest in the same sacred land they loved, and where they spent their lives. The moon and stars continue to shine brightly in their memory.

51

LONG BRANCH SCHOOL

Still sets the school house by the road, a ragged beggar sunning, around it still the Sumac grows with Blackberry vines a running. This is part of a beautiful poem, the title is "School Days", written by John Greenleaf Whittier sometime around 1865. You can find the complete poem by going online. However, there is some difference in the wording of the first stanza. This is the way most of the people believe it was printed in the poem book.

We don't know if this poem represents a true story in Mr. Whittier's life, or if it is a product of a very active mind. At any rate, considering the time in our history, I feel certain that his school house was very similar to the Long Branch School which I attended from the first grade through the eighth grade. My dad was the teacher my first two years, all the children referred to him as Mr. James.

I am sure you have seen pictures of the early one room schools that were so common in the early settlement days of our country. Long Branch was typical of most schools in Butler County in those days. They were in the neighborhood of twenty six feet wide and thirty feet long with five large windows down the back side, and one near the corner in the back end, and one entrance door up front. Due to no artificial lighting in those days, large windows were necessary to let in as much light as possible. The blackboard was about four feet wide and ran the length of the building with a molding ledge top and bottom. The bottom rail was a little larger so you would have a place for the chalk and erasers. The writing surface was made of wood and required painting a few times each year. I recall one day we were painting the blackboard, and Essie Cardwell was holding the quart can of black paint, and it slipped from his hands and dropped to the floor. By some stroke of luck, when the can hit the floor, it did not over turn and spill the paint. However, some of the paint was propelled upward and Essie's face was covered with paint, which meant we had to find some turpentine and give Essie's face a good scrubbing.

Discipline in our school was no problem. On the first day of school my dad would bring in a hickory branch about five feet long and lay it up on the top rail of the blackboard. You would not believe how quiet that school room was. The hickory branch in those days was referred to as a scantling. Scantling was a term used in the early days of our country to describe a piece of wood of small to moderate size.

The Long Branch School was built in 1907. It replaced a log school house that stood there in earlier times. As a child it was a mystery to me why they chose that location as there was absolutely no playground for the children. In later years I learned that it was build it among the trees so it would stay cooler in the hot summer months.

For a playground we used the Long Branch School Road that ran along side. There was a level spot in the road as it passed the back section of the school. With a bat improvised from a slat that was at one time part of a slat and wire fence, and a ball of knitting yarn, we would play ball. Of course, you would need two teams, and the method of choosing the teams was performed with a small stick of wood, approximately eighteen inches long. One team member would grip the stick with one hand near the bottom part of the stick, then the other team member would place his hand above the first, and when they reached the top, the person that was unable to get his hand on the wood stick lost, and the winner got to pick his team. Of course we played other game like Hide and Go Seek, and Fox and Hounds. And if you wanted to play alone, you could always go and swing on a grapevine.

School would begin at eight o'clock, and after we stood and said the Pledge of Allegiance, we would start studying our lessons. Almost everyone brought their lunch, and we placed the pails in one corner of the room. We did have a water well out in front of the school with a wood box around it to keep debris from getting in the water, and to keep any one from falling in. The job of going to the well was assigned to some of the older boys. They would take the water pail, tie the rope that was there to the handle on the pail, drop it down, let it fill up, then pull it up by hand. Some of the more prosperous schools had a permanent oak bucket with a pulley arrangement which made the chore much easier.

Since there were no bathrooms or out houses, there was a system that we used. When one needed to go, he or she would raise their hand to get permission to go outside. They would take one of their books and place it on the floor at the doorway entrance. While the book was there, no one else was allowed to leave the room. It certainly was a large bathroom as the whole outside county was available.

Pioneer children are no different than other children as we loved Christmas, and looked forward to it with great anticipation. When it arrived we would go out and cut down a large cedar tree as they were plentiful in our area, nail a couple of cross boards to the bottom, stand it up in the corner and nail them to the floor. This structure was strong, I don't remember one of our trees ever falling down. It's a good possibility that the nails used were somewhat rusty, and had been picked up at some building project and straighten to make them usable. One more plus for the Christmas tree was that it stood in the corner used to punish the naughty children. The tree prevented them from standing there. Since there was no money to purchase anything, decorating the tree was done by the children and their families. Popcorn and red berries from holly bushes were strung on thread and then draped around the tree with some bows and ribbons that were left over from the prior year. It was a very exciting time and I can recall how sad I was after the festivities were over.

I had the reputation of being a good student and loved to go to school. One of the most trying times I had was when my dad purchased several pair of knickerbocker pants for twenty five cents each, and insisted that my brother and I wear them to school. It's difficult to explain how humiliated I was with all the other boys my age wearing long pants. With all the remarks and giggling, I am surprised that it didn't destroy my self-confidence, but somehow I managed to live through it without any noticeable damage.

In the early days, teachers would live, or board, with one of the students' families. When I was about eight, the teacher lived with us. She was a young lady about eighteen. Due to limited facilities, it was necessary for me to sleep with her. Life can be very rough when your peers find out that you are sleeping with the teacher. But again, I managed to pull through.

As in the School House by the Road poem, there was a great deal of love demonstrated between the boy and the little girl. That is also true in my case, as I was deeply in love with a little girl named Pauline. At that time it appeared to be so real. But the world took us in different directions, and the strong love soon faded away.

The school is gone now, has been for a number of years, but I have pictures and some boards from the building that will always keep my memories alive.

52

MAPLE SYRUP

We all know that the state of Vermont is well known for its maple syrup, however, Butler County has produced some of that delicious pancake topping, as well. Not in the large quantities that Vermont does, but a few gallons for family consumption, and a few gallons to sell to our friends in Morgantown. The Martin family was the only family in our immediate area that got involved in the making of maple syrup.

There is a very narrow window of opportunity when it is possible to produce maple syrup. Only in the early spring when sap begins to run, usually a few weeks in March when the weather freezes at night, then warms up above freezing in the daylight hours.

Most maple syrup farms have what is called a Sugarbush, or a considerable number of maple trees in a group. Our farm didn't have a sugarbush, rather we had perhaps a dozen trees scattered over 36 acres of woodland, which meant more work was necessary when it came time to pick the sap up and carry it to the backyard where we would do the boiling. The commercial producers, I'm sure, have large automated evaporators to condense the sap down to syrup. Our method of condensing was totally different. First we would put together two 6-foot long green logs, preferably oak, approximately 8 to 10 inches in diameter, and lay them side by side approximately 12 inches apart, and that was what we set the cans on for boiling. The reason we used green logs was to prevent them from burning too rapidly. We used empty lard cans for boiling. These cans were plentiful and would hold approximate 10 gallons of sap. In our area it was understood that if you didn't have a 50 pound can of lard in your house, you didn't have anything to eat. Usually our operation required two or three cans. Once this was all set, you were ready to build a fire between the logs.

Each maple tree would produce two or three gallons of sap each day, depending on the size of the tree, and how many vertical slits were opened up. Too many slits would injure the tree, and in a few years it could die. The sap was extracted from the tree by cutting a horizontal slit in the tree, driving a spile into the slit, and then adding the vertical cuts as mentioned above. The sap would gather down at the spile and drip into a pail.

I don't have any hard facts about this, but my guess is that it takes about 10 gallons of sap to make 1 pint of syrup. As the cans evaporated you would have to add additional sap. Sometimes the cooking would extend into the evening hours. The condensing of sap, as you might imagine, would require a considerable amount of wood to complete the project, but we could always depend on white chestnut wood to do the job. Once the sap in the cans was reduced to near syrup consistency, it was taken inside the house and run through a strainer, than on to the kitchen stove, where it was cooked until it reach the correct viscosity of syrup. The syrup was then transferred to quart fruit jars for safekeeping until it was needed for the breakfast table.

Making maple syrup was such a memorable and rewarding experience for me. I can still recall the sweet aroma that filled the air around the boiling cans. I have often wished that every young person could at some time in their lives have the opportunity to experience this very rewarding work of nature.

53

MEMORIES OF LONG AGO

We are all familiar with the old platitude, "There's no place like home." When I was a boy growing up in our little two room house there on Long Branch School road, I was for the most part very happy with my life and the surroundings. However, being an average teen age boy, I longed for companionship with friends of my own age. Of course, this was impossible in the drab winter months. Most of the people my age lived a few miles away. The inclement weather, the gloomy landscape, the muddy road, all added to the bleakness of the day. A visitor of any age would have been a welcome sight. I remember my feelings standing on the high ground in back of the house, looking across the school house bottom land at the dark hills and leafless trees on the other side. My feeling at that time is somewhat difficult to explain. Lonesome, lonely, depressed, or perhaps, some of all of that would be true. It was about that time that I had check out a book from the school library. One passage in the book advised that if you suffer from loneness, you should "chop wood, and stop fretting." That's what I did, and to my surprise it did help.

It's safe to say that happy times in that part of my life over shadowed the sad times by a wide margin. Attending Long Branch School was my greatest pleasure and satisfaction. My memories of that school are treasurers that have lingered in my memory as bright as a sunny day. The school is gone now, but

I love to visit the location and ponder the past. I can recall the names and faces of the young people who were fortunate enough to attend that institution of learning.

Across the road from the school was two towering black oak trees, a reminder of the great forest that once covered this land. These trees provided shade, and on hot summer days, they were a favorite spot to have lunch. At one time our teacher was Mr. Gordon Tyler and I can still see him sitting with his back against the big oak tree having his lunch. Mr. Tyler and I appreciated each other's company and I usually had my lunch nearby. I can recall a time when he defended me. One girl that attended school was Marie Wolf, and she was about the same age as me. In back of the school was a grapevine swing that us boys would take turns swinging on. When it came to my turn, Marie stood at the bottom of the hill and refused to move. Pleading with her was unsuccessful. "You don't dare!" was her comment. But I did dare, and Marie got quite a bump. Of course, she went crying to the teacher. Mr. Tyler was not sympathetic. He said, "Marie, I witnessed the whole thing. It was all your fault."

Mr. Tyler and I had no problems. However, that was not the case with several of the other pupils. I recall a confrontation between him and one of the older boys who threatened him with a baseball bat. He was tall and very thin, with a light and willowish demeanor. Some of the kids gave him the nickname "Ichabod Crane." However, they were very careful not to mention it when Mr. Tyler was around.

The name comes from a story called "The Legend of Sleepy Hollow" written by Washington Irvin in 1820. Ichabod was a school teacher. He rode a gray horse named Gun Powder. He was chased one dark night by a headless man riding a large black horse and carrying his head in his hand. This was very frightening to Ichabod. As the story goes, his horse was found the next morning grazing in a field, but Ichabod was nowhere to be found. People in the village believed he was spirited away by supernatural means. There were rumors about his sighting in other towns, but never confirmed. Guess we'll never know what happened to Mr. Crane.

54

MOONSHINE WHISKEY

The year was 1932 and the making of moonshine whiskey was big business in Butler County Kentucky. About half of all the families that live along the Long Branch School Road were in the moonshine business, either making it or transporting it. Every hollow in this area, at one time or another, had a still except the Possum Hollow. I suppose the reason was because there was no way in or out without passing by our house.

But setting stills up in the hollows was very necessary. Water was a very important part of the process. The 55 gallon barrels that were used to ferment and sour the mash required lots of water, and all hollows have a branch or creek running through them. Also, wood was another necessity. It took a considerable amount of wood to boil the mash and produce the distilled product. In order to get the mash to sour, and for other reasons, lots of sugar was needed. The sugar came in 100 pound white bags with very little markings. Since the bags were plentiful, and there was no money to buy dresses, the women folks used the bags to make dresses.

Life was difficult in the days of the Great Depression, however, I have some fond memories about the making of moonshine. One nice August day when I was a boy, 13 or 14 years old, I visited some of my neighbors and friends that had a moonshine still up one of the hollows just up the road from our farm. They were in the process of building the fire under and around the big 55 gallon copper boiler, and a soft summer breeze fanned the fire. In a short time White Lightning was filling up the gallon jugs. The first of the run has a very high alcohol content, but the longer it runs the lower the alcohol content becomes, so it is necessary to mix these two together.

Most moonshine was sold at 130 proof. One method used to get a proof reading was to put some moonshine in a can, then swish or stir it with a small stick. If the beads or bubbles stayed for a minute, it was 130 proof. The finished product sold for about one dollar per gallon. If you were a neighbor and only needed one gallon there was no charge.

In stories we are tempted to glorify the making of moonshine, but I will not. In the first place, it is against the law, and I have witnessed many lives that were destroyed by either making or drinking it. It has been said that moonshine is the tears that mothers have shed over the past ten thousand years. My advice to everyone is: don't make it, and above all, don't drink it!

55

MY COUSIN ROLLIE CHILDERS

My cousin Rollie and I were about the same age; he was my senior by a few months. He was the third child of Columbus Alley Childers and Eva Martin Childers, who was my dad's sister. There were five children in his family: Butrice, Charles, Rollie, Cleo, and Thurlo. We all attended the Long Branch School. They were all good children. I cannot remember an occasion when there was dissension between our families. As their mother passed away early, the oldest Butrice, who was perhaps 18 years at that time, did a splendid job of looking after and taking care of her younger siblings. I don't know if she ever received the thanks she deserved for the unselfish work and dedication she provided.

Rollie and I were very close, and it appeared that we shared many of the same values and principals. We have heard that some people are born with an old soul. They are the people who are able to distinguish between right and wrong at a very early age, and continue to do so for the balance of their lives. Rollie had an old soul and my association with him had a positive impact on my life.

The Childers home was located on Pea Ridge Road, near the Buzzard bluff that overlooked the Green River. It provided a great place for outside activity. Rollie and I spent many happy days fishing and boating on the river.

Saturday was the big day in Morgantown when we were young. I can recall the sidewalks being so crowded that it was difficult to walk down them. One day Rollie and I were there on Main Street, and some of our friends were across the street on the courthouse lawn. In an effort to cross the street, Rollie evidently didn't look to see if there was any automobile traffic, and he ran into the side of a car that was passing by. Fortunately, he was not injured, rather it just sort of spun him around. However the teasing was quite heavy. Being the strong person he was, he pulled through without any noticeable damage.

Rollie loved to play the guitar and sing western songs. One of his favorites was, "Riding Down the Canyon", introduced by Gene Autry in 1935, along with "Tumbling Tumble Weeds". Gene was our favorite cowboy, and when his films were playing in our little theater in Morgantown, we would try our best to find a dime somewhere so we could watch Gene take care of the outlaws. The theater was on Main Street, near, or just north of the current city hall. Just when we thought that everything was going well, and our friend Gene was the most popular cowboy on the planet, there was suddenly a new cowboy by the name of Roy Rogers. It took us a while to warm up to Roy.

In my opinion, the month of May is one of the most beautiful months of the year. It's a time when God's work is most apparent. It also just happened to be the time when strawberries are getting ripe and need to be picked. One year when Rollie and I were about 17, we got approval from our elders to go to Richardsville in Warren County to pick them. Of course we had to walk to Richardsville, and cross the Green River at Woodbury on the ferry boat. It took us most of the day to walk the 20 miles. We found a place that would provide us with room and board, and Mr. Miller, just down the road, had a large strawberry farm and was happy to have us pick for him.

It been some time since that happened, and I'm not sure how much we got paid for our work, but something tells me that it was around three cents a quart. It was a very pleasant place to work, there were several lovely girls about our age working there. It stands to reason that in an environment like that, boys of 17 would be fortunate to remember their names.

The work lasted three or four weeks, and soon it was time for Rollie and me to go home. But before that happened Mr. Allen Minton, who lived there in Richardsville with his family, and owned and operated a large sawmill, came by one day and ask if Rollie and I would be interested in working for him. The wages were big, a dollar a day, with room and board. I said yes immediately as my previous jobs had paid fifty cents per day without room and board. Rollie was unable to stay, due to a commitment that he would come home and help his dad in his building business. I was sad, and had a lonely feeling about losing my friend. But the feeling subsided after I got to know the Minton family. I will always be grateful to Allen and his wife Stella, and all the Minton family, because they treated me like one of their own.

At another time in history, Rollie and I would have probably remained in Butler County. But the world was changing. War appeared to be imminent, which made everyone restless, and we both had our dreams that were very important to us. As mentioned earlier, Rollie had a great love for the west. The dream that he polished most, was that someday he would be able to live in the west. That was a dream that become a reality. He spent most of his life in Arizona, working in the field of education. I am sure that he did an outstanding job in his field. He was blessed with an extraordinary amount of wisdom, which I feel certain is benefiting his former students today. Although we lived far apart, in different part of the country, we always remained friends. I have never had so many friends that I could afford to lose one.

56

MY DAD'S OVERLAND CAR

I know you have heard people complaining about their current automobiles. Their comments are usually, "They don't make them like they used to." For myself, having been exposed to cars made in the good old days, and the way they are made today, I have no desire to go back to the way they were made then.

Similarities between my dad's 1925 Overland and today's cars is like comparing a shovel to a bulldozer if you needed to move a large mound of dirt. Of course there were some similarities. They both have four wheels, but the Overland's wheels had wooden spokes, and in the hot dry weather it was necessary to splash water on them to keep them from drying out and becoming loose. They both have gasoline combustion engine. The Overland had a four cylinder engine, and looking down at it from the top, it appeared to be about the size of a shoe box. I never knew what the horsepower was, but I recall my dad driving it wide open downhill, and asking my mother how she liked the speed, which was 35 miles per hour. Like cars of today it had a steering wheel. The wheel of the Overland was made of wood dovetailed together to make a circle. I can still remember seeing the pieces when it fell apart. After that, Dad would steer with the spokes. The tires were somewhat larger than the balloon tires we find on bicycles today. The rubber would peel off when driven on a rocky road.

In the early days of Butler County, there were only two kinds of roads, rocky, or muddy, usually both. Where we lived on Long Branch School Road, the car could only be driven in the summer months, May through October, because the dirt roads were impassable in the winter months. However, with all its shortcomings, the Overland was still head and shoulders above the Model-T Ford, which was the most popular car at that time.

I failed to mention that the Overland was a one seater, and there were six in our family. My two younger sisters were small enough at the time that they could ride in the seat. My brother and I would ride by standing on the running board and holding on to the frame that supported the windshield. The windshield pushed open and closed, with a couple of wing nuts to hold it in the desired position.

Most of the time the car was parked outside under the big Sycamore tree. This was necessary due to the fact that my dad raised chickens, and the garage was usually full of chickens. The car had a canvas top. It wasn't long until the cloth top deteriorated, and was completely removed, allowing rain and snow to enter the inside of the vehicle.

I don't intend to be critical of this car, it left us with lots of memories, some beautiful, some not so beautiful. One day our neighbor was riding with my dad on the stretch of road just beyond the school house, on Long Branch School Road. The road was muddy with deep wheel ruts, and the car was being whipped from side to side due to this condition. Our neighbor was a large man, and sort of top heavy. The moonshine that they had been nipping on had left then both very relaxed. The momentum caused the side of the car to fall off, dumping the side of car and our neighbor into the mud. Fortunately, no one was hurt. When we were in the process of putting the side back on, we found the reason why it had fallen off. There were wood two by fours attached to the frame with some bolts, and the body was crimped at the bottom and nailed to the two by fours. Of course, when the wood got wet and deteriorated, that side of the body fell off.

When my brother and I were about eight and ten years old, we were checking out the car one day. We found out that if we put the car in gear, and turned the ignition key, the car would move from the power generated from the battery. My brother wanted to see if he was strong enough to hold the wheel. He suggested that he sit down in back of the rear wheel, put his legs on either side, and lock his hands around the spokes. I was to do the driving. For some reason the car happened to be in reverse, and it rolled back upon my brother's stomach. He screamed and yelled. By some miracle, l was able to get the car in a forward gear and roll it off his stomach. We surveyed the damage that it had done to his body. Bruised, battered, with some skin peeled from his body, but didn't appear to have any broken bones. We decided to keep the accident a secret from our parents. We were afraid of the consequences we would suffer for playing with the car, running the battery down, and my brother getting injured. As I remember, the threat that parents used most in those days was "I'm going to skin you alive." Rather intimidating to boys of eight and ten year old.

Boys are such an unpredictable group, causes one to wonder how they ever survive to become men.

57

MY SISTERS

I was always grateful that I had my sisters, Bonnie and Irene. Bonnie was a couple of years younger than me, and Irene was a couple of years younger than Bonnie. Along with my brother Otis, who was the oldest, we all grew up together in the little two room house on Long Branch School Road.

When we were children, all the land in that area was cleared and used for farming. The view was rather extensive. One could see down the road and all the land in front of the house for at least half a mile. When one topped the hill after passing the school house, our house would come into view. I can still remember how my heart string would sing with joy, and the warm fuzzy feeling of security would override any fears that I may have previously had. I have often wondered what made the family love that very modest little house so much. Was it because it was located in the sharp curve of the road? Or was it because it stood at the mouth of Possum Holler with a babbling stream running alongside? Maybe it was the large Sycamore tree that decorated the front yard. I feel certain that all the above contributed something to the happiness we all experienced while living there. However, if I had to make an educated guess, I would say that love of family was the main ingredient that made our little house a happy place to spend our childhood years. I firmly believe that love is the fiber that hold our world together. Of course, growing up in the years of the worst depression our country ever experienced was a challenge in itself. At times, food, clothing, and the necessities of life were in short supply. But I have always believed that trying times, and adversities, bring people closer to gather.

As far back as I can remember, everyone in our family had some sort of a nickname. My dad was called "Bun", my Uncle Odel was called "Mance", and my Uncle Clifford was called "Chess". Wish I did, but I have no idea why or how these names developed.

In our immediate family, both my sisters were tagged with names other than their own. Irene was called "Diggie". The nickname was given to her by our cousin, Edison Hudson, although I don't remember why. When Bonnie was small, she broke a sewing needle trying to pry open a hickory nut. Of course, she was scolded for breaking the needle, and when ask what she was trying to do, she said she was trying to open a hickernurk. After that, she was called "Needlenurk". These names were around until they become teenagers. After that you would have a fight on your hands if you even mentioned them.

My sisters became teenagers when the permanent wave fade was at its peak. In those days a teenage girl was a nobody if she didn't have a perm. I can recall how dad would cry and complain when he had to dig up the money to pay for them. Perms were quite expensive compared to the price of most everything else at that time.

As mentioned, the view was good from our house. We could see the family home of Alonzo and Lily Burden from our place. It was easy to tell when the family was preparing supper by the amount of smoke escaping from the stove pipe of the wood burning kitchen stove. The Burden children were about the same age as our family. We were all friends, and spent considerable time together. When Bonnie and Irene become old enough to be interested in boys, my parents, for whatever reason, forbid boys from coming to the house. With the help of the Burden children, they set up a clever little clandestine operation, where the boys would come to the Burden home, and the children would hang out a white sheet to signal that the boys were there. You could be sure that my sisters would find some reason to go visit with the Burden family.

Both my sisters were talented singers and could play the guitar to the point that they were invited to perform on the radio. I have always felt that they had the talent to succeed. Had there been anyone available with the knowledge and desire to promote them, and with some help and lots of good luck, they could have been the famous Martin Sisters. They could have competed with the McGuire Sisters for the number one spot on the charts.

Due to the fact that I was somewhat older, there were times when I worked away from home and would come home only on weekends. For the most part, my sisters had only the basic necessities of life and very few luxuries. And because I loved them, I made it a habit to spend a little of my $2.50 weekly salary and bring then some candy. I'll never forget how happy and excited they were to receive this modest gift.

As in most cases, kindness has a tendency to forge love and respect among all God's creations. Both my sister have passed away and I miss them very much. It was a blessing to have known them, and I cherish their memories.

58

MYSTERIES OF LIFE

Some people believe that from the moment that we were born our path in life has been established by our creator. Others have a different approach and believe that our pathway in life is determined by each of us. One thing is for certain, this very wide disagreement is likely to continue for some time. I happen to be a believer that the path we follow in life is not established by our creator, but God gives each person the ability to choose the path of life he or she would like to follow. To add value to this belief, we need to look closely at the Earth and all the living creatures that we share it with.

It might be reasonable to believe that God in His wisdom designed a survival plan for all creatures He placed on Earth. God gave the fowls of the air strong talons and eyes that can detect a small movement as much as a mile away. The rabbit was blessed with strong legs to speed away from danger. The lizard can change his color to match the surroundings. The list goes on and on. Genesis 1: 27 tell us that God made us human in His own image, male and female. Perhaps He was a little partial and gave us dominion over every living thing that moved on the Earth.

The path of life is much like climbing mountains. When you reach the top of the first one, you see the plateau that stretches out to the next mountain, which appears to be more difficult than the one you have just conquered. Take a look backward at your accomplishment. This will give you the strength and courage to climb the next mountain on your path of life. Grit and determination to succeed is one of our greatest assets, to make us worthy of this monumental task.

In the midst of the garden, God planted the tree of knowledge. He used the tree of knowledge to provide us with a brain that has the capacity to think, plan, and reason, and a conscience that tells us good from evil, right from wrong. Later on He must have thought that the path of life was in need of more light, so He added the Ten Commandments. It would be difficult to overstate how important it is for us to use the tools that we have been blessed with. It is the responsibility of each person to chart a path of life that is happy, and full of love and kindness. Kindness is the language that the deaf can hear, and the blind can see, and is one of the cornerstones of civilization. God would be pleased if we used these talents to their fullest extent.

I have often thought that at the end of our lives, when we stand before God, we could feel that we had no talent left, and could safely say to Him that we had used every bit of talent that He had given us. From experience, most of us adults know that charting the correct path in life has not, and never will be easy. One of the problems is that so many of the important decisions must be made when we are young. Finding our place in life when one is young is a very lonely spot to be in. It's been said that no other animal goes through the unbelievable and unpredictable things that teenagers come up with. We were all teenagers once in our lives. It's very important that we forgive them. It would be a mistake not to do so.

There are a couple of things that us grownups should consider as we continue to chart our path of life. One is to think before acting, and the other is don't continue to think, and never get around to acting.

59

MYSTERIES OF THE EARTH

Have you ever given serious thought to this mysterious rock planet that we live on? Scientists tell us that the Earth in its orbit around the sun, leaps through space at 66,600 miles per hour, and makes a complete circle of the sun every 365 days, while spinning counter clockwise on its axis at 1,000 miles per hour, making one complete circle every 24 hours which gives us night and day. It is also tilted on its axis 23.5 degrees from vertical, which gives us our four seasons each year.

I was taught that the Earth was round when I attended Long Branch School, even though there were limited facts at that time to prove that it was true. Earth is the third planet in distance from the sun, and the fifth largest of the eight in our solar system. It is sometime referred to as The World, Mother Earth, the Blue Planet, or by its Latin name, Terra. The Earth is estimated to be about 4.5 billion years old, and life of some type appeared on its surface about one billion years later. Over time, the Earth has significantly altered its atmosphere and other conditions. The formation of the ozone layer, together with the Earth's magnetic field which blocks harmful solar radiation, making it possible for life to flourish on its surface. As far as we know it's the only planet in our solar system that has water, and while we have an abundance of water, only 3 percent of it is fresh water.

As mentioned, the Earth travels very fast. If we drove our cars as fast as the Earth spins, we would cover the Earth's diameter every seven seconds, and the distance to the moon in four hours. On its orbit, it is closest to the sun on January 3rd, and the farthest away on July the 4th. This sounds a little strange, even though it is further from the sun in the summer month, the tilt of the Earth causes the sun to have a more direct impact on the Earth. The tilt of the Earth does undergo a slight irregular motion over short periods of time. This is caused by the varying motions of the sun and the moon on the equatorial bulge. Yes, astronomers tell us that there is a bulge around the equator of the Earth that causes the Earth to be 26.5 miles larger, this is probably due to centrifugal force.

Let's don't forget the gravitational pull that keeps us and everything else firmly attached to the Earth. Every planetary body, including the Earth, is surrounded by its own gravitational field. The strength of gravity at any given point depends on the planetary body mass of the Earth, and other factors, such as the sun and moon. Gravity is usually measured by how fast an object will fall per second. It is believed that gravity is what keeps planets from crashing into each other. We certainly hope that the Earth doesn't crash into any large objects on its orbit around the sun, even a glancing blow could cause the Earth to lose some of its gravity field, and that would be a disaster.

As we all know, the Earth is very complicated. There are so many things that it must depend on in order to continue to be a life sustaining planet. The sun, the moon, its orbit around the sun, the spinning on its axis, the 5.3 percent tilt from vertical, the gravitational pull that keeps everything in place.

With its many forms of life, vegetation, oceans, mountains, and plains, it's a very beautiful world. It provides all living creatures with the necessities of life. We humans live on it, abuse it, but the facts are, at this point in history, we know very little about it. Perhaps, only God would be able to explain its many unknown mysteries.

60

MYSTIC WINDS

Meteorologists tell us that the differences in density between two air masses produces wind. The same is true with the jet stream. The difference in heating between the two poles and the equator produces the jet stream. Our meteorologists of today are very intelligent, know their job, and are very essential to our safety. It would be difficult to imagine life without our weather people. That being said, they are pretty much in the same situation as the rest of us when it comes to understanding the mystic winds that roam the Earth.

Wind is the symbol of freedom, like each life, it should enjoy the freedom that God intended. The mythology of the mystic wind has been around since the beginning of civilization, and has been passed down from generation to generation. As a child, I can recall my parents and neighbors discussing their thoughts about this mythical wind that blows through the hills and hollows of Butler County. If the myth is true it carries the secrets of long ago, and the reason that it blows so softly is that it is trying to share its story with us, if we could only understand the language.

The mystic wind appears to have favorite places where it likes to whisper its story, and these locations are chosen by each of us. The best place is an old familiar spot where one can ponder the past, and let our mind wander back in time. A generous amount of nostalgia will be helpful. Some of my favorites are the old homestead where I grew up, the location where the Long Branch School once stood, Welch's Creek, and Main Street in Morgantown.

The old homestead, when visited, provides a mental picture of the landscape and the family life we experienced there. When standing alone at the school house location, I can mentally see the children, their smiling faces, and hear their laughing voices. When walking on the banks of Welch's Creek, I'm flooded with memories of all the happy days and hours spent there with the family, especially my brother. And now, the almost vacant Main Street in Morgantown causes me to remember when it was so crowded that it was difficult to walk down without bumping into someone.

I feel certain that the mystic winds travel with us in our journey through life, and that our connection may be much greater than most of us realize. Every life has a book, the book tells the story of each person's life. That leaves one to wonder who is looking after, and caring for the books. One possibility is that each person's book is nearby but is invisible to our eyes. If we stretch our faith and imagination, perhaps we can visualize this beautiful book lying on a table by an open window, and the mystic winds of time are blowing through and turning the pages. When the pages are all turned, it will be time for the soul to return back to the Lord who gave it in the beginning. Transportation will be provided by an angel with snowy white wings. Under these angel wings will be the mystic winds that have been blowing through this world from the beginning of time. When the final destination is reached, the Lord will say, "Welcome, my child. Step inside, and we will review your book of life."

Next time you have an occasion to visit one of your sacred spots, listen closely, you may be able to understand what the mystic winds are saying.

61

NOT FORGOTTEN

If you watch television at all, you have probably seen the very interesting Allstate Insurance commercial, where the father and son appeared to have a fender bending accident. It made me think about my friend Robert Lee Clark, better known as Bob to his friends. Bob and I worked for the same company. Our company supplied trim parts to the automobile industry, such as tail lamps, radiator grills, handles, hardware and thousands of other parts. Bob was our Chief Mechanical Engineer, while my title was Marketing Engineer. It was necessary for us to spend a considerable amount of time together visiting our customers, purchasing, and engineering divisions. In the process, we become very close friends. I told him about my life growing up in the Kentucky hills, how my mother had seen the Tarzan movie where the star's name was Elmo Lincoln, and how impressed she was with him, and when I was born a few months later, she gave me that name. Bob was born on Hall Street in the city of Grand Rapids, Michigan. At the time he was born, he had three older sisters. As ultra sounds had not been invented, there was no way of knowing if the baby would be a boy or a girl. Of course, his father wanted a boy to carry on the family name, so he said to the doctor, "Give me a boy, and I will name him after you." The doctor's name was Robert Lee.

While in the military service, Bob was a navigator in the Air Corp. He would tell me the story about his first assignment after graduating from the navigation school. They assigned him to a B-17 Flying Fortress. The colonel said, "Lt. Clark, here's your orders. Take this plane and its crew to India." Bob said it was an experience he would never forget, and he felt that he must have aged ten years in a couple of days, but he was very proud of the fact that he set the plane down on the runway in New Delhi.

Bob was married to Jackie, a very beautiful and likeable person. They had four or five children and lived in what was considered to be an up-scale neighborhood. One day, Jackie called Bob at his office and said that the neighbors would like to have them go to dinner with them this coming Friday evening. Bob said, "That will be great. Tell them we'll go." It was fairly easy for them to have an evening out. Both families had teenage boys to babysit the younger children. As I recall, the boys were somewhere near the ages of twelve and fourteen. As Bob told the story, they had finished a very enjoyable meal and were having some dessert, when the waitress stopped at their table and asked, "Are either of you gentlemen Bob Clark?" Bob said, "Yes, I'm Bob Clark." She said, "You have a phone call Mr. Clark. The police would like to speak with you." The police relayed the bad news to Bob. There had been an automobile accident. No one was hurt, but both cars were severely damaged. As everyone learned later, Bob's son took a car from their garage and the neighbor boy took one from their garage and went for a little joy ride. Somewhere in their travels they managed to smash them together. Bob and Jackie refused to provide details of the punishment the boys received. Is it any wonder that parents turn gray before their time?

Bob and Jackie retired to St. Helena Island, near Beaufort, South Carolina. Beaufort is known for its Tabby Cement. Tabby was the first concrete made in America. It's made from lime, sand and oyster shells. The lime is made from oyster shells that are heated until they pulverize into lime powder. As there are no rocks in that part of South Carolina, crushed oyster shells were used in place of gravel. The incentive that the builder used to get their building job was that you would get a mailbox post made of Tabby cement. When we visited them, Bob would always tell me story about the post. From what Bob told me, there was only a few craftsmen left with the skill to do the job properly.

Both Bob and Jackie have passed away. I miss them very much. Especially, Bob. He never bought into the misconception that if you were born and raised in the hills of Kentucky, or some other southern state, you would be unable to think, and your mind was impaired to some degree. Many times when Bob needed help to solve a problem, he would ask me to come and review it with him. I recall the time when he was unable to get the heat staking machine to produce a good part. We reviewed it together. I suggested that we move the heating element from the top of the press to the bottom, where the metal was thinner. Perhaps it would heat the metal to the required temperature. It worked. I recall Bob looking at me, and using the king's English, said, "Elmo, you are as smart as hell, don't know why I didn't think of that."

Another instance was when Chrysler had requested that we make an engineering change to one of their parts. It was a small change. We billed them $5069 dollars to make the change, expecting to be paid in the normal thirty day period. That didn't happen. Our billing office contacted Chrysler, but they gave some type of excuse: "They were still reviewing it." This dragged on for months. We sent just about everyone with any authority down there, and they came back empty handed. One day the plant manager called me to his office. Elmo, he said. "Bob Clark was just in here. He wants me to send you to Chrysler and see if you can collect $5069 dollars they owe us for an engineering change.

Don't think I ever told anyone the method I used, but I came back with the check. In a few days, the engineering department presented me with a gold star award, attached to some blue ribbons, with words of praise for a job well done. It hangs on my trophy wall. It's one of my most precious possessions. When I see it, it makes me wonder why a city boy would strive so hard to become the friend of a hillbilly boy that grew up on Long Branch School Road in Butler County, Kentucky. Looking back, I feel that the world is a better place because of him. I'm blessed and honored to have had him as a friend. In my life, he will never be forgotten.

62

OF BRILLIANT COLORS

Autumn is the time of year when nature provides us with one of its most beautiful shows, the brilliant color of the fall leaves. I remember being told by a biology professor that a dry summer will produce foliage with above average color and brilliance. This is based on the complex chemical interaction between weather and leaf color. Leaves produce more yellow and orange pigments for photosynthesis in response to the stress brought on by dry weather.

The southern Appalachians is the home to some 100 tree species, most are deciduous which accounts for our fall leaf color. Kentucky's fall color season usually peaks around the last two weeks in October, a few days after the first frost. Sourwood, Dogwood, Sassafras, Black Gums and Birch trees are among the earliest to change leaf color. The best way to view the colors is to find a high spot so you can look across the valleys. Maples, with their beautiful gold and yellow colors, typically change color at the peak of the season, while Oaks come on later in the color cycle, usually in early November.

Butler County is blessed with many Maples and other trees that produce great colors, which brings leaf watchers in search of finding the most beautiful locations. More than a million people visit the Great Smoky Mountains National Park each October to view the fall colors, making it the third busiest month of the year.

A great location for any leaf watcher to consider visiting would be the Big South Fork National River and Recreation Area that straddles the Kentucky and Tennessee line on the Cumberland Plateau. It doesn't have the high elevation that Smoky Mountains have, but I understand that the river gorges and valleys are lovely in the fall and the park is much less crowded. The driving distance from Butler County is also considerably shorter at approximately 140 miles, which makes for a wonderful weekend adventure. Should you decide to make the trip and haven't already been there, I would also suggest visiting the Yahoo Falls, which is in the same area near Whitney City, Kentucky. This is where the Indian massacre took place in the fall of 1810. I visited it one spring after the snows had melted and new buds flowered and it was beautiful. I imagine it would be even more beautiful in the fall when the leaves are in color.

Most of us don't pay much attention to leaves. We enjoy looking at them when they display their vibrant colors each fall, or complain when we have to rake them from our lawns. However as trivial and tedious as they may seem to be at times, leaves are one of the mysteries of nature. Deciduous trees would not survive without leaves to catch energy from the sun and convert it into chemical energy and produce oxygen, carbohydrates, glucose and starch, which trees must have to survive.

I believe there is also a nostalgic feeling about leaves that come from the old home place where one had lived when they were a child. Sometime back, I noticed a young lady picking up leaves in the Bowling Green City Park. When she came near me, I asked her what she needed the leaves for and she mentioned that Bowling Green was her hometown, but she had moved to some faraway place and the leaves gave her comfort.

I will admit that I have a couple from the big Sycamore trees penned to my garage wall.

63

OLD SPINNING WHEEL

"There's an Old Spinning Wheel in the Parlor" is a song that was written by Williams J "Billy" Hill in 1930. It's a very beautiful song that I first heard when I was ten or twelve years old. We were having a Christmas party at the Long Branch School House where Gordon Tyler was the teacher. Mr. Tyler was a very fine teacher. He taught school for many years in Butler County where he lived with his son, Robert, who was about nine at that time. Robert's contribution to the party was to sing "There's an Old Spinning Wheel in the Parlor." He did such a splendid job in his performance that I have remembered the words and tune my whole life, even though I did not hear it again until I was well into my retirement. Feeling nostalgic, I decided to do some research to find it, and I was happy to find that it is still available. It sounds just as beautiful as I remember…just listening to it brings back a flood of memories from my childhood days.

The artist rendition I most recently listened to was Slim Whitman, whose real name is Ottis Dewey Whitman. Mr. Whitman is a left-handed guitar player, but it was not always that way. He lost the second finger on his right hand while working in a meat packing plant and learned to play left handed while in the Navy. After he came home from the service, he played baseball for a class C team in Tampa, Florida. On his days off from his post office job, he sang on a local radio station in 1948 where Colonel Tom Parker heard him sing and secured a recording contract for him at RCA. Parker changed his name to "Slim" following the record deal.

In the USA only two of his 230 recordings made it to the Top 40 charts, however, in the United Kingdom, Australia, and Europe they rushed to buy everything he sang.

If we look back at these two individuals perhaps we can use them as an example of courage and determination. Robert, who was just a child, stood up before his classmates and their parents to sing this song a cappella style. This must have taken a great deal of courage. Mr. Whitman, who appears to have had a considerable amount of setbacks in his life, showed great determination in overcoming his problems and go on to become a very successful entertainer.

This story has a happy ending. Everyone loves stories with happy endings.

64

ON THE WINGS OF A DOVE

There are many different types of doves in our world. They are found on every continent and many islands in the oceans. The Mourning Dove, a beautiful bird, is a native of America. They range from Canada through Mexico, and Central America. They have been called several names such as Carolina Pigeon, Turtle Doves, and Rain Doves. They are known as American Mourning Dove to distinguish them from the African Mourning Dove. Its plaintive woo-oo-oo-oo call gives this bird its name.

Mourning Doves were abundant when I was growing up in Kentucky. We could hear their cooing call quite often in the spring and summer months. My mom had been taught that when the doves cooed they were calling for rain, which is why they were call Rain Doves. Scientist tell us that the doves coo is the male's way of attracting a mate.

The male and the female both work together in preparing the nest. The male picks out the location and shows it to the female for her approval. The nest usually contains two eggs. Both parents incubate the eggs; the male in the morning and into the afternoon, the female the rest of the afternoon and the nighttime hours. It takes about two weeks for the eggs to hatch. Both parents feed the young dove milk for the first three or four days, then gradually augment their diet with seeds. The young will leave the nest in ten to fifteen days, although the parents will continue to feed them for some time. They will be fully matured in approximately 85 days and be ready to produce their own family.

Besides being one of God's most beautiful creations, the dove is recognized as the bird of peace. The legendary story tells us that once upon a time in the Far East, the leaders of two kingdoms held grudges against each other and over the years become angrier and angrier. Finally, one of them announced that he was going to war with his neighbor. It had been a number of years since the threatened leader had been to war and he had almost forgotten where his armor and battle clothes were. The day before the battle was to start he asked his mother to bring his helmet. His mother went away, but soon returned empty handed. "Why didn't you bring my helmet?" he complained. "I couldn't lift it. It was too heavy for me," she replied. The son was surprised and decided to go get the helmet himself but his mother stood in the way, blocking his path. "Please, please, don't touch the helmet" she pleaded. "But, Mother, I'm the leader of our country. How can I go to war without my helmet?" His mother had to tell him the secret. "A dove has built a nest in your helmet." Inside the nest were three baby doves. "Please don't touch the helmet," she begged. "If we disturb them, the mother will go away and never return. Then the suffering of the baby doves might bring misfortune and disaster to our land."

Her son listened and decided to go to war without his helmet. The warring leader could not believe what he was hearing, so he sent one of his men to see if it was true. The man returned and said it was. The warring leader agonized for a while, then extended his hand to the helmetless leader, and said, "Let's make peace together. Your mother didn't want you to destroy a tiny nest of three doves, how could we go to war and destroy thousands of homes?" So they signed an agreement to keep the peace forever and from that day forward the dove has become known as the symbol of peace.

I once found myself in a situation similar to the above story. We had purchased some land out in the suburbs with the intentions of constructing a new home for the family. The family was excited and anxious to get started. I wasted no time. As soon as possible I contacted the excavating company and made arrangements for him to bring his equipment and clear the land where the house would be located. The vegetation was a couple of feet high, and as we were walking on the sight location, a dove flew up. And would you believe it, there on the ground was a nest holding two fuzzy little baby doves. As you can imagine, a thousand thoughts raced through my mind. What will I do now? But in a few minutes, I decided to postpone the work for a couple of weeks until the doves were able to leave the nest. Of course, explaining this to the person that had used his time and equipment was no easy task. He must have been a very fine person, because he appeared to understand. Even though I tried to compensate him for his time, he refused. Leads one to believe that there are many people that do care.

There is also the biblical story about the dove and the olive branch in Genesis 8:11. Noah sent out a dove from the ark in an effort to try and determine if the flood waters were receding from the land. In his first attempt, the dove returned because she found no resting place for the soles of her feet. Noah waited seven days and sent her out again. This time she returned with an olive leaf in her mouth. Noah knew then that the water was receding. Over thousands of years there has been considerable disagreement about which one represents the symbol of peace, the dove or the olive branch. In the past few centuries, most scholars have leaned toward the olive branch. We are all familiar with the legendary term, *I extended an olive branch in pursuit of peace and friendship.* Personally, I think that both the dove and the olive branch represent a symbol of peace, and they should share it equally. It's easy to see that doves represent peace, love, and kindness, and should be protected.

When I visit the old home place in Butler County, I always listen for the gentle cooing of the doves as they call for the rain.

65

ONLY GOD CAN MAKE A TREE

Woodman, Woodman, spare this tree. Touch not a single bough! In my youth it sheltered me, and I'll protect it now. When as a little boy I sought its grateful shade. Here too was where my sisters played. These are a few words from a poem written by George Pope Morris in 1837. Mr. Morris was inspired to write this poem when someone suggested that the large oak tree that his forefathers had planted near their home be removed due to its age. My inspiration to write this story comes from the large Sycamore tree that stands near my old home place on Long Branch School Road, where like Mr. Morris's sisters, my sisters, Bonnie and Irene, played when they were young.

Mr. Morris and I have a few things in common. We were both born on October 10th and our love for trees inspires us to write poems and stories about them. I consider it safe to say that most of us love trees. This is evident by the fact that many of us have at some time in our lives planted a tree and expressed our love by providing them with water and fertilizer, as well as a hope that God will bless them and make them grow into beautiful trees.

The one person I have known in my life whose love for trees was unconditional was my brother, Otis. He could never find a reason big enough or strong enough, to cause him to cut down a tree. The acres of forest land in the Possum Hollow that he inherited from our parents was, and is still, covered with large Oaks, Beeches, Poplar and many other types of trees. It's been at least 80 years since any timber has been harvested from that site. In that group of trees is a large poplar which has a diameter of between forty and forty five inches at the trunk, and is in the neighborhood of eighty to ninety feet tall. The family always referred to it as "Tommie's tree", which was his nickname. My brother was approached many times with offers to purchase the land but he always refused to sell. In his lifetime, he received advice from many people, who challenged the wisdom of his convictions to leave the trees as they were. When pressured to reconsider he would usually say, "Trees are beautiful and they provide many benefits to the Earth. They are a home to the birds and wild animals. They stabilize the land from washing away and clean the air that we breathe. God put them there, God will take them away when He is ready."

I was always proud of my brother's stance regarding trees and the many other challenges he faced in life. In recent years, our society has coined the phrase "Stand for Something." When my brother stood for something, there was very little room for compromise. Over the ages, the forests that covered America have been essential in making it the greatest nation on Earth, though we should all recognize that over the past several hundred years our American forests have been severely abused. In an effort to be better, we now have laws that prevent over-harvesting, and the replanting program has been very successful. This is not so with the rainforests across the world. It's my understanding that they are being destroyed at a rapid pace. Rainforests can be characterized in two words, warm and wet. They are found along the equatorial zone of the Earth. Some of the larger ones are found in South America, Africa, and Malaysia. It is such a tragedy, and there is so much to be said about their pending demise that the whole world should be concerned.

66

OUR LOVE FOR CARS

My life and the invention of the automobile both started at about the same time. This could be why I have such passion and love for them. I don't think that I'm an exception to the rule as most Americans love our cars, and it's easy to understand why. Their contribution has been enormous, perhaps greater than any other invention, as they have added so much comfort and convenience to our lives. I'm grateful that I have been privileged to witness the development and engineering achievements that have taken place in the automobile industry in the last 50 years.

Some of my observations have been quite interesting. In 1927, the Model A Ford replaced the Model T, a car that had been a very popular car for a number of years. The Model A was a giant step forward in automobile engineering with its four wheel brakes, safety glass, a three speed sliding manual transmission, and a top speed of 65 miles per hour. It was a great success and set the stage for the beautiful and dependable cars we drive today. Everyone wanted to have one. My dad's sister and her husband, Clarence Allen, owned a 1931 Model A Deluxe Coupe. It was easy to tell how proud he was and how much he cared for his car. He would tell everyone who would listen stories about his car; what a comfortable ride it provided, how it would start every time the starter button was pressed, and above all, how it was the perfect car. Try as they may, automobile companies would never be able to make further improvements in design and dependability of automobiles from that of the Model A in his opinion. It would be interesting to hear Uncle Clarence's comments if he were here to see the automobiles we drive today.

The Model A made its debut at the beginning of the Great Depression, however, that didn't stop people from buying them. Ford produced approximately 5,000,000 of these legendary vehicles. The selling price ranged from $385 for the Roadster to $1400 for the Town Car. As popular as these cars were, there were times when they could be purchased at a fraction of their selling price. Some of our neighbors would find a way to visit Detroit and drive back in a car. The ones I recall seeing regularly were the Roadster, which were new or basically new, and could be purchased for $35. I'm not sure if this was due to over production on Ford's part, or people had purchased them and were unable to maintain them due to the economic conditions at that time.

Things certainly have changed over the years. At the turn of the century, $35 will get you a tank of gas.

The Model A made such an impact on the motoring world that in 1979, Mr. Harry J. Shay founded the Model A Reproduction Corporation Car Company in Battle Creek, Michigan. Mr. Shay had an agreement with Ford to produce 10,000 Model A's and Ford would let them place them in their showrooms. For a while, it appeared that the reproduction company might be a success. They were able to produce approximately 5,000 units before the government decided to step in with new safety rules and regulations. The small company was unable to cope with all the extra expenses, in addition to 125 lawsuits, and was forced to file for bankruptcy on July 6, 1982. Through Mr. Shay's vision and intellect, he was able to live out his dream, if only for a little while.

There are numerous Model A Clubs in America and throughout the world. They hold the title of being the most customized and rebuilt of any other automobile. Each year there is a the national tour held in the spring along the 444 mile stretch of the Natchez Trail, between Nashville, Tennessee and Natchez, Mississippi. If you have a chance I would encourage you to visit.

67

OUR SEARCH FOR WISDOM

As a child growing up on Long Branch School Road in the early part of the 20th century, it was not uncommon to find people that were unable to read or write. When it was necessary for them to sign a document, they would place an X on the line where their signature was required, then someone would witness the transaction, and it would become a legal document. In unusual circumstances, someone else would make the X and the would-be signer would touch the pen. Although these people didn't have any formal education, the majority had common sense, which is one of the basic ingredients of wisdom. A wise man once said that it's better to be uneducated and have common sense, than to be educated and have no common sense.

Wisdom is sometimes expressed in platitudes, commonly known as common sense. Most of us are familiar with them. Just to mention a few: *"If you are in a hole stop digging." "People who fight fire with fire usually end up with ashes." "Never put off until tomorrow what you can do today." "Never spend money before you have it." "Character is doing the right thing when no one is watching."* There are many of these platitudes, they go on and on. They may be old, tattered and worn, but they embody the experience of the human race.

Since the beginning of time, people have been trying to understand the foundation of wisdom, where it comes from, how it is acquired. Some scholars believe that it is a gift from God at birth, and wisdom is divine, that it's more about the heart than the head. Others believe that there is an overlap between knowledge, understanding, and experience. There is also a consensus that adversities, and the storms of life, cause people to seek and attain wisdom. Regardless of how it is achieved, it is believed to be one of the greatest assets available to the human race.

People who have attained wisdom have a considerable advantage over those who have not. It is reported that that they live more useful and happier lives, they are revered by their peers for their unselfish help and advice for their neighbor, and those who have stumbled on life's rough and rocky road, their ability to understand human nature, and some sense of what may happen in the future.

Our founding fathers were men of wisdom; they were capable of looking into the future and provided the frame work to protect the country from its enemies, both foreign and domestic. For their vision and hard work, we Americans should be grateful.

For people of the Christian faith, our greatest teacher of wisdom was King Solomon. His teachings are found in the Old Testament book of Proverbs. They are as true today as they were 2000 years ago. One thing I have always found interesting about his philosophy, is that he indicates that wisdom is female. Chapter 1 verses 20 & 21 of Proverbs reads as follows. *Wisdom calls aloud outside. She raises her voice in the open square. She cries out in the chief concourses. At the opening of the gates in the city. She speaks her words.* I'm not going to disagree with the king. Women of the free world have demonstrated wisdom and courage that is to be applauded.

It saddens me to give you this news, but wisdom and common sense have become a very scarce commodity in our world at this time. It would be a better place if each of us had more of Solomon's wisdom, and a generous supply of Job's patience.

68

POKE GREENS

I felt that I needed to write a story about poke greens in order to keep this very important southern culture alive. Poke is known by many names: pokeweed, poke bush, pokeroot, and inkberry just to name a few. It is a plant that grows in abundance in and around Butler County, and in many other places in the world. Poke for food purposes should be picked early in the spring when the plants are small and tender. Since they are one of the earliest plants to sprout, us pioneer folk along Long Branch School Road were always grateful for some something green after a long winter.

We have heard many stories about this plant being toxic. From what I have heard over the years, I'm not sure it's true. I have eaten it all my life, so have many of our neighbors, without suffering any ill effects. However, to be on the safe side, my family has always taken precautionary measures to parboil it at least two times, changing the water each time, then we would fry it in bacon grease. This method of cooking is recommended by most people who have had experience in its preparation. Once completed, this dish is called poke salad. In the deep south it is sometimes called poke salet. Salet is the German word for salad, and preparing poke may have started in the Ozark Mountains from German settlers.

Poke is reported to be loaded with vitamins, especially vitamin A. Records indicate that the Native Americans used the poke plant for food millions of years ago, even before corn was introduced. They said it had the ability to drive away the evil spirits and cleanse the body. This may have been because they learned about its purgative properties.

Our family and neighbors picked other edible greens such as lambs quarter, water crest, and plantain but poke was the favorite of most everyone. In addition to the poke plant providing healthy and tasty food, the poke root is also used for medical purposes. It is said to be one of the better medicines available for the treatment of rheumatic conditions, plus creams that clears up rashes and skin problems. It is currently being studied as a medicine for the treatment of AIDS and cancer. Who knows, someday this lowly plant may become a miracle plant and save many more lives to add to the ones it has already saved from starvation in and around the Appalachia Mountain region during the years of the Great Depression.

In addition, when the poke stalks reach maturity they produce flowers which are a greenish and white color. These flowers turn into purple berries. These berries were used by Native Americans to paint war colors on their bodies. The berries were also been used as a source of ink. Reports, indicate that many soldiers during the civil war used ink made from pokeberries to write letters home. Most historians feel certain that our Declaration of Independence was signed with pokeberry ink.

No matter what the season, spring will be here soon, and it will be time to go out and pick some poke, which is part of God's free harvest. Make sure you prepare it properly, and when that is done, by my reckoning, poke greens should be saturates with vinegar, piled on top of a piece of buttered cornbread, add a dash of pepper, and then enjoyed by everyone.

69

PRECIOUS MEMORIES

Precious Memories, How they linger, How they ever flood my soul, in the stillness of the midnight, precious sacred scenes unfold. A beautiful song written by J.B.F. Wright in 1925. Mr. Wright was born in Tennessee on February 21, 1877. He had very little musical training. He would write from inspiration in his own words.

It would appear that Mr. Wright and I have one thing in common: we both have a memory that is capable of producing a mental picture of the past. That's the way people used to see pictures before cameras were invented. I can recall the first time I heard the song, *Precious Memories*. It was sung by the choir at the little white Belmont Baptist Church, which was across Welch's Creek from our farm. There was no bridge that crossed the creek near the Long Branch School Road. To get across, we had to depend on Mother Nature to make a bridge by blowing down a tree that would reach from one bank to the other. Mother Nature was kind. Most of the time, she provided us with a foot log that we could walk across in the daylight hours. However, on the return trip home it was usually dark, and the safest way to keep from falling into the creek was to feel your way and crawl on your hands and knees.

Most of us boys from our side of the creek loved to go to church there. We become acquainted with some of the beautiful girls that attended the church. In those days it was customary to walk your girlfriend home. Of course, her parents were usually walking nearby, which had a tendency to keep us boys in line. Some of those friendships developed into lifelong relationships.

The Belmont community has a beautiful new church now. The good people of that community are to be commended for their loyalty and dedication to the area in which they live. All churches are a symbol of peace and love. I drove past the original church a month or so ago, which is currently being used for other purposes at this time. It still occupies the same location as it did when us boys attended service there. Seeing it again caused my mind to be flooded with memories of the past.

I have a CD in my car, and *Precious Memories* is one of the songs. The artist singing it is Roy Acuff. Roy does a fine job, and I listen to it a lot. However, sometime in the near future I intend to visit the new Belmont Baptist Church and see if I can talk the Reverend Gray Embry into having the choir sing *Precious Memories* for me.

Memories are precious and beautiful. Perhaps they are divine, a gift from our Creator, something to turn to for strength and comfort, when the road to the future looks dark, stormy, and difficult to travel. Perhaps it would be beneficial to each of us if we would take time to pause, and ponder the past, and listen to that small voice inside of each of us. It guides our lives, and tells us things that no one else can.

70

PRESIDENT'S DAY

Our calendars remind us that two of our most admired presidents were born in February: George Washington and Abraham Lincoln.

George Washington was our first president and served two terms from 1789 to 1797. He fought in two wars, the French and Indian war, where he was captured by the French army, but was released when he promised not to build any more forts along the Ohio River. Later, he become the commander of the Continental Army at the beginning of the Revolutionary War. The war was a long and bloody struggle. Our country was young at that time and ill equipped to fight a war. Washington's men suffered severely from food shortages, warm clothing, and equipment. However, George Washington was a leader of men. He understood the seriousness of the situation and eventually was able to drive the British from our shores.

In addition to being a very patriotic person, history indicates that he was a very caring and compassionate person. In his army was a young soldier by the name of Nathan Hale. At a time when the British appeared to be winning all the battles, Washington felt that he needed someone to go in back of the enemy lines to monitor what the British were planning to do next. Captain Nathan Hale volunteered to go. As in most wars the Americans were divided—some were not in favor of breaking away from Great Britain. That being the case, someone snitched on Nathan and he was taken into custody by the British Army. After they found out who he was, the British Army sentenced him to death for spying. On September 25, 1776, at the young age of 21 years, he was hanged there in the city of New York. However, his last remarks have been a strong rallying cry for patriotism here in America: "I only regret that I have but one life to give for my country!" It been said that General Washington was very distraught about the loss of his young friend, and the method they used to punish him. Many of the policies used in our government today were set in motion when he was president. Due to his bravery, patriotism, and love for America, he earned the distinctive title as the father of our country

Abraham Lincoln was born in Hardin County, Kentucky, on February 12, 1800. When he was seven years the old, the family moved to Indiana. He lost his mother when he was nine. His father later married Sarah Bush Johnson. The story has it that she was a very bright person and encouraged Abe to seek an education. Young Abe would study his books by the light from the fireplace. She would always defend him when he was at odds with his father. When Abe was 21 the family moved to Illinois. After moving to Illinois, he built a flat boat and made several trips down the Mississippi carrying produce. Later, he become a self-educated lawyer in the state legislator, and was elected to congress in 1846. In 1854, he become the leader of the new Republican Party, and was elected president in 1860.

It was a time when the country was facing many problems, and was in the act of becoming divided. On April 20, 1860, South Carolina legislators voted to secede from the union. Within six weeks, six other southern states followed South Carolina's lead and the war between the states erupted. It's safe to say that no other president of our country has ever faced the monumental task that Mr. Lincoln faced when he became president. It was a bloody war that lasted four years, fought on American soil, and 620,000 Americans lost their lives, more than in any other war. Not only were the states divided, the families in America were divided. Brothers chose different sides and faced each other on the battle fields. It was a time that challenged the spirit and souls of men. If we look at their pictures made at that time, it's easy to see the hurt and sadness in their eyes.

Kentucky tried to take a neutral stand, but that didn't keep hostile armies from tramping over most every hill and valley in our state. So much for "neutrality." I never heard of them traveling on the Long Branch School Road. Perhaps they were unable to find that historic little spot. However, armies from both sides helped themselves to the use of Kentucky land. Sugar Grove, Morgantown, Woodbury, Russellville, and other location were used by both armies.

Kentucky was fortunate compared to states in the Deep South. Most everything of value in these states was destroyed, including families and the southern way of life. The government was very slow in providing help for the destitute. It took approximately 100 years for the South to fully recover. President Lincoln was assassinated just a few days after the war ended. It is believed that if he had lived, the South would have recovered much sooner. Being a very kind and compassionate person, he would have done everything in his power to improve their standard of living.

It's fitting and proper that we here in America honor these two great men who gave so much of themselves to make our country a land of freedom and opportunity.

71

RABBIT TRACKS

The severe winters we have had recently, and the fact that we have been blessed with a considerable amount of snow, caused me to remember the snows we had when I was a boy growing up in Butler County. Trying to predict when it would snow was difficult. Some winters the snow was very light, and we didn't receive enough to cover the ground, and then there were other winters when there was an abundance of that white stuff. I can recall times when we had as much as twelve inches on the ground.

My brother and I were always hoping and praying for snow that would provide us with the opportunity to go out and track rabbits. At times, one can be fooled when tracking rabbits in the snow. When a rabbit is running fast, the foot prints from their long back feet and legs land ahead of their front feet. They can run at speeds up to eighteen miles per hour—a gift from God that has helped them survive.

Rabbits are very intelligent animals. However, making tracks in the snow put them at a considerable disadvantage. By following their tracks, the hunter is able to find the location where they will be hiding in the daylight hours. They usually choose a briar patch, fence row, or a dense patch of under growth which we called a thicket. Once you followed the tracks until they entered into one of these hiding places, you could walk around and see if there were any tracks leaving, if not, it was a good bet that the rabbit was still in there. Rabbits have a tenacity to stay in their nest as long as possible. Sometimes they wait until they are almost stepped on before they decide to run. If the vegetation was not heavy, you could look inside and see them. And by using a .22 rifle, the hunter had meat for the table, and had saved the cost of a three cent shotgun shell.

This was something that my brother and I would do when times were hard. It made us feel that we were contributing something to the welfare of the family. Some of our neighbors were fortunate enough to have a dog that was capable of trailing rabbits. A good dog improved ones chances of not coming home empty handed. However, this process was not an easy chore for the dog. As mentioned, rabbits are very intelligent. If the dog was in hot pursuit, the rabbit would use one of his tricks to confuse the dog by back-tracking down the trail that he had just used. Then the rabbit would leap as far as he could to the right or left, and go off in the other direction. The dog would become very confused because there was no trail to follow. It would appear that the rabbit had disappeared into the air. Some of the older dogs were wise to the trick. They would make a wide circle and pick up the new trail.

There are several types of rabbits in the world. Rabbits in our area are called cottontails because when they run they show their white powder-puff tail. They are found all the way from Canada, through South America, and in other parts of the world. In the winter months they eat bark and buds from small trees. In the summer months they feed on grass and other green plants. They are especially fond of what grows in your vegetable gardens. When I was just a small lad, my dad had hired a fellow to construct a barbed wire fence around the school house bottom land. I'm not sure, but I believe his name was Tilford West. I was there helping by handing him the tools he needed. Suddenly, he stopped, looked at me very seriously, and said, "Go tell your dad that in order to finish this job, I'll need a box of rabbit tracks, and a dozen cross eyed needles." I didn't tell my dad, but I have never forgot what he said.

72

REFLECTION

Stephen Collins Foster certainly described Kentucky very well when he wrote the song about how the sun shines bright in "My Old Kentucky Home." In the song, he reflected on many other beautiful attributes of our great state. In order to write such a lovely song, he must have had a special place to go where he could reflect and ponder the many things that were flooding his mind. It would be nice if everyone had such a spot to use for this purpose.

When I was a boy growing up on Long Branch School Road, there was a bridge over the branch where I would go to reflect and ponder my thoughts. Having a bridge was a little unusual. Most of the time everyone waded the branches. However, the banks were quite steep and my dad was having problems getting his little overland car across. My Uncle Clifford Martin was staying at our place at that time, and he helped my dad build the bridge. He was young and strong, and a very good workman who had helped build the Aberdeen Bridge over the Green River. One day, I heard that we were going to build a bridge over the branch. It caused great excitement at the time, and in a day or so, we were up in the Possum Hollow cutting timber. The bridge was constructed of four logs, eight to ten inches in diameter, and approximately fourteen feet long. These logs were used as stringers to span the branch. We used our mule Jim to snake the large logs to the building site.

For the floor, we used six inch diameter poplar logs that were split down the center. They were placed across the stringers with the flat side down and nailed to the stringers with number twenty spike nails. It was a very substantial bridge. Before it was complete, they attach baling wire to each corner and tied the other end to a tree or post. This was necessary to keep it from floating away when the backwaters covered the land.

On warm spring and summer days, it was an ideal place to lie on your back and look up at the brilliant blue sky, watch the fleecy white clouds slowly passing by. It would be difficult to find a better spot to think and ponder one's thoughts. On top of my list were the lingering thoughts: what would we children do if something happened to our parents? Will I ever become a man? Time seemed to move so slow. Will I be more successful in life than the people that surround me now? Is it possible that when I grow up, I will be lucky enough to find the right person to swim with me in the stream of life? I had heard many stories about the great farms that existed in Illinois, and Indiana. Perhaps, when I get a little older, I should go to one of those states, and get a job on some big farm. Work hard, and just may be, that farmer would have a beautiful daughter that would take a liking to me. I feel certain that this thought came from watching Gene Autry in our little Morgantown movie theater. Gene always got the girl. This was just one of the many things I reflected on.

I never managed to get to the big farms in Illinois and Indiana. However, most of the good thoughts become realities. If I became tired of looking at the sky, I would turn over and watch the little fish swimming in the water below. I would drop some earth worms in the water and watch them fight each other for the food. Made me wonder what it was like out in the big world.

Due to the damp conditions and the wood not being treated, the bridge began to decay and stared to fall apart. A few years later, it floated away on the backwater. Perhaps it got caught up on some of the trees along Welch's Creek, and the beavers used it to build a nice beaver lodge.

73

REMEMBERING UNCLE SYLVESTER BURDEN

Uncle Sylvester lived around the road about one half mile from our place. He wasn't our uncle, but due to his advanced age, everyone called him uncle. He was an elderly gentleman when I was just a child or eight or 10 years old. I believe he was in his late 80s or early 90s at that time. He must have been a young man at the time of the Civil War, however, I don't recall him speaking about it. He did tell some stories about the Ku Klux Klan, which was very active just after the war.

In his younger years he was the owner of a Hopkins and Alan single barrel shotgun. He told many stories about that gun. How it was the first breach loader in that part of the Kentucky. How it would break an egg every time at a distance of 100 yards, and how he had used it to kill the last wild Turkey in Butler County. He said that this took place up near Burnt Cabin Point. I became familiar with the gun after he had passed it along to his son, who was our closest neighbor. My brother Otis and I would borrow it when we needed an extra shotgun to go rabbit hunting. It was like no other shotgun we had ever seen. It was a lever action like a rifle and the breach dropped down so it could be loaded. Our vocabulary at that time did not contain the word recoil, so we always said she kicked like a mule. I always wanted to have it for my gun collection. One of the grandsons tried to help me find it, but our last information was that it was in some unknown attic in Louisville, with the stock broken off.

I believe the most unique thing about uncle Sylvester was that in his 90 some years he never was out of Butler County. It was rumored that he once went to visit a friend who lived on the Butler-Edmonson County line. If they stayed in the front yard and didn't go to the back yard, he would not be out of Butler County. However, no one will ever know for sure if they visited the backyard.

He would speak about trains, and said he always wanted to see one. The train passed through the next county, about 30 miles away. On a few rare occasions, when we had a high pressure system in place, you could hear the steam whistle.

Looking back through the misty veil of time, one would wonder what Uncle Sylvester would think if he viewed our country today. The lonesome wail of the steam whistle is gone forever and wild turkeys are in an abundance now. I can remember the nice warm sunny day he was baptized in Welch's Creek, in a well-known location called the Horseshoe Bend. That creek has stood the test of time, and it still looks the same today. It is where my mom and dad were first married, and where they went fishing and caught some yellow bellied catfish. It happened on the first day of May 1918. It's one of God's most beautiful creations.

74

SAD AND PERSONAL

I have always had love and admiration for each and every tree on Earth. Of course, there are some trees that are special, and occupy a very special place in my heart. One of these would certainly be the big triple trunk Sycamore that stands like a mighty giant on the bank of the creek that flows past our old home place on Long Branch School Road. It certainly represents a statue in time and history. However, what happened to my car on Sunday, April 11, 2015, caused me to temporally lose my love for trees.

On the above mentioned date, my daughter, Linda Sue, and I visited the old home place. The purpose of the visit was to check and see if there were enough sugar maples available to produce some maple syrup, since making maple syrup was one of my favorite things to do when growing up here. Doing so again was an attempt to recapture some pleasant moments of my childhood. It was a very pleasant day, warm and sunny. We parked where we usually do, just north of the big Sycamore on the road that runs up the Possum Hollow. We walked up the hollow and circled back around the bluff. We were excited because we found several nice sugar maples trees. This trip must have taken an hour or so. When we got to within sight of the car, something didn't look right. I could see this big tree laying near the car. When we got a little closer, we could see that it had fallen across the top of the car. I've had some shocks in my life, but seeing this big tree on top of my favorite car with the top caved in ranks near the top. Doors all twisted out of shape and glass everywhere. The sight left me numb and speechless.

In the first thirty seconds, my mind must have processed a thousand thoughts. What do you do when the closest place to get help is twelve miles away? This place is so remote that only God and the Internal Revenue Service knows where it located. A place where cell phones don't work.

It so happened that I wanted to see if my chain saw was working, and I had brought it along. I said to Linda, "We will use the saw and cut the log off." But she objected, pointing out the remaining log on the roof would roll down on the hood of the car and cause more damage. Of course, she was right. She got out her cell phone and started calling. By walking up and the road, she found a spot that produced a broken signal. With the signal fading in and out, she finally got enough information to my cousin Iris, and her husband Ron Webster, so they were able to determine where we were, and that we were in big trouble.

They showed up in a few minutes, and as luck would have it, Lynden Baines Johnson and his wife were out walking as well. With their help, we were able to remove the log. With the log out of the way, our next chore was to find a way to get inside the car and to see if it would run. To our surprise, it started, and it was mobile. Ron with his infinite wisdom could tell that I was a basket case and insisted on driving the car back to Morgantown. By lowering the seat and bending his head to a forty five angle, he was successful.

I have always thought that I have lived a charmed life, and my guardian angel has watched over me. I mentioned to Iris that he must have been taking a nap when this happened. Iris disagreed and explained that he was still looking after Linda and me, otherwise we would have been in the car when the tree fell, and we could have been seriously injured.

My thanks to my guardian angel, and to each of you for your help and kindness in my time of need.

75

SANDSTONE CLIFFS

Kentucky has many sandstone formations. The Red River Gorge, located in the Daniel Boone National Park, is perhaps the largest and most beautiful. Geological information indicates that the sandstone formations in Kentucky are in the neighborhood of three hundred million year old. Sediment, sand, and gravel from the ancient Appalachian Mountains were carried by a great river and deposited at a delta at the edge of a large inland sea, which covered most of central North America at that time. The sediment turned to rock and the inland sea receded. Gradually, streams began cutting through the sedimentary rocks. Since the sandstone rock is harder than the shale and siltstone, it resisted the erosion, and that is why we have so many beautiful sandstone cliffs in Kentucky.

All my life I have been impressed with the sandstone cliffs that decorated our homestead on Long Branch School Road. In early times, they were referred to as the Possum Hollow Bluff. They are located on the top of a rather steep hill that ran southeast along our property line. When the leaves had fallen in the winter months, they were visible from our house. They formed the east ridge that defined the Possum Hollow. Besides the main range of cliffs, there are a number of boulders scattered at the foot, some as large as a small house. Sandstone color varies, depending on the geographic location. In this range, the color is considered to be an off red, or light orange.

The climb from the bottom is steep, but the rewards are great. At the base of the cliff, you will be impressed with the beauty that surrounds you. A lovely forest of hardwood trees, moss growing in every conceivable location. The configuration of the rocks that time has crafted. I tend to become very emotional when visiting this location, partly due to my childhood experiences of growing up there. However, the history and majestic beauty of the cliffs are worthy of consideration. We can let our thoughts wander back millions of years to their formation, and to the people that dwelled here over the centuries. The American Indians were the latest people to inhabit this land before we came. There are numerous indications that point to their social habits and lifestyle.

The vertical face of the cliff is in the vicinity of thirty five feet high. There are some breaks in the face of the wall that lead to the top, but they are very difficult to negotiate. It was a challenge for us as teenage boys, but we were able to succeed. Now days I take the longer way around. Since it is the highest point in the area, it provides a great view of the surrounding country side and the Long Branch Valley below.

There are some things about nature that I fail to understand. If you take a walk around the cliff, you will find trees growing out of small cracks in the rocks, and they appear to be surviving quite well, where there is not a handful of soil to be seen. Makes me wonder how this is possible. My experience with planting trees has been poor. I follow the instructions, water them, fertilize them, spray them, and most of the time they don't survive.

Aside from the beauty and history of the cliff, it had a tangible value to our family. My dad was always in the chicken business. Chickens need a considerable amount of sand or grit in their diet. This is necessary to process their food and to make shells for eggs. Sandstone was ideal for this process. Chunks could be easily broken off from large rocks and crushed into fine sand. The rocks are still there, scarred with the hammer marks. This is one of my favorite places to visit.

76

SENTIMENTAL JOURNEY

Memorial Day is a United States federal holiday. With the passage of the National Holiday Act of 1971, it is celebrated on the last Monday in May, providing a three day weekend for federal employees and most everyone else. It was formerly known as Decoration Day, and was celebrated on the 30th day of May to commemorate Civil War soldiers that had lost their lives in battle. However, after World War II it was extended to include soldiers of all wars.

There are many stories as to its actual beginning, with more than two dozen towns laying claim to being the birthplace of Memorial Day. History indicates that organized groups of women in the south were decorating soldiers' graves before the end of the Civil War. While Waterloo, New York, was officially declared the birthplace of Memorial Day by President Lyndon Johnson in May of 1966, it's difficult to prove conclusively the origin of the day. It is more likely that it had many separate beginnings. Some people continue to observe it on the original May 30th date. Several bills have been introduced in congress to restore observance back to the original date, but so far they have failed to get any support for change.

Although, Memorial Day was designed to honor those who had lost their lives in war, our society has carried it a step further. Today, most of us honor our loved ones as well, by visiting cemeteries and placing flowers on their graves. Like most everyone else, some of my grandparents and some of their children passed away before I was born, or was old enough to remember them. I have always felt that not knowing them left a blank spot in my life. I'm sure that most everyone has that same feeling at times in their lives. However, come Memorial Day, we can partly fill that blank spot by visiting their resting places which will give us an opportunity to express our love, and to reflect and ponder on what we have missed by not knowing them.

My grandparents on my mother's side, George and Lily Napier Oller, their youngest daughter Mattie, my sister Bonnie, and her husband Gavin Flener, my uncle Clifford, my aunt Kate and her family are all buried in the Morgan Smith Cemetery. My grandparents on the Martin side, Vander Wright and Mary West Martin, along with many great-uncles aunts and cousins are buried in the Fannie Rone Cemetery. Both are located in Butler County. Most of my immediate family rest in the Fairview Cemetery in Bowling Green, Warren County.

In memory of all our loved ones that each of us have lost, join with me in visiting their resting places and let them know how much they are missed and remembered. If you are like me, you probably miss them most in the rebirth of spring; in the blooming of the flowers; in the beauty of autumn; in the soft blowing of the wind, and when we have joys we yearn to share. As long as we live, they will be alive in our hearts, for they are part of us, as we remember them.

As I recall, it was impossible to keep my mom from going to the cemeteries on Decoration Day, and paying her respects. I'm sure she would be pleased to know that her children and grandchildren have followed in her footsteps. Even though it may be a sentimental journey, and will take some time and effort, we must remember that anything worthwhile takes some effort. The American people are to be complimented for the love and kindness expressed for their families and friends that are not with us anymore. I have always felt that the caring people of Butler County set the standard for others to follow.

77

SHADOWS OF THE SYCAMORE

In past stories I have mentioned a few words about the majestic Sycamore that decorates our old homestead on Long Branch School Road. I've been trying to make an educated guess as to how old this stately tree really is. I can recall my dad telling me it was a large tree in the year of 1916. He was very familiar with it at that time. It was the year that he started courting my mother, who was sixteen at the time. It's no wonder that my dad fell in love with her; she was a very beautiful girl. My dad lived on Bull Creek, and mom lived with her mother and sister Kate on the extreme north end of Long Branch School Road. I'm sure that my dad visited the log home where she lived very often. The following year they slipped off to Gallatin, Tennessee, and got married.

Taking into account that it was a large tree 98 years ago, and seeing how much it has grown in that length of time, I'm convinced that it was a sapling when the pilgrims landed at Plymouth Rock in the year of 1620, which makes it 394 years old this year. To say that this tree is massive is an understatement, besides being historical and a legend in its own time.

Due to its age and size, it reigns king over all other trees in the Long Branch Valley. When the sun begins to set in the west, it casts a long shadow over this very quiet land. Something it has done for the past several hundred years. It has also provided shade for those who sacrificed so much to save the world from tyranny including Jonnie Elmore, Essie Cardwell, and many others. It's sometimes called the friendship tree. It was sort of a gathering place where the neighbors could come and visit with each other. A place where one could find some happiness, and have their picture taken.

The gentleman in the picture below is Will Childers and was taken using an old fashion box Kodak camera. I believe it was taken by my brother in the middle '40s. If you look closely you can see the corner of the brooder house in the upper right hand corner. This building was removed sometime near this date. We usually called him Uncle Will, because he was married to my dad's Aunt Laura West. Uncle Will was a small man in stature, but a giant when it came to responsibility, honesty, hard work, and common sense. Times were hard in those days, and Uncle Will eked out a bare existence farming his Welch's Creek bottom land. It would be safe to say that every dollar he ever had, was earned from the sweat of his brow. His extended family can be proud to say that that they are part of his family.

The Martin family is happy that the Sycamore is still surviving, especially me. The thought and memories attached to it are very precious. It's my hope that everyone will be able to enjoy its graceful beauty for many years to come.

Will Childers,
Long Branch School Road, KY circa 1940

78

SILENT WINGS

An owl hunting at night is a bit like a stealth bomber. Both are capable of flying undetected and attacking their target by surprise. The owl's highly specialized wing feathers enables them to fly silent and invisible in the dark of night and sneak upon their prey. The feathers on the leading edge of an owl's wing are serrated, it is believed that this breaks up the turbulence and reduces the sound of air over the wings. Feathers on the trailing edge of the wings have a tattered free flowing edge that reduces noise by breaking up sound waves. There's other advantages to silent flight. Silence makes it easier for an owl to listen and to pinpoint the exact location of its prey. Owls have great hearing abilities because their ears are set forward in their face, and the facial feathers funnel the sound directly into their ears. Their ears are offset with one ear slightly higher than the other which creates a 3-dimensional hearing system.

It's been reported that an owl can capture its prey by sound alone, without ever seeing it with its eyes. Their eyes are large which lets in lots of light. However their eyes are fixed in their sockets and will not rotate from side to side. To compensate for this, they are able to turn their head more than 180 degrees which makes it possible to see their total surroundings very quickly. This superb binocular vision, exceptional hearing, and the strong crushing power of their talons, which is said to be two or three hundred pounds per square inch makes the owl a very efficient hunter.

Owls were plentiful in Butler County when I was growing up there. They could be sighted most days perched on the top branches of a dead tree, or surveying the landscape from high in the sky. We referred to them as hoot owls, or night owls. Their hooting calls could be heard at twilight time in the spring and summer months. They would carry on a hooting conversation with each other across the valley. The species I remember were the Great Horned Owl, Barn Owl, Snow Owl, and the Screech Owl. No doubt there were others around that I wasn't aware of. It is estimated that there is more than 200 different species throughout the world.

The food they eat depends on the size of the owl. Small owls, such as the Screech Owl, feed on insects. Barn Owls eat rats and mice which are found in abundance around barns. Large owls catch rabbits, squirrels, muskrats, and your chickens if they can get to them. My mom was aware of this and every night after going to bed, she would get up and go double check the rock that was used to close the opening in the chicken coop. It is said that with their massive wings span, they can carry up to three times their weight.

As a rule, owls don't build their own nest; they use old crow nest, squirrel nest, holes in hollow trees, and ledge shelters in cliffs. The nests usually contain too or three eggs. The young owls leave the nest before they can fly, and the parents try to look after them on the ground. This creates a very unsafe condition. It is estimated that only one in 100 of these young owls survive to become adults. Most mature owls that have a mate remain in the same location. Younger owls that are not mated, tend to seek out new territories in search of food and a mate. In some parts to the world, owls are looked on with suspicion and darkness. We in America generally associate them with wisdom. This goes back as far as Ancient Greece, which was noted for art and scholarship. Athens' patron goddess of wisdom had the owl as a symbol.

79

SONG OF THE WHIPPOORWILL

Those of us who have listened to the sad and mournful song of the whippoorwill are very fortunate indeed. The last time I saw, or heard one sing, was about fifteen years ago. My brother Otis and I were visiting our old home place, and had went on down to Welch's Creek to see it we could catch a few of those nice yellow bellied catfish. Since we were in a place that we dearly loved, we may have lingered a little too long. We had left the car up on top of the hill, near where Gettie West lived. It was twilight by the time we reached the top of the hill, and setting there in the sandy part of road, with its head pointed down near the ground, was this whippoorwill, singing to the top of its voice. We were within ten or twelve feet, but it paid us no mind. After it finished singing it flew a little distance down into the Possum Hollow and started singing again.

There were an abundance of them when I was growing up in the Long Branch Community. All country boys in those days were familiar with the call of the whippoorwill. There have been many songs written about the whippoorwill. Hank Williams wrote and sang, "I'm so lonesome I could cry," which all country music lovers enjoyed. The Delmore Brothers had a big hit song when they released "When it's Time for the Whippoorwill to Sing." And there are many more songs that make reference to this lovely bird.

Some folks say that it makes their heart stand still when they hear a whippoorwill sing. Our house was located at the mouth of the Possum Hollow, and there were wooded hills on either side, these hills appeared to be one of their favorite locations to sing their song. In the twilight hours, and at dawn, one or two would begin to sing from one hill, when they had finished, the group on the other side would begin. It would cause one to believe that they were communicating with each other. It stands to reason that they would communicate with each other. However, at this time I'm not enlightened to the point where I am able to explain it properly. It's possible that they were just telling the folks in the neighborhood that spring is here, and summer is just around the corner.

The whippoorwill is a small nocturnal bird, brownish in color with very short legs that make them waddle when they walk. Their range is mostly the eastern part of the United States, from Southern Canada, south to Central America. It appears that they are not too fussy about the quality of their nest, a couple of leaves on the forest floor, or a small amount of sage brush in a field is all that is required to start raising a family. Most nests contain two eggs, which are laid in phase with the lunar cycle. The eggs hatch on an average of ten days before the full moon. And since they feed on insects, moths being their favorite food, it's possible for the adults to forage all night and find more food for their young.

It's been reported that the whippoorwill population is decreasing, and that in recent years it's become difficult to find a location where their songs can be heard. These birds have played a very important part in American history and culture, and have had a positive effect on the lives of many people. Everyone should wish them well in the future.

The legends about them are many and varied. When love is young and in full bloom, their songs add momentum and reinforces the thought that their loved is being blessed, which adds to the wonder and beauty of being in love. However, when love stumbles, and has a tendency to fall apart, their sad voice in the twilight appear to be sympathetic to a broken heart. There is also folklore stories that have followed them around for ages. If one sings to close to your house, it an omen that someone close is going to pass away. If a group lingers around a house where death is approaching, the story is that they are hoping to catch the soul of the departed. If the soul eludes them, they disperse in quiet disappointment.

Some of my friends tell me that they have experienced situations where the above appeared to be true. Since I grew up with the whippoorwills, and have a long standing relationship with them, I have never been near or witnessed any of the above happenings. However, that doesn't mean that they are not true. Taking everything into consideration, I'm going to continue to believe that every departing soul will be in the arms of an angel with snow white wings, and under those wings will be the mystic winds of time that will speed them on their way.

80

SPRING WATER

Early settlers in Butler County depended on springs for their water supply. Springs develop when the aquifers are higher than the land surrounding them. The water gravitates through openings in the Earth until it reaches the surface. These types of springs are known as non-artesian springs. The amount of water that a spring will produce depends on the pressure from the aquifer and the opening in the Earth that the water traveled through. In some instances where the water supply is abundant, they are dammed up to make a pond or small lake.

As a child growing up in Butler County, there were two springs that played an important part in my life. One was what we called the Sylvester Burden Spring. It was about three quarters of a mile from our house. It produced a considerable amount of water and continued to do so in severe drought conditions. The water was heavy in minerals, to the point that it would color the ground an orange color. Not being an expert on water, most of us would say that it was heavy with iron. Another unique thing about it was the casing. It was formed by a tree stump that was about fourteen inches in diameter and extended down into the ground approximately two feet and appeared to be somewhat petrified. As far as I know, it was the work of nature that produced it.

The second spring was located on our farm. It was just a few steps from our house, perhaps fifty steps from the big Sycamore tree. It was a large spring and produced a large amount of clear, mineral free water. My brother and I planted it with fish, which grew and thrived. Due to the fact that there were very few things for boys to do, we would tie earth worms on a string and drop them into the water for the fish to grab. Some of those fish would hang on until they were totally out of the water. Great fun for boys that were eight or ten years old.

This spring like the Sylvester Burden Spring was a perpetual flowing spring. In the hot dry months of summer it's where my mom would do our laundry, as would many of our neighbors. We had a well in our back yard, it was about twenty feet deep, and the walls were lined with flat rocks stacked on top of each other. Of course, it was mostly surface water and would go dry in the hot months of summer. I suppose we have all had mysteries in our life that we struggled to understand. Supplying water for the Martin family after the well had gone dry, was, and still is, a mystery to me. Each summer, when there was a water shortage, it was the job of my brother and me to carry water from the Sylvester Burden Spring for drinking and cooking. As mentioned, it was three quarters of a mile each way, so this was a considerable chore for small boys. I could never understand why our parents didn't utilize the water from our spring. It was nearby and wasn't hard with minerals. It would have been so simple to upgrade it to a beautiful water supply. All that was needed was to put some small stone in the bottom, set in an eighteen by thirty inch tile, and fill around it with dirt.

At this time in history, chances are, this mystery will never be resolved. However, Butler County is to be complimented on their water system. It appears that everywhere one travels in Butler County, community water is available. Great progress has been made since 1904 when the Eberman Brothers installed the first public water system in Morgantown. Looking to the future, there may never be any public utilities in the Long Branch School area. Perhaps that is good. Some places on Earth should remain as God made them. Where the serene silence is only broken by songbirds, or watching deer, and other wildlife, drinking from the springs. Something they have been doing for thousands of years.

81

STORIES WE REMEMBER

Some things that happen in our lives have a tendency to be remembered. That is true about the two following stories. It's imposable to know the exact date. My guess is that it happened sometime in the mid-1950s. My wife Ruth bought me a ring for Father's Day. It is a very nice ring called a double headed Spartan, due to the two Spartan heads that it displays. I have always been very fond of it, and received many favorable comments on how beautiful it was. We always said Ruth purchased it at a time when we couldn't really afford it.

In 1996, we lived in Florida but were building a new home in Pawley's Island, SC. Of course, we made many trips to Pawley to check on the progress of the new home. One trip we made was in the winter, and the weather was unusually cold for that part of the country. The trip being something in excess of 500 miles, took most of the day.

When we reached Georgetown, which is about ten miles south of Pawley's Island, it was getting late. We decided to stop at Shoney's for dinner. Ruth wasn't very tall, so she used a pillow cushion to sit on. When she got out of the car her cushion fell out. I picked it up and brushed it off before putting it back in the car. When we reached the motel I realized that my ring was missing. I was concerned but I didn't mention it to Ruth for fear she would stay awake all night fretting about it. The next morning, I told her it was missing, and I thought it may have fallen off when I brushed off her cushion, and that I would run down to Shoney's and look where we had parked. When I arrived, there was an employee cleaning up the parking lot with his broom and dust pan. He was just about ready to turn the corner at the back of the building when I jumped out of the car and yelled to get his attention. I told him I was searching for a ring that I might have lost in the parking lot last evening. He reached into his dust pan and pulled it out. "Would this be it?" he asked. It was difficult to believe that it was back in my hands. Five seconds more he would have been gone forever, and my chances of ever finding it would been lost. It's another example that my guardian angel was looking after me, as he has always done.

My second story is about a maroon nylon sweater that was purchased sometime in the early 1960. It was purchased from the Herpolsheimer's store in Grand Rapids, Michigan, which makes it about fifty some years old. It was actually my sweater. I've worn it off and on for many years. When my Ruth's health failed in the early '90s, and she needed a light wrap, she always wore it. In the past eight years that she has been gone, I have used it every winter to keep myself comfortable inside the house. There must be something magic or unusual about this sweater, it keeps you comfortable, but never too warm. The label is still attached. It reads, "Medium size, Ban Lon. Full fashion knit." I read the label quite often, because I repair it quite often. I've come to a sad conclusion that it is now beyond repair, and that makes me feel like I'm losing a very close friend. It really deserves a place in the Museum of Natural History in Washington, DC, but the chances of that are very slim. Maybe a glass display case would be an appropriate final resting place for this very historic piece of cloth. Perhaps it inherited its quality and durability from that store with the unusual name. My dad was intrigued with the name, and when he come to visit, would always ask if we had visited Herpolsheimer's lately.

82

LONG LIVE THE SYCAMORE TREE

In previous stories we have mentioned the large Sycamore tree that stood just a few steps from our house. This tree was a real asset to our family, the shade it provided in the hot summer days was priceless. In the early days there was no electricity to run fans or air conditioning. Our family spent many summer days under its shady branches. It was a very pleasant place to while away the hot summer hours. In addition to the shade, the creek that ran past created a very relaxing noise as it flowed over the rocks and the roots of the Sycamore. There was a number twenty spike nail driven into the tree which supported a water pail and a community dipper. The reason I refer to it as a community dipper is because it was used by everyone, even thirsty strangers that passed by could help themselves. I don't think it would be appropriate to comment on the sanitation practiced in our country at that time. However, it was the place to go if you had a chore to do, file the ax, replace the handle in the hammer, string some ginseng roots on a thread, chew some tobacco, or sip on some moonshine with your neighbors.

This tree was large when I was a small child. It had three trunks growing from the ground in close proximity. At that time, each of them were approximately twenty inches in diameter. Put them all together and you have a massive tree.

Sycamores are one of our oldest clans of trees, dating back millions of years. They are noted for their long life. Some have lived to be five and six hundred years old. Sycamores shed their bark, but the process is different from other trees. Their bark is rigid, and will not stretch as the tree expands, therefore it falls off, leaving the trunk and branches in several different colors, usually green, tan, and cream. The seed balls they produce are a very complicated process, starting with a bloom and ending up with a fuzzy ball about one inch in diameter that remains on the tree all winter, then falls apart in the spring. The wind scatters the seeds in a wide area.

In addition to all the benefits this tree provided, the fuzzy balls made great targets for us boys and our .22 caliber rifles.

Sycamore wood has not been considered a good wood for building. However it gets high marks when made into butcher blocks.

Our family is grateful that this beautiful tree is still standing, and looks about the same as it did when we were children, except considerable larger. The wound it suffered from the spike nail is still visible in the form of a bulge, but is much further up the tree. I am reminded of the poem "Trees" written by Joyce Kilmer. "Poems are made by fools like me, but only God can make tree."

I agree with Mr. Kilmer.

83

THANKSGIVING MEMORIES

In my childhood years, Thanksgiving was a very special day. Looking back, I am not sure that I appreciated this holiday for all the right reasons. Did I thank God for my many blessings? Was I grateful that I lived in a country with freedom and opportunity? Did I thank President George Washington for signing the proclamation that made it a legal holiday for every American to appreciate and enjoy? At that time in my life I am sure that these very important questions crossed my mind. However, something makes me believe that I was more interested in the festivities that it generated, than in all its other important values.

Things were quiet there on Long Branch School Road, but when a holiday rolled around, one could be sure that there would be something happening at the school house. Like most children my age, socializing was a very important thing in our lives. For Thanksgiving, we would have a party at the school house, our parents would gather in, and we children would put on a little show for them. There were always some treats for us kids, as I remember, popcorn balls were served quite often. They were made by cooking some sorghum molasses until it was very thick, almost reaching the candy stage, then the molasses was poured over the popcorn, and pressed it into balls. These balls were very tasty. Some folks referred to them as the poor man's Cracker Jacks.

At one of our Thanksgiving parties, Ralph Burden, our neighbor, who was a little younger than me, recited the very popular Thanksgiving poem, "Over the river and through the woods to grandmother's house we go." Ralph did a splendid job. What made it so memorable was his great southern accent. I have always had a soft spot for southern accents. It is part of America's culture and it would be a great loss to our country if it ever disappeared.

We should also thank the pilgrims for their courage. They, and the Mayflower, have a very special place in our history in their effort to flee persecution from the English government. They first went to Holland, but were unhappy there and returned to England. They set sail from England on September 6, 1620, with 110 people aboard. The trip took sixty-five days. They first sighted land off Cape Cod, but went on to Plymouth, which had been named by Capitan John Smith in 1614. They were concerned about the Indians, but the Indians were very friendly.

The first winter was very cold, with lots of snow which hampered the building of the settlement, only 50 of the original group survived. Among the Indians that helped the most was the one named Squanto. He could speak English, and taught the pilgrims how to make maple syrup, what plants were edible, which ones were poison, and which ones made good medicine. He taught them how to grow corn by heaping up the dirt in a row, and adding some fish that acted as fertilizer.

Since those early days, Thanksgiving has been a symbol of gratitude, love, and sharing here in America. I find it a great privilege to live in the most caring nation on Earth.

84

THAT LONESOME ROAD

Walk down that lonesome road all by yourself. Don't turn your head back over your shoulder, And only stop to rest yourself when the silver moon is shining high above the trees.

This is part of a song sung by James Taylor. He became a very popular entertainer and was inducted into the Rock and Roll Hall Of Fame in in the year 2000. His Lonesome Road song never become very popular. Perhaps it had a difficult time competing with the original Lonesome Road song that was released in 1927. The lyrics were by Gene Austin, and the music by Nathaniel Shikret, and since that time it has been recorded approximately 200 times by different artists.

The original Lonesome Road is a folk song with religious connotations, and is linked to the road of life. If we check the meaning of the words, lonely and lonesome, we find them very similar in meaning. If one decided to walk down the Long Branch School Road, it could be described as being very lonesome, very lonely, or both. However, the road of life is much more complicated than the Long Branch School Road.

When Mr. Austin wrote the words *"Look down, look down that lonesome road. Look up, look up, and seek your maker before you travel on,"* he felt that he was loaded down with the burdens of life, and the load that he was toting was more than he could carry. In addition he was unable to understand what had begun as a true love with his partner appeared to be falling apart. It's an example of the many problems we all face as we travel down the road of life.

Eddie Arnold explains in one of his songs: *"The road to that bright happy region is a narrow and dim trail they say, But the broad one that leads to perdition is posted and blazed all the way."* Makes it easy to understand why so many of us stumble on the road of life. In addition, the road of life presents many other personal problems that we have no control over. Our mobile society makes it difficult for us to stay in one location. The lure of a better place to live, the opportunity of a better job half way around the world causes us to pack up and leave our neighbors and friends that we have loved and shared our lives with over many years. Saying goodbye in these situations causes hearts to break, and many tears to flow.

Of course, there is the most dreaded time when our Heavenly Father calls, and we must say goodbye to someone we love so dearly. For the most of us, saying goodbye is one of the most difficult things we have to do in our lifetime. Perhaps if we doubled our faith, and looked a little closer at goodbye, we may find some hidden blessing in our goodbyes. It's a shortened version of "God be with you." If you have faith and the person you are saying goodbye to has faith, then God is the link that will keep you together forever. It will give us added spiritual strength, while we hold on to our many beautiful memories.

According to Mr. Taylor we should not turn our head back over our shoulder. I'm going to completely disagree with him about looking backward. I have, and I think most people I know, find it to be a very rewarding experience. Recall the old adage: If you don't know where you have been, how will you know where you are going? And as long as possible, myself, my friends, and my loved ones will continue traveling down the road of life, and on into that lonesome valley, and ask that He keep our steps steady according to His promise.

85

THE TWELVE DAYS OF CHRISTMAS

We have all heard the Christmas carol about the 12 days of Christmas. And if you are like me, you may have been baffled about what in the world do leaping lords, French hens, swimming swans, and especially the partridge that won't come out of the pear tree have to do with Christmas?

History indicates that from 1558 until 1829, Catholics in England were not permitted to practice their faith openly. During that era, someone wrote this carol as a catechism song for the young Catholics. It has two levels of meaning: the surface meaning, plus a hidden meaning known only to members of their church. Each element in the carol has a code word for a religious reality that children could remember.

1   The partridge in the pear tree was Jesus Christ.
2   Two turtledoves were the Old and New Testament.
3   Three French hens stood for faith, hope and love.
4   The four calling birds were the four gospels of Matthew, Mark, Luke and John.
5   The five golden rings recall the Torah or law, the first five books of the Old Testament.
6   The six geese a laying stood for the six days of the creation.
7   Seven swans a swimming represented the sevenfold gifts of the Holy

Spirit: Prophesy, Serving, Teaching, Exhortation, Contribution, Leadership and Mercy.

8   The eight maids a milking were the beatitudes. The eight declarations of blessedness made by Jesus in the Sermon on the Mount.

9   Nine ladies dancing were the nine fruits of the Holy Spirit: Love, Joy, Peace, Patience, Kindness, Goodness, Gentleness and Self Control.

10   The ten lords a leaping were the Ten Commandments.

11   The eleven pipers piping stood for the eleven faithful disciples.

12   The twelve drummers drumming symbolized the twelve points of belief in the Apostles' Creed.

I'm sure that there are other thoughts and stories as to how and why this Christmas carol was written. This history story was recently shared with me, and I believe it's the best explanation I have heard as to its origin.

86

THE BEGINNING

It's safe to say that everything we touch or see had a beginning, including our lives. The first ten words in the Bible reads as follows: "In the beginning God created the heavens and the Earth." We haven't been able to see how beautiful God made heaven, but we all can see how beautiful the Earth is. Perhaps, when he was creating heaven he had more beauty than heaven could hold, and some of it spilled over on the Earth. The Earth we live on is blessed with beauty—the oceans, mountains, lakes, rivers and streams, many of which are bordered with all types of vegetation, trees and wild flowers of every imaginable color. If we look closely, beauty can be found on most every spot on the Earth. Considering the fact that God had only three basic materials to work with, animal, mineral, and vegetable, we should applaud Him for doing an outstanding job.

We are surrounded with many beginnings, some are provided by Mother Nature. The rising of the sun each morning, which is the beginning of a new day, the beginning of spring, and the other three seasons.

I'll put the emphasis on spring. It's so beautiful and refreshing when it arrives. It would appear that the Earth has had a new birth. It's one of the many mysteries that we enjoy here on Earth. Beginnings, in the broadest terms, are largely started by the effort and ingenuity of the human race. When school begins, when two people are married, it's the beginning of a new way of life. Starting a new job, or a new business. The list goes on forever. We know that some of these beginnings are very important and they have contributed greatly to our way of life.

Speaking of life, most of us feel that the greatest beginning of all is when a new baby is born. "The beginning of a new life." We should all pause for a moment to consider how important the miracle of birth is. Without new babies, the human race would cease to exist. Besides, from being sweet and cuddly, babies are a very important part of God's plan for His children here on Earth. Children are such a blessing and bring love and happiness to the parents and grandparents.

Most parents have great hope and expectations for their children. It's their hope that they will follow in their footsteps, when they become adults they will become responsible citizens, and contribute to society, and leave the world in better condition than they found it. However, in some cases this doesn't happen, and much to the parents' surprise, some choose a different path to follow.

Remember the old adage: *Just because you are following a well beaten path doesn't mean that you are on the right road.* Some of our greatest achievers followed no path at all. Just their dreams. We are fortunate to have these people who chart their own course. Since we have only one life to live, it's important for everyone to lead a life that makes them happy. Scholars are going to have to dig much deeper into the basket of life to find the answer to the many questions that surround the mysteries of our lives. All life is absolutely priceless. It's the only thing on the Earth that we cannot put a price on.

87

THE BLESSING OF FRIENDSHIP

Friendship plays such an important role in our lives. To love truly and devotedly is the noblest gift with which a human being can have, and true friendship walks hand in hand with true love. People that are blessed with these attributes have a much better chance of overcoming the many adversities that are sure to plague their lives.

The definition of a friend is broad, and in some cases very complicated. Most newborn and children three or four years old are very devoted to their mother. They view their mother as their friend and protector. Most of us were very serious about the friends we made in school, and would go to great lengths to protect them. We would make up stories, make false statement to our teachers and our parents in an effort to keep them from being punished. That type of behavior must fall in into the category of true friendship.

As we become adults, our opinion about friends change. Most of us have a wide array of friends. The family friends are very important. That's because they are bound together by love. As mentioned, love and friendship walk hand in hand. Many families make great sacrifices when members of their families need help, both personally and financially.

Another group are the ones that we know well, they are the ones for whom we have warm regards and affection for. These friends are sometimes found with the people we work with, or have worked with in the past. My experience over the years has generated some very strong and lasting relationship with the people I have worked with. However, I once faced a difficult decision about trust with a certain person that said he was my friend. He certainly appeared to be my friend, he treated me with great respect. Would go out of his way to be helpful, even ask me to join his company and sit on the board of directors, which I refused. The reason I refused was because I had watched the way he had treated other people that were supposed to be his friends. He tried very hard to destroy them, in some instances he was successful. My thoughts were, if he would turn on his supposed friends, I was afraid that he would have no problem doing the same to me.

I'm a strong believer that friendship gained by chance or accident is truly a gift. It was by chance that the stories I was writing for my children about growing up in the hills of Butler County were first published in the Banner Republican newspaper. It has brought me great pleasure and happiness that the people of the county welcomed the column with open arms. But what's most important to me is all the new friends I have made in the process. With many of them I have developed a personal friendship that I cherish very much, and they have added considerable happiness to my life. It was made possible by chance, or accident. Perhaps fate helped. Fate has a way of producing miracles. One of the best things in life is to hold onto your friends. I've never had so many that I could afford to lose one.

88

THE BUTTING RAM

Once there was a silly old ram, Thought he would punch a hole in a dam. These were some of the lyrics in the song, "High Hopes", sang by Frank Sinatra many years ago. This is a story of another ram that must have been related to the one that Frank sang about, because this ram wanted to butt everything that came near him.

He was a large animal, larger than most other rams. Due to his size and temperament, he was considered to be dangerous. He belonged to a farmer that had a farm on Pea Ridge Road. This was the road that went to Morgantown. This road was graveled and was for the most part in good condition. Our farm was on Long Branch School Road, about a mile from Pea Ridge Road. The problem was that in the winter time it was a muddy mess. If you did not have a horse or a team of mules, walking was the only way to get to Morgantown. Morgantown was, and still is, the county seat for Butler County, Kentucky. It was the only place where the surrounding people could get supplies and transact business. It was essential that my dad went there once or twice each week. It took approximately one hour to cover the four mile distance, if the ferry that crossed Green River did not hold you up too long.

One cold winter day my dad was on his way to Morgantown, and was passing the farm and pasture where the ram was kept. Guess my dad was not concerned because he had traveled that road many times before without having any problems. However, this time was different. As he rounded the curve, there in the center of the road stood this big white sheep. Of course my dad was surprised and startled at the sight of this big sheep. They sized each other up for a few seconds, then the ram lowered his head and charged full speed at my dad. My dad tried to sidestep him, but received a glancing blow that knocked him back near the high bank on the right side of the road. The ram turned around and charged again, this time my dad stepped aside and the ram missed him. However, due to the high bank the ram had to stop near my dad. My dad reached out and grabbed the ram by his wool. Much to my dad's surprise, he just stood there, making no effort to pull away. My dad tried to push or pull him down the road toward the place where the fence was broken, and where he had gotten out in the first place, but to no avail. The ram refused to move. My dad knew if he turned him loose he would continue his butting rampage. As you can imagine my dad was in quite a predicament. He could see the break in the fence were the ram had gotten out. How was he going to get him back to the opening?

After some thought, he decided to see if he could ride him back to the opening, so he climbed on the ram's back and with a little nudging, the ram started walking down the road toward the opening in the fence. Once my dad had guided him to the opening and his head was on the inside, my dad slid off his back and pushed him through the opening. He then repaired the fence so the ram would not get out again. It must have been an unbelievable slight to see a man dressed in a black hat and a long black overcoat riding a big white sheep down the middle of the road. We heard later that a man and his wife witnessed some part of this. The husband said he thought he was going to have to give his wife some smelling salts as she was about to faint. She thought she was seeing a ghost.

I know this story is somewhat difficult to believe. I would not blame you if you don't believe it. But it really did happen, just this way, on a cold January day in 1934, give or take a year or so either way.

89

THE CARBIDE LAMP

Kentucky has always been a coal producing state. Butler County, which is included in the Western Coal fields of Kentucky, had several active mines when I was growing up on Long Branch School Road. As I recall, most of them were small vanes, thirty six to forty eight inches in height which made extracting the coal from the mine a very undesirable and difficult job. I recall seeing some of our neighbors returning home from a day in the mines, their faces were so covered with coal dust that it was difficult to recognize who they were. They all had carbide lamps attached to their caps, which left their hands free to use the pick and shovel, the necessary tools for digging coal.

The carbide lamp was what all miners used to light up the inside of dark mines. The lamp was developed and first sold around 1896, and become the standard light for miners, and cavers, and is still preferred by cavers today. They use the soot produced from the open flame to mark their trail on the rock walls. The carbide lamp is made up of two chambers, and a bright polished reflector which projects the light forward. The lower chamber is filled with calcium carbide and the upper chamber is filled with water. A valve is used to control the amount of water that drops into the lower chamber. There was a small lid on the top of the upper chamber that was called the water door, it would lift up so it could be filled with water.

When calcium carbide comes in contact with water it produces acetylene gas, which is very flammable, and produced the flame that makes the light. The amount of water that drops into the lower chamber controls the amount of acetylene gas, which also controls the size of the flame. It was a very efficient light; it produced its own energy to light up the darkness. To light the lamp, and get the flame burning, there was a spark wheel and flint attached to the reflector, similar to that of a cigarette lighter, that was operated by a quick spin of the wheel, using the heel of the hand. Since the flints cost money, finding a way to conserve them was important. The miners developed a method so that only one swipe of the wheel would be necessary to light the lamp. I recall watching them hold the palm of their hand over the reflector for a few seconds to trap the gas, and one swipe usually lit the lamp.

It my understanding that the carbide lamp is no longer manufactured in the United States, but is still produced in England. In our country they are considered to be a valued antique item. For us boys growing up on Long Branch School Road, we found another use for calcium carbide. Since we had no money to purchase fire crackers, we used it to make a loud bang. This was achieved by using a Clabber Girl baking powder can. At that time they were made of metal and had a recessed lid that fit very tight. Punch a small hole in the bottom of the can, drop in a small amount of calcium carbide, add a drop or two of water, pound the lid on tight, light a match to the small hole in the bottom, and it produced a loud bang.

I understand that in the Netherlands they use this same method to make loud bangs. Their reason for the bang is to scare off evil spirits. Makes one wonder what reason boys have for playing with things that make a loud bang.

90

THE CENSUS TAKER

The year was probably 1930. As I recall, the weather was not very pleasant in Butler County Kentucky at that time: cold, bleak, and wet. But regardless of the weather conditions, my dad had signed on to take the census in part of the county. In the beginning, he walked to cover the families that lived nearby, but as the distance become greater, he needed some type of transportation. Motor vehicles were very scarce in those days, and even had they been available, the dirt roads were a muddy mess and impassable to cars. With not many options available, my dad decided to rent a horse. I'm not sure that renting a horse in those days was as popular as renting a car is today. Now days when we rent a car, we insist that it be fully equipped for comfort. The same was true for horses, they came equipped with saddle and bridle. I'm not sure what the rental charges were. I would venture to guess it was near fifty cents a day. Considerably different from the fifty dollars or so we pay for a rental car.

I remember very well the day that our dad came home riding the horse. He was very large, sixteen or seventeen hands in height, and his color was grey. We children were very excited as our family had never owned a horse; this was a new experience for us. Our dad probably told us what his name was, but we were not concerned with that. The moment we saw him, we knew that his name should be Gunpowder, like the grey horse that Ichabod

Crane rode in the story of the Headless Horseman. We kids were familiar with the story because it was in one of our books at the Long Branch School at that time. It was a very interesting story due to all the problems that Ichabod had when the headless horseman scared him out of the county.

However, just because dad had Gunpowder didn't mean that all of his transportation problems were over. Mother Nature has a way of using her power when we least expect it, and at the most inconvenient time. At this time in history, she must have thought that Kentucky was too dry, and decided to dampen it up a tad. Well, dampen it up, she really did. It must have rained for the better part of a week, and soon Welch's creek was flooding the bottom land, and in a few days the Green River was over flowing its banks, and the backwater was so great that it was only a few feet from our front yard. The reason that this water created such a problem was that some of the census territory was on the other side of Welch's creek. The bridge, and the bottom land where the main road crosses Welch's creek, was all under water. With the final census report due within a few days, dad had a real problem on his hands. He felt it absolutely essential that a way be found to get to the families on the other side of the creek. There were many suggestion as to how this could be accomplished. Find a boat. A check with the neighbors, found no boat available. Build a raft from logs. No boards or nails large enough to hold a raft together.

Then, someone in the family remembered that the loft floors of the barn were rough sawed eight by twelve inch boards. That would solve the problem. By moving the corn and hay to a different location, we removed enough boards to build a four by eight foot boat and fashioned a paddle from a poplar board that may have come from the house siding. With some black tar to seal the nail holes and seams, she was sea worthy.

The trip across the water was about a mile and one half. Dad was gone a couple of days. We were all happy to see that it was a safe voyage. We kids named it Noah's Ark. We thought Noah would have been proud of it.

91

THE CHICKEN HAWKS

The hawks, that were most common in Butler County when I was a boy, were the Cooper Hawks, Sharp-shinned Hawk, Red Tailed Hawk, and a very small hawk, that was referred to as the Blue Tail. Each of these are carnivores, meat eaters, known as raptors, or birds of prey. Because they would prey on their chickens, everyone in those days gave them the nick name of Chicken Hawks.

They are all predators, and feed on small animals, such as chipmunks, all types of rodents, birds, and even snakes. They are well equipped, and have the proper tools for hunting their food. It's been said that their eye sight is eight times better than us humans. Their claws, or talons, are long, curved, and very sharp, and are used to catch and kill their prey, and if necessary, they can rip their catch to shreds with their strong hooked beak. In our neighborhood, anyone that was able to kill one of these chicken stealing thieves was considered to be a hero. Since our family was involved in the poultry business, it became quite a chore to protect our flocks from those predators.

One nice morning I was asked to stand guard over a flock of chickens, and was told to take the shotgun along, just in case any hawks ventured to close. As I recall, there was a fence made from what we called poultry netting, which was anchored on each corner of the brooder house, and extended out approximately 25 feet. There was quite a group of chickens, somewhere between 50 and 75. As mentioned, it was a beautiful sunny day so I sat down on some straw and rested my back against the brooder house wall. I can recall how important I felt, doing a man's job, protecting the chickens with the big .12 gauge shotgun laying across my lap. It must have been very comfortable, because I fell asleep.

Suddenly, I was awakened by the noise chickens make when they are frightened. There, in front of me, was this very large hawk. He or she was two or three feet above the ground, and the chickens were running in all directions. It was my first experience being so close to such a large hawk. The wing span was three or four feet wide. I could see those red and gold eyes, the big hooked beak, and those large talon claws, all spread out with the intention of grabbing a chicken. It all happened in a split second, the Hawk must have realized that I was there and became frightened, and got out of there without a chicken. I was so excited that I forgot that I had the shotgun, and above all, missed my opportunity to become a hero. I was very disappointed about letting the hawk get away.

As time has passed I have become very pleased with the way it all ended. The hawk, the chickens and I all survived. However, there is a question that remains. Did the hawk fail to see me sitting there? Or did he or she feel that it was just a boy that was sound asleep, and it will be easy to grab a chicken before he wakes up? With their sharp eyesight, it's hard to believe that I could not be seen.

Hawks are now protected by law. We have learned that they play a very important role in keeping our ecology in balance. Otherwise we could be overrun by rodents. Hawks have all the characteristic of eagles, that noble bird that we have adopted to be the national emblem of the United States. It's my hope that they will all find a safe haven here in America.

92

THE CROSSCUT SAW

The crosscut saw played a major role in my life, my family, and most everyone else in Butler County at the turn of the 20th century. It was the primary tool for cutting wood which was the energy source available for heating homes and cooking food at that time.

My brother and I were very familiar with the crosscut saw. It was our assignment to keep an ample supply of wood available at all times. It was basically a full time job in the winter months. The improvised barrel stove we used for heating would devour a rick of wood in a very short time. Of course, we complained about the amount of work at the time. However, looking back, we were fortunate to have a crosscut saw. Otherwise, we would have had to chop the wood with an ax which would have required much more work.

History indicates that rudimentary saws have been around for quite a while. They were in use in ancient Egypt, and the Roman Empire, a few hundred years BC. In the 17th century, the European countries made great improvements on the crosscut saw. That was about the time that they started immigrating to America. I'm assuming that when they viewed the size of trees in America's virgin forest, they were convinced that the big crosscut saw was an absolute necessity.

There are several types of crosscut saws but the ones that I am familiar with are the one-man crosscut, two-man crosscut, or bucking saw. The one man crosscut was a six foot felling saw designed to cut down standing timber. These are that big old strip of thin metal saws with an elaborate set of teeth. A two-man saw had a handle on each end. Most have anywhere from two to four cutting teeth in a groups, and one raking tooth. The design is simple: the cutting teeth cuts the wood and the flat raking teeth rake out the sawdust to prevent clogging. They are also designed with a curve on the tooth side, as well as on the back side, this makes it easier to drive in a wedge. Wedges are used to prevent the saw from binding and to make the tree fall in the proper location. The bucking saw is thicker and heavier, and is designed to cut horizontal logs.

Using a two-man crosscut saw is a team effort, both workers must pull and push in rhythm, if one doesn't do his part the other person will become aware of it immediately. I know from firsthand experience that this can lead to very heated confrontation.

Saws like most other cutting tools become dull and need to be sharpened. They also needed to be reset on occasion. Resetting becomes necessary when the cutting teeth become worn and the kerf is not wide enough to keep the saw from binding. I understand that there were tools available to help in this process. Due to economic conditions, these tools were not available at the Martin farm, so the job of resetting the saw was assigned to Grandpa Martin. He made his own tools by cutting a slit in a board that would accommodate the handle of the old time flat iron inserted upside down, that way he had a flat steel edge to lay the teeth on. By striking them with a hammer and using the correct amount of force, he could reset a saw to like new condition.

I believe that America would not have become the greatest nation on the Earth without the help of the crosscut saw. In the building of our nation it was used to clear the land for farming, build cabins and villages. Basically every railroad in America was built with ties cut by a crosscut saw.

If we look back at the crosscut, and the people that built our country, we get a sense of courage, strength, and patriotism. Something that our country still needs. The crosscut is fast disappearing from our land. If we see one today, it most likely will be decorating the wall of a rustic cabin.

93

THE DANCE

As mentioned before, Aunt Kate was my mom's sister, and she and her family lived just up the school house road from our place. Although they were sisters, they were so different. My mom was content with her life and family and there were only a couple of things she struggled to change. One was to try and improve our way of life, and the other was to light a fire under our father's ambition and get him to do some of the things that he was capable of doing. But I don't recall a change of any size.

Our aunt Kate was totally different. She was a fun loving person, excitement and socializing was very important to her. Unfortunately, Butler County had very little to offer a person that was interested in this type of lifestyle. In order to brighten up her life a tad, one day she announced that there would be a dance at her house on Saturday night, September 22. Invitation was by word of mouth, and within a week or so, everyone within a five mile radius was aware of the big dance.

I would estimate that I was about six years old at that time, and the first thing that I remember was a group of men on horseback riding down the Possum Hollow, and the road, such as it was passed near our house. Of course, all of us children ran out to see what was happening, but we didn't recognize any of them. My dad spoke to them, they told my dad that they had heard about the big party at Aunt Kate's place, and had come to join in on the fun. I can still visualize them setting there on their horses with cigarettes hanging from their lips, and the corks from moonshine whisky bottles visible from their pockets. As small as I was, they didn't leave a positive impression on me. I recall my mom and dad discussing whether we should go or not. It appears that they decided that it would be alright to attend, because the next thing I remember we were there.

My memory is a little vague about the number of people that were there. My guess is that there were somewhere between fifteen and twenty. Must have been quite cozy as Aunt Kate's house only had two twelve by fifteen foot rooms. I recall seeing a couple of guys doing some type of solo dance. But I was small and sleepy, so my mom put me on one of the beds so I could get a nap. The next thing I knew was my mom getting me off the bed and on my feet, and pushing me toward the back door. I was still half asleep, and ended up in back of the door. While I was back there, some big fellow was knocked or pushed against the door and almost crushed me. But we must have made it home alright.

The following day there were lots of stories floating around about the big fight, and some visual evidence of just how brutal it was. Carley Napier, who was related to us on my grandmother's side of the family, stopped in at our place. Carley had been an active participate in the slugfest, and had plenty of scars to prove it. Besides cuts and abrasions, someone had crashed a chair over his head, leaving deep wounds and two black eyes. However he was still able to laugh about the situation, because Carley had a reputation for loving a good fight. It was said that more than once, when Carley was out drinking in a bar, and some big guy would stand up and announce that he could whup any S.O.B. in the room. Carley would stand up and say he was ready to challenge that statement.

Another story was that some of the fighting drifted out into the back yard, and whoever was fighting with John Kat Phelps, grabbed a grubbing hoe that had no handle, and was hanging on a nail on the side of the house, and chopped John Kat in the head several times. Of course, there were no doctors available. Had there been one available, the injured would have been afraid to see them, for fear the Sheriff would want to know how and where it happened. As I recall every one lived in fear that the long arm of the law might find out about the fight, but if they ever heard about what happened, they never pursued it, which made everyone involved happy.

Being small at the time, I don't recall what comments my Aunt Kate had about the outcome of her party but I am sure she was disappointed. In the early days, people like my Aunt Kate who liked to have fun and socialize, were looked upon as a little different, and did not fit into society as it was view at that time. As I have grown older and reflected on my Aunt Kate, I have concluded that she was ahead of her time, and was born 75 years too soon. It appears that most people today set a high priority on having fun and socializing. I am afraid that if we picked only friends today that were against having fun and socializing, we would have very few friends. I would like to say to my Aunt Kate, if you are listening up there, I'm defending your right to live your life the way you did. You would fit like a glove in our society today.

You have heard the saying that no matter how bad something is, something good can come from it. John Kat, the fellow who got his head chopped with the grubbing hoe, is a testament to how factual this is. It was reported that the hair on John's head was straight, but after the chopping it got, it grew back nice and wavy. All I can say is that that is a tough way to get wavy hair.

94

THE EVENING SUN

Today, when the sun sets in the western skies of Kentucky, as it has done every day from the beginning of time, chances are good that there will be no one there in the Long Branch School Community to witness the beauty of its setting. As it hides its face behind a few billowing clouds, the rays from the sun will turn them into a multitude of splendid colors. When this all happens, we know that the day is finished, and twilight is approaching.

Twilight is sometimes considered the most peaceful, pleasant, and rewarding part of the day. It was a time when neighbors would come to visit, and perhaps bring some news about what had happened in and around the immediate area. If news was scarce, my dad could always get out the guitar and pick and sing a few songs. I recall two of his favorites. *"Rabbit stole a pumpkin, and started down through town, when he heard them dogs a coming he laid his pumpkin down."* And if there were children in the group, or if Christmas was near, he would sing the Christmas song. *"Children would you like to go up to Santa land, where the Christmas dollies grow, and it's Christmas all the year."* It's the only time in my life that I have heard those songs. Wish I could give you more information about them. However, at this time I have been unable to find any history as to where and when they originated. Perhaps the ever flowing tide of time has washed them away forever.

If you are like me, you have a tendency to keep looking back over your shoulder in an effort to recapture segments of history. If possible, I would like to find out who the people were that lived on the land where I grew up, before it was occupied by the Martin family. I'm angry with myself for not asking this question when there was someone around to answer them. I'm sure that my grandmother Lily Oller, or Uncle Sylvester Burden, could have explained everything I wanted to know about these early settlers.

It's easy to tell that there were people living there before we did due to the many signs that remained. There was an apple orchard with a number of trees one of which was an Arkansas Black. It produced some of the most delicious apples anyone ever tasted, but like the rest of the trees, it was getting old and died within a few years of our moving there. Also, there were a number of plum bushes that grew near the spring. They produced yellow fruit the size of a fifty cent piece. They lingered on for a number of years. I keep looking to see if some sprouts might come up from the roots. But nothing so far. There were no roots or stumps in the cleared land which indicated that it had been farmed for a number of years.

All this confirms my thoughts that they were there but I wonder who were they, and why did they settle there? Could it be that they liked the beauty of the land, the hills and valleys, the songs of the birds, the abundance of wild life, and the serene quietness, and at the closing of the day, they could look westward down the Long Branch Valley and watch the going down of the sun, which is captivating in its beauty? I'm sure these early people were happy living there, laughed when things were going well and cried when misfortune and tragedy came calling. As in the scheme of life, the sun has gone down on their lives, and we miss them. We who came after them are grateful that they were good stewards of the land and left it very much the way they found it. I venture to say that if Goldilocks was out picking wild flowers, and happened to stumble into this Long Branch location, she would say "This is just right."

95

THE FALLING OF THE LEAVES

"Autumn Leaves" is a much recorded popular song. It originated in France in 1945 and at that time was called "The Dead Leaves". In 1947, Johnnie Mercer wrote the lyrics in English, and Jo Stafford was among the first to sing this version. "Autumn Leaves" become very popular in both languages, and was made into a movie in 1956 starring Joan Crawford. I always thought the lyrics were very beautiful. *"The falling leaves drift by my window. The autumn leaves of red and gold. I see your lips, the summer kisses. The sun-burned hand I used to hold. Since you went away, the days grow long, and soon I'll hear old winters song. But I miss you most of all, when autumn leaves began to fall."*

In addition to being a sentential time, fall is a time when Mother Nature displays some of her most beautiful work. The bright orange, red, and yellow leaves mixed with a swath of green never fails to delight us. In order to display these beautiful colors, trees must go through a long and technical process. Like all other living things, trees must have water. They get water from the ground through their roots. They take a gas from the air known as carbon dioxide. Trees use sunlight to turn water and carbon dioxide into oxygen and glucose. Oxygen is a gas in the air that we all breathe. Glucose is kind of sugar that trees and other plant use for food, energy, and building blocks for growing. The way trees turn water and carbon dioxide into water and sugar is called photosynthesis. That word means letting the sunshine and the light in. Chlorophyll is the chemical that gives leaves their green color.

As autumn approaches, and the days become shorter, tree recognize that it's time to begin getting ready for winter. In the winter, there is not enough water and light to grow. The tree will rest and live off the food it has stored in the summer months. When that happens, the green chlorophyll will disappear from the leaves, and we begin to see the bright orange, red, and yellow colors start to appear. A small amount of these colors were there all the time. However, we were not able to see them in the summer, because they were covered up by the green chlorophyll. As far as I know, wherever you see a green leaf, or a bright yellow, orange, or red one, they have all followed this same plan that nature provided for them.

The trees along Long Branch School Road are no exception. I recently spent some time there at our old home place where I grew up. There is a large sugar maple tree standing in what was once our front yard. It was getting ready for winter; its leaves had turned yellow and gold. It presented a very striking and beautiful picture with the late afternoon sun enhancing its brilliant colors. This tree occupies a very special place in my memory. My brother Otis and I had transplanted it there when it was approximately three feet tall. I was somewhere in the vicinity of twelve years old at the time. If we calculate the time that has passed it would be seventy eight years old at this time.

It was a beautiful day, very calm and still, with no wind. However, around four in the afternoon, a very soft whispering breeze suddenly developed, and leaves began falling. The wind only lasted a couple of minutes, and passed on. I am inclined to believe that the mystic wind of time was paying us a visit, and was trying to communicate its story with us. How interesting it would be if we could only understand what it's trying to tell us.

96

THE GHOST OF RED HILL

In the early days, thirty years or so before the bridge at Aberdeen was completed, to reach the Red Hill from Morgantown it was necessary to cross the Green River on the ferry boat. From the Morgantown ferry leading north, you would travel on the Leonard Oak Road. It takes you across the river bottom land, over the big iron bridge that crossed Welch's Creek, and on to the forks of the road where Noah Johnson and his family owned and operated a small grocery store. At this point, you had traveled approximately four and one half miles. Then you continue on Leonard Oak Road for an additional two miles, and you will be in the vicinity of Red Hill. On this leg of your journey you will have passed other landmarks, such as the Eland Coleman Store, and the road that runs down to the quaint little village of Martindale, and Bull Creek. Just before you start to descend Red Hill, look to your right, and you will see the Brush Arbor. In your travel you will be mostly on a dirt road. However, this was a time in history when gravel roads were becoming more available, and you may have found some sections of the road improved. If it was a very beautiful spring day, you were able to enjoy the scenery along the way. However, if you were going to Cedar Grove, or Jetson, and got delayed, and found yourself traveling back after dark, you could encounter the Ghost of Red Hill, as several people in the neighborhood had spoken about.

One night Clora Cox was riding her horse down Red Hill on her way to visit her relatives that lived on up the road a few miles. As she was riding along, she noticed what appeared to be a woman dressed in white, walking along side of her horse. Now, Miss Clora was of pioneer heritage, and as a rule not easily intimidated. However, the magnitude of what was happening sent chills through her body, and then stark naked fear took control. She lashed her horse with the ends of the bridle reins, and sent him full speed down the road, and didn't slow down until she reached the home of her relatives. Not only was Miss Clora very frightened, she almost killed a good horse in the process. Her daughter, Miss Alice Cox, tells me that for the rest of her life, Miss Clora would never go near Red Hill after dark.

At this time in history we had a very competent medical doctor in Morgantown named was Dr. George Estil Embry. Most people referred to him as Dr. Estil Embry. He opened his office in Morgantown in the winter of 1911. Dr. Embry and my dad were friends and were both members of the Masonic Lodge in Morgantown. When something of interest happened to either of them they would usually discuss the situation.

It appears that one day the good doctor was on a medical call to see a patient up near the Temple View area. He had some trouble locating the residence where the patient was, which caused him to have to drive back to his office in the dark. The doctor was driving the most widely used car at that time, the Model T Ford. The doctor was trying to negotiate the car up the Red Hill and due to the darkness and the road conditions, he was going very slow. Suddenly a woman dressed in white stepped from the roadside, and took hold of the front fender of the car. According to the story, the car hesitated, and tried to stop, but in his frightened condition, the doctor gave the car all the gas available and left the lady in white behind.

This story may sound a little unbelievable. However, I have never been one to dispute the word of a fine Christian lady and a good doctor.

97

THE GINSENG PLANT

The ginseng plant is considered to be one of the world's greatest herbal healers. The roots of this slow-growing plant have been used in China and other Asian countries for thousands of years, and the therapeutic qualities of ginseng is recognized the world over. It's found growing here in the eastern part of the United States and in Canada, and has been harvested and exported to Asia for the past 300 years. Native Americans were aware of its medical properties and would chew the roots as a method of extracting the medical juices.

Growing up on Long Branch School Road, we were always searching the Possum Hollow woods near the sandstone cliffs for the ginseng plants, and when we were lucky enough to find a dozen or so, we would bring them back to the house, sit under the big Sycamore tree, and, using a needle and thread, we would string them on the thread so they would dry. I don't remember which one, but one of the stores in Morgantown would buy the ginseng roots. I'm not sure, but chances are good that it was the produce store operated by Clyde Guffy. In difficult economic times it was one way to make a dollar now and then.

Ginseng is a green leaf perennial plant that changes its appearance in the early years of its life. In its first year after sprouting from a seed, it will have a tiny stem about three or four inches tall with three leaves, and will disappear in the winter months. In its second year it generally has two leaf prongs and grows to a height of five or six inches. The third or fourth year, there is usually three leaf prongs, and a yellow greenish flower will develop from the stem which produces the seeds.

Like most of our neighbors at that time, we had no knowledge about how this very important plant reproduced, therefore we gathered all plants large or small. Over the years, this practice has almost eliminated the wild ginseng plant in many states, Kentucky included. I understand that most states have passed laws controlling the harvesting of this plant. Some of the most important features of the law makes it a violation to harvest any plant that is less than five years old, and then not before the month of September, and that the seed be replanted if it is still clinging to the stalk. The age of the plant can be determined by feeling the stem just below the surface of the ground. You will find an enlarged area on the stem just above the root, it is called the rhizome. If the rhizome is half inch or longer, it indicates the plant is mature and can be harvested.

Recently, I read a short story written by Jesse Stuart. Jesse grew up in the mountains of Greenup County, Kentucky, and is considered to be one of our state's greatest writers. His writing was mostly about early life in the mountains. His short story titled "The Pullover Sweater" inspired me to write this story. The setting of the story began at the Greenup County High School, where two boys, Shan Stringer and Roy Tomlinson, were competing to become the football star. Roy had his pullover sweater with two strips, and it was being worn by Jo-Anne, the girl that Shan was in love with. There was another girl by the name of Grace Hilton, the neighbor girl that Shan had walked to school with in both grade school and high school. Being the caring person that Shan was, he would carry her books and walk the path in front of her in case there were any snakes. Shan's performances on the football team had won him three strips, but he was too poor to buy a sweater to put them on. Shan turned his thoughts to his family, perhaps they could lend him the ten dollars which was the cost of the sweater. But after serious consideration, he could not think of anyone in the family that had ten dollars. So, in desperation, he went to the bank and ask Mr. Cole if he could borrow ten dollars. Mr. Cole asked what he needed the money for. Shan told him he needed to buy a sweater. Mr. Cole had him sign a note and then gave him

$9.75, keeping twenty five cents for interest. The note had a duration time for six months, and Mr. Cole indicated that he expected him to pay it back in full at that time. Shan was very excited and went and purchased the sweater immediately, then had his mom sew on the big G, which was the logo of the Gladsen High School, and the three red stripes on the sleeve, and gave it to his girlfriend Jo-Anne to wear.

Everything went well until Shan noticed that the six month date for repaying the note was fast approaching. He had no money to pay it back, and knew no one, or any place where he would be able to obtain the ten dollars. This started to worry him and pressed on his mind until he become very despondent, which continued to get worse. Then Jo-Anne offered some harsh criticism, and gave him back his sweater, which made the problem worse. After several efforts, Grace finally coaxed him into telling her what the problem was. "The note was due in ten days and I don't have the ten dollars to pay it off," he said. "I don't have it either," Grace said quietly. "If I did, you could have it. But that doesn't help. Maybe I will think of a way. " On their way home from school the next day, Grace asked, "When is the note was due?" Shan replied, "Ten more days." So Grace said, "We'll have it by then." Shan was taken back by her statement until she explained that she had noticed a sign at the Dave Darby store indicating that they were paying a good price for ginseng and other wild roots. Shan thought that it was too late. However, Grace insisted that on their way home, they go down in the cove area and look for ginseng. Much to their surprise they were able to find a reasonable amount of ginseng and yellow root. So every day after that, on their way home from school, they would visit the cove and try to fill up their lunch pails. Shan would carry it home, string it on thread, and hang it on a nail above the stove to dry.

On April 27th, one day before the note was due, Shan took a small sack of dried May-apple and yellow root, and more than a pound of ginseng roots to Mr. Darby's store. When Mr. Darby was through weighing and figuring, he said, "It all comes to sixteen dollars if you trade it out in the store." "How much if I take cash?" Shan asked. "Fifteen dollars," he said. Shan took the cash and went to straight to the Citizens Bank and paid his note. On the way home, Shan told Grace how much the roots had brought, and there was five dollars left which he gave to Grace. "We'll dig some more to make up your share," he said "Wonderful," she said, smiling at him. Shan looked at Grace and wondered why he had never noticed how beautiful she was, beauty such as Jo-Ann would never have. Grace was as beautiful as the mountains in springtime.

Then Shan asked if she would do one more thing for him. "Take off Roy Tomlinson's sweater," he said. "But what will I do without it?" she asked. "It keeps me warm." Shan started to pull off his sweater, then he felt her hand on his arm. "No, Shan," she said. "Keep it a while. I couldn't wear it yet." That was all the promise Shan needed. He was proud of her. She was not going to discard Roy's sweater in the same manner that Jo-Ann had treated his. Shan didn't know what she was thinking, but he was thinking that school would soon be over, and he could build a house, if she wanted it, there on Seaton Ridge on the path that leads from her family's house to his.

We are aware that ginseng has great medical benefits, but it also appears to be a purveyor of love and romance, as well. Remember the old adage: "I love you because you are beautiful, or you are beautiful because I love you."

98

THE GREEN RIVER

The Green River rises in Lincoln County, Kentucky, and flows southwest through south-central Kentucky. I am not sure how it got its name. Perhaps, when it's in its normal state it does look green. On its journey to the Ohio River, it passes through Butler County. If one went up Long Branch School Road and continued over the hill it would be about a mile and one half from the Martin farm. Butler County is fortunate to have this beautiful and historic river flowing through its land. It has contributed substantially to the wealth and welfare of this county.

It has a long history of activity over the past 100 years. Before highways were built, it was the lifeline of commerce. Most everything moved on the river in barges pushed by tugboats. The big Stern Wheelers that carried passengers, mail, and smaller items were called packets. They were a splendid and beautiful sight to see. The ones I recall seeing were usually painted white with two large black smoke stacks and a large rear paddlewheel painted red. Once or twice each year, the showboat would visit Morgantown. It would anchor near the ferry boat crossing. The bridge across the river was not completed until sometime in the early 50s. Before that everyone had to use the ferry. At times, when the river was running wild, it was a time-consuming and life threatening event, to say the least. But the showboat would arrive when the river was quiet and on its best behavior. You would know that it was there when you heard the calliope music. A Calliope is a musical instrument made up of a number of steam whistles and played from a keyboard, sometimes called a steam organ. Its music was so loud it could be heard for several miles in all directions. I was never on the showboat because it cost money, and in the time of the Great Depression the expression was, "dollars were as big as a wagon wheels."

The river played another important role in the lives of the Martin family. My grandfather, Van Martin, built a house boat on the river and moved the family in as a permanent living quarters, which they occupied for a number of years.

One way to make some money was by catching railroad ties that were floating down the river. At that time, railroads were being built at a rapid pace and ties were in demand. When ties were made in the forest they needed to be sold, so they were transported to the river and neatly stacked upon the banks, where they waited for the boats to pick them up. Many times before they were picked up, a large amount of rain would fall, and the river would overflow its banks, sending the ties floating down the river. Since the Martin family was down there, they would use a johnboat to capture them, restack them on the river bank, and put the Martin name on them. Then they would sell them when the next boat came by.

Of course, there was no power to propel the houseboat up and down the river. They used a system called a windless. This consisted of a rope, and a large bobbin with a crank handle attached. One end of the rope was attached to the bobbin, the other end was carried up the river and secured to a tree. By turning the crank the rope was wound around the bobbin, and this would propel the boat upstream.

The stories that I heard from my dad and uncles was that they enjoyed the river life very much.

99

THE HONEYSUCKLE VINE

Springtime is the time of the year when God's work takes center stage, and for all of us who are fortunate enough to live here in the south, we are blessed with the beauty and sweet fragrance of the honeysuckle vine. This woody climbing vine grows in abundance here in Kentucky and neighboring states. There is a beautiful song, titled "Kentucky Babe," written by Richard Henry Buck in 1896. It has been recorded by Bing Crosby, Perry Como, Eddie Arnold, and many other artists. What makes this song so special is that it's about Kentucky, the honeysuckle vine, and a baby. While we hold Kentucky and the honeysuckle flower high on our priority list, it would be difficult to find anything more precious and valuable than a baby. If you don't have a recording of this song, do yourself a favor and try to find one. I consider it a national treasure.

I had my first contact with this remarkable flower when I was a child. My dad's Aunt Laura and her husband Will Childers had a vine that grew on a trellis in their backyard. I can still recall how beautiful it was, and what a sweet smell it had. I'm am sure that around Butler County, there may be some vines still growing that were taken from Aunt Laura's original plant.

There are approximately 180 species of honeysuckle vines in the world. China has the largest amount. Europe and North America have approximately 20 each. Some of the most common ones growing in our location are the European Woodbine, the Japanese White, and the Trumpet. These blooming vines have many amenities, they also have some liabilities. Sometimes they spread so fast that it becomes a full time job to keep them under control, and if they climb a small tree or shrub, they can wrap around the tree trunk so tight that it prevents the sap from flowing up the tree, and if this happens, the plant will die. However, these problems are small compared to all the pleasures they provide. Some folks believe the fragrance they emit is unmatched by any other flower, and of course, they attract many of our favorite friends, such as the hummingbirds. It appears that they think the nectar in the honeysuckle flower is the sweetest of all flowers. And of course the honeybees and many other members of the bee family feed there as well.

At this time in my life I am blessed with honeysuckle vines by the hundreds. Due to the fact that there is practically no homes being built in the last few years, there are a number of vacant lots in back of my home. These lots are saturated with honeysuckle vines. Some small trees are so completely covered with vines that it's impossible to tell what type of tree it is. It looks like such an ideal place for hummingbirds to gather and feed. Much to my surprise, very few are seen feeding there. Makes one wonder if hummingbirds are becoming a scarce commodity. We hope that isn't the case. Perhaps these particular honeysuckles are stingy with their nectar.

It's been said that in the early days, children would suck the nectar from the flowers, and that's how the honeysuckle got its name.

100

THE ICE PLANT

The last time I visited Butler County, I decided that I should drive down and look at the sight on the Green River where the Morgantown Ferry once operated. It's a place where I spent considerable time when I was young, waiting to cross the river. The first thing I noticed was how steep the hill is leading up to Morgantown from the river. Looking back in time, I don't recall being concerned about having to climb two very steep hills in order to reach Morgantown from our place on Long Branch School Road. I suppose being young has some advantages. Next, I noticed the location where the ice plant was once located. There is some structure, cement footings, and other debris which show where it once stood.

In the last part of the 19th century, and basically the first of the 20th century, ice was a very important product. When things settled down after the Civil War, Texas and Kansas became leaders in supplying beef to the rest of our country. Since refrigeration had not been developed to any extent at that time, ice was used to keep the meat from spoiling. In the year of 1900, there were 677 ice plants in the United States, and the biggest share of them were in Texas. I understand that the one in Morgantown belonged to the Eberman brothers, who were also responsible for providing the first public water and electric service for Morgantown citizens.

As a child I had the opportunity to be inside the plant on a few occasions.

As best I can remember, the building housed a large generator and a large one cylinder gasoline engine that was sometimes referred to as a one lunger. It provided the power to drive the generator that produced electricity, which was necessary to drive the compressor in the ice making process. When the gas engine was operating, it made a somewhat muffled bang that could be heard for several miles. We could hear it at our place on Long Branch School Road. The ice was frozen in metal containers, and I would estimate that they were thirty inches by twelve inches by sixty inches long, and each block of ice would weigh 300 pounds. The containers were in a pit all together. They stood upright, and the top ends were near the main floor level, and the ends of the frozen ice was visible.

The plant was operated by our neighbor, Mr. Homer House. His daughter attended Long Branch School. Since there were no refrigerators at that time, many people used ice boxes to preserve their food. The ice was delivered to the homes by horse or mule drawn wagons. There was a time when the cost of ice was more expensive than the food that it saved. But that changed when manufacturers discovered new and more economic methods to produce it. As I recall, the cost of ice was of no concern to the Martin family. When we wanted to keep food from spoiling, it was put in a pail, a rope was tied to the handle and lowered down in the well. Temperature near the bottom of the well was approximately fifty five degrees, which helped some.

Since the early days, great changes have been made in refrigeration. We now have outstanding quality and convenience in home refrigerators, with ice dispensing, and cold drink machines everywhere we travel. Last but not least, air conditioned homes, and cars. How did we ever live without air conditioning? Ice is now considered a food item and is controlled by the Food and Drug Administration, I believe we would all agree that is a good thing.

101

THE DARKNESS OF VIOLENCE

Growing up in the early part of the twentieth century on Long Branch School Road in Butler County, violence was a concern of most people in the county. Next to having enough food for survival, violence was upper most in the mind of most everyone.

It was true that some parts of the county had the reputation of producing a considerable amount of moonshine whiskey. While this occupation was unlawful, it was not a violent crime. However, it is believed the over consumption of this product was guilty of leading to more violence.

As far as I can remember, there was several fatal shootings and other shootings that left people wounded in the county at the time we lived there. I don't recall exactly where it was, but one of the shootings took place a few miles north of us in one of the churches. To the best of my memory, the minister and a lady that sang in the choir lost their lives. The second shooting happened in Morgantown, where a man that ran a restaurant on what was then called Dog Walk St. was fatality shot. It was reported that both shootings in some way were tied to the moonshine business. My memory tells me that these shootings took place in the mid-1930s.

At that time in history, there was a very popular song, titled "Twenty One Years." For some reason, that was the sentence most people received at that time for committing violent crimes.

While these were violent crimes and shouldn't have happened, they were small and isolated compared to what has happened in our country recently. A few of these incidents include the shooting in Fort Hood which took thirteen military lives, the shooting in a Colorado theater where twelve people died, the church shooting in Charleston which left nine church members dead, and the recent attack on the military post in Chattanooga that killed five military people. If we look close at the violence in our country in recent years, it's easy to see that it is the innocent that are suffering the most.

The etymology of the word violence comes from the Latin word "violare" which gives us "violation." There are many types of violence. Murder, rape, theft, starvation, and abuse, both physical and mental. They are all forms of violence that violate and dishonor the dignity of the human body and spirit. Life in this world is given by God, and violence that destroys life is against God's teaching. He must be very disappointed in the way that so many of His children have strayed from His teaching.

There are many opinions about the reason that we have had so much violence in our country in the last few years. Some believe that America is drifting back into the dark ages and may soon become a barbarous state. Their belief is based on the fact that Christianity, which is considered to be the foundation of civilization, is under attack. Law and order, which is necessary for a free society to function, and is designed to keep its citizens free from harm, is also being criticized when that branch of public service attempts to enforce the laws of our land.

Many Americans take these situation lightly and feel that there is nothing to worry about. However, some of our brightest citizens are concerned. And their advice is, "If you are not concerned, you should be."

102

THE LINCOLN PENNY

The Lincoln penny has a very long and interesting history. The penny gets its name from the British coin, pence, and the British influence was still notable when I was growing up in Butler County, Kentucky. I was five or six years old, and one of the neighbor girls who was about the same age politely informed me that her mom was not going to buy an item from my dad because he wanted a dime for it, and her mother had only two pence she could spare.

Benjamin Franklin designed the first one cent piece for America in 1787. It was much larger than the pennies we have today. In fact, it was about the size of our current one dollar gold coin. In the 64 years that it was in circulation, it had several designs: the flowing hair, the flowing hair wreath, liberty cap, just to name a few.

In 1857, the small penny was introduced. It was known as the Flying Eagle design, which was later replaced by the Indian Head penny, which was in circulation until 1909 when it was replaced by our current Lincoln Head penny. When Theodore Roosevelt was president, he was of the opinion that the American coinage needed to be updated. He was the friend of a well-known sculptor by the name of Augustus Saint-Gaudens, and asked him to redesign the American coins. Unfortunately, Mr. Saint-Gaudens passed away before his work was finished. Had he lived to finish the designs he had started, history indicates that our pennies would be totally different today.

The task was taken over by a sculptor by the name of Victor David Brenner. At that time, the chief engineer of the U.S. Mint was Mr. Charles Barber, who had his own thoughts about what the one cent piece should look like. He was also unhappy that Mr. Brenner was an outsider, and not part of the U.S. Mint establishment, and was very critical that Mr. Brenner had included his initials V D B in a very conspicuous manner on the reverse of the coin. Due to so much criticism, the initials were eventually removed. However, the president had seen Mr. Brenner's rendering of President Lincoln, he was impressed, and gave the order to use the image of the slain president on the obverse, and the wheat straws on the reverse of the new penny.

The Lincoln penny is unique in two ways. It has been in circulation longer than any other coin in the United States. When the prototypes were made, they found that there was too much space on the coin above President Lincoln's head. It was decided to fill in the space with the motto "In God We Trust." It was the first time a coin of such a small denomination had been honored with that motto. Although the obverse has featured the profile of President Lincoln since 1909, the reverse has gone through many changes. It featured the wheat straw from 1909 to 1958, and then the Lincoln Memorial from 1958 to 2008. In order to commemorate Lincoln's bicentennial birthday, in 2009 the U.S. Mint struck four new designs on the reverse side of the penny coin. One displayed his childhood, one his formative years, one his professional life, and one and his presidency. These were circulated for just one year. In 2010, they were replaced with the Union Shield which continues at the present time.

It is estimated that approximately 300 billion pennies have been produced. Pennies have played a very essential part in our American culture. They have made it possible for retailers to price products in odd numbers, as well as even numbers. However, I'm not sure it has been a benefit to us consumers.

For the most part, pennies have been, and are, a highly respected coin. For most people finding one is a token of good luck. I'm a firm believer in this old legend. When I find one, I polish it up and carry it around in my pocket for months. In the movie *Three Coins in the Fountain*, the setting for the move was the Trevi Fountain in Rome, three young American girls that were working in the American Embassy in Rome were seeking romance. Each of them tossed a coin in the pool on the theory that they would be lucky in love. It's been a very long time since I last seen the movie, however, I still have a mental picture of seeing three bright shining pennies at the bottom of the pool. Chances are good that the girls used pennies, most everyone did because of the good luck legend.

Of course, most of us are aware of the shoe that we called the penny loafers, they have no laces and you can just slip them on. There is a diamond type slit in front just above the instep where you can insert a penny. It has always been considered a good luck token for the person that had pennies tucked into their loafers. This type of shoe was first produced in Norway, and exported to England in 1930. Americans that visited England took a liking to them, which caused American shoe companies to start manufacturing them. The loafer gained its popularity in the '50s, when prep school students in the east, wishing to make a fashion statement, started to insert pennies in the diamond slit of their loafers. From that, the penny loafer name was born, and still remains very popular today.

Like me, I'm sure that you have heard people say that if they see a penny on the ground, it's not worth the effort to bend down and pick it up. Perhaps it's the namesake that pennies and I share that causes me to have such high respect for them. A wise man once said, "Take care of your pennies, and your dollars will take care of themselves."

103

THE LONG SHADOWS

When the Earth tips on its axis, and the sun sinks lower into the southern horizon, that is when the long shadows start to invade our landscape. Due to the many hills and valleys in and around the Long Branch School area, there's no shortage of long shadows. The shadows give us our first indication that summer is fading, and the fall season is approaching. It wouldn't be necessary to look at the calendar to know that the season is changing from summer to fall. All one needs to do is walk outside or survey the surrounding countryside from your window. You will notice that the shadows are growing longer. Fleecy white clouds linger in the azure blue sky, and there is something about the atmosphere that takes on a quiet and serene look. When these signs are prevalent, it's time for all creatures on Earth to prepare for the coming winter months which will arrive shortly.

In my front yard is a large hickory tree. In the hot summer days it provides shade for my garage in the morning, and shade for my neighbor in the afternoon, that makes us both happy. Most years it produces some hickory nuts. On occasion, a squirrel or two will stop by and help themselves to a few nuts. There has always been a chipmunk or two living in the shrubs around our house. While looking out the window one day, I noticed one of these little fellows flitting across my driveway. In a few minutes, he returned in the opposite direction. This got me wondering what this little fellow was doing.

Finding a spot where I had a better view, I found that he was gathering hickory nuts from under the tree and transporting them to the shrubbery at the end of the garage, where he probably had an underground lodge to store them in for winter food. I was impressed with the work ethics of this little guy. First he would peep out from the shrubs to check and see if there was any danger around, then he would dash out and grab a nut, then run back to the cover of the shrubs, travel under the shrubs as long as possible, then make a dash across the driveway at full speed.

He was well aware that being out in the open is not healthy for little chipmunks. There are cats, hawks, and other predators waiting to gobble him up. I got to thinking how intelligent this small animal was, and how God had prepared him to survive in a very hostile environment. First, he could tell by the long shadows that winter would soon arrive, and that it was essential to have food enough to last through the cold snowy months. Second, he was well aware of how dangerous it was to remain out in the open any longer than necessary. Makes one wonder if God divided intelligence equally. So many of us humans fail to have the instinct to properly prepare for the difficult days that lie ahead in our lives, or to protect ourselves against the many dangerous conditions that we face daily in this fast moving world that we live in.

When I was a child growing up in that little house there in the sharp bend of the Long Branch School Road, sometimes in the winter months the cold north wind would make a whistling noise around the corners of the house. My mom would say that it is asking, "What have you done with your summer wages?"

Thanks, Mom. I have always remembered your advice.

104

TILL THE SOIL

Tilling the soil, planting the seeds, and watching what the Earth and Mother Nature produce is a miracle so great it is difficult to comprehend. As a child growing up on the farm in Butler County, I was subjected to about every conceivable garden plant available. And at that time in America, being able to grow your own vegetables was the difference between having enough food and going hungry. My mom always said that when you till the soil, it puts you close to God, and even closer when you are down on your knees digging in the dirt with your hands. Then she would remind us to be careful not to get the knees of our overalls dirty.

Besides the many vegetables we grew, the flat land surrounding the house was usually planted in tobacco. Tobacco plants grew into a big sturdy plant, four to five feet tall, with heavy leaves eight to ten inches wide. This was before pesticides, and if you didn't pay close attention, the tobacco worms would destroy the plants. My brother and I were assigned the task of removing the worms from the plants. As I recall, it was a chore that no one appreciated. To begin with, it had a bad odor, and the leaves had to be turned up to find the worms, and they were somewhat sticky and gooey. Some of the worms were three and four inches long with a horn sticking up from their tails, a sight that would cause a ten year old boy to have nightmares.

When the tobacco reached maturity, it would go from dark green to a more yellow or golden color, which meant that it was ready to be harvested. From there it went through more processing before it was ready for use. As I recall, it was considered a very important commodity at that time. Most men chewed tobacco, and some grandmothers smoked it in their corncob pipes.

Our farm consisted of fifty acres, more or less. Thirty acres were wooded, and twenty acres were cleared and suitable for growing most any type of crops. One section which contained approximately fourteen acres was what we called the School House Bottom Land—so named because the south end extended up near the school house and the Long Branch ran through the center. This land was usually planted in corn, and due to the fact that this was very rich in nutrients, it produced better than the average bushel per acre.

In those days we gathered the ears of corn by pulling them from the stalks by hand and placing them in the wagon which was pulled by two mules. There was no money to purchase gloves and my mom wanted to protect her little boys' hands from the frost, and the very abrasive corn husks. To accomplish this she would wrap our hands in rags and tie them with strings to hold them in place.

I recall one frosty morning when me, my dad, my brother, and our neighbor, Alonzo Burden, and his two boys were gathering the corn. The neighbor's older boy wanted to see if he was strong enough to hold one of the wagon wheels. Somehow, he got his hands locked around the spokes and was unable to let go. It created a considerable amount of excitement when someone noticed that he was being dragged along by the wheel. He was very fortunate that he was not injured.

Sometime later, my parents sold the fourteen acre School House Bottom land, which left the family with approximately six acres of land that was suitable for cultivation. As my dad had majored in agriculture in college, we were able to use some modern and some antique farming methods to do a reasonable good job of producing what we needed from the land. This was an achievement my family still takes pride in.

105

THE LOVE OF A BROTHER

My brother Otis was two years older than me, and for the most part we got along very well. There was a considerable amount of love and affection displayed between the two of us. What caused some problems was his tendency to be a big tease, and to play jokes on people. I recall one instance when he was teasing me real heavy, to the point that it caused me to lose my temper. Of course he was larger than me, and so he ran away. I was unable to catch him, and in my anger, I picked up a goose egg size stone and threw it at him. The stone struck him with a glancing blow and he fell to the ground and pretended he was hurt. Of course, I was frightened until I found out that he was just pretending. My parents took a very dim view of what I had done, and the marks from that hickory switch stayed around for several days as a reminder not to throw stones at my brother.

I was not the only one he teased. He loved to tease our father. I recall some of the things that he did to him. It was neighborhood gossip that the school house was haunted. Reports of strange sounds from inside the school at night were very common. My brother decided to use some of his teasing talent on our dad. On occasions when he knew that Dad would be late walking back from Morgantown after dark, and knowing how superstitious he was, he would go get inside the school house, and when dad arrived he would shake together a couple of steel pieces which made a sound like chains rattling. Dad would hurry on home and make some remarks about the strange noise he had been hearing coming from the school house. If my brother had not been at home, I am sure that dad would have blamed him, knowing his reputation for doing such things. However, when Dad got past the school house, my brother would jump out the rear window and run across the bottom land and be home when Dad arrived.

This went on for some time, until one night when Dad and some of his friends had been sipping on some of that 130 proof moonshine. To say that the moonshine gave him some additional courage, is very much an understatement. This time, when my brother made the noise, Dad swore some kind of a wicked oath and charged into the school house, seeing my brother as he was exiting the window. Getting caught made my brother's life very miserable for quite a long time.

At times, brothers are essential for survival. I recall one rainy day when a group of us boys had gathered in one of our neighbor's garages, when one of the larger boys decided to give my brother a good beating. I just could not stand by and let that happen, so I joined in to help my brother. In the end, it was the big guy that got beat up, he got either knocked or pushed against the wall, where there happened to be a protruding nail which scratched his head up quite a bit. One of the older boys that had witnessed the fight, and had older brothers that had some problems with the law, took me and my brother aside and advised us that we could be in trouble if the boy decided to press charges. He said that the charges could be banding and confederating together to do bodily harm. I don't know if there is or was such a law, but it sounded very serious. We were frightened for some time, but we never heard any more about what happened.

I was always grateful that I had a brother, not only to grow up with, but share memories in later life. Brothers are not just anyone. You are bound together as friend and family, someone you can trust and confide in when you have goofed up and need a sympathetic ear. Of all the people I have loved in my life, my brother rates near the top. If you have a brother, be kind to him and hold him close in your heart. If you are like me, you will always remember the happiness and pleasures you shared together.

106

THE MIGHTY OAKS

On our farm in Butler County, Kentucky, just down Long Branch School Road, there on the banks of the creek that flows down from the Possum Hollow, two large oak trees grew. One of them had BB shot in it. When I was about 10 years old, I talked my father into letting me shoot his shotgun into one of those large oak trees. At that time, I was allowed to shoot and handle the .22 rifle. This was my first time for me to shoot the shotgun. It kicked so hard that my shoulder was sore for several days. The trees were at approximately 36 inches in diameter and were very similar in stature, actually they looked like twins, they both had a canopy or crown 30 to 40 feet wide.

If you think about that, there are many reasons why they should look alike. The tiny acorns that gave birth to each of them probably came from a giant old tree that stood in or near that location two or three hundred years ago. In that case they would be brothers or sisters. The fact that they stood on the banks of the creek which provided plenty of water for each of them meant they received the same amount of moisture that was necessary for them to excel. They both enjoyed a Southern exposure, which gave them plenty of beautiful Kentucky sunshine, and the soil there was rich in nutrients. We have heard the legacy saying, "Mighty oaks grow from little acorns."

I remember a story that begins on a bright sunny morning, which just happened to be the first day of May. The weather is always beautiful in Kentucky on the first day of May. In previous stories, you will recall that Grandma Lillie Oller divided the land between my mom and my Aunt Kate. Aunt Kate's house was up the road near Aunt Lara's and Uncle Will's place. Some of her land was the field directly across the road from our house. It was a nice level piece of land and my Aunt Kate always had her garden there.

When Aunt Kate moved to Bowling Green, she rented her house to a young couple who also had their garden in the same spot. That morning, the husband was working in the garden. My dad, being the sociable sort of a person he was, asked the young man if he would join him for a drink, which he agreed to do. My dad brought out the quart of moonshine and they took a couple of chairs and sat under the big Sycamore tree to have a few drinks. It so happened that Uncle Bill came along. Uncle Bill was known for never refusing a drink. I believe that he and my dad had discussed Uncle Bill's desire to buy the large oak tree. It was such a beautiful tree, Uncle Bill thought it would make beautiful oak shingle. This appeared to be the ideal time for them to go down and look at the tree, and to engage in further discussion about the sale.

So the three of them took the moonshine and went down and sat under the tree. I feel certain that they made a deal regarding price and everything while they sat there under the tree. A short time later, three of our neighbor boys came along. They were young men, about 18 years old and up. To be sociable, they joined in and had a few drinks. By this time the quart of moonshine was depleted. As I recall, I was there listening to all the conversation. My dad called me over and handed me a fifty cent piece, and instructed me to run up to the top of the hill where a fellow lived that was in the moonshine business, and buy a quart of moonshine.

For some reason in those days, when parents wanted children to do something, they would always say, run and do this or that, they would never say go do this for me. So I ran as fast as I could to the top of the hill, which was about a mile, got the quart of moonshine, and hurried back.

To my surprise, several more of our neighbors who lived on the other end of Long Branch School Road had joined the party. I would estimate that there were approximately eight or ten people there at that time. As you can imagine, the quart that I had brought down didn't last very long. So they had my brother go and get them another quart. And when they had polished off the quart that my brother brought for them, they sent me back to fetch the third quart.

I can recall what the fellow said who was supplying the moonshine. "What are they doing with all this booze? Are they using it to take a bath in?" Now whiskey is aged in charcoal barrels and kegs. This process tends to make it more mellow and taste better. The person we were purchasing it from was trying to age it, but it was being drank up before it had time to age. I can still recall seeing the charcoal pellet floating around inside the quart jar.

By this time, it was getting over into the afternoon. And if you can imagine, every one of them were intoxicated, inebriated, or even worse. Remember, the stuff that they were drinking was 130 proof. If any of them had taken a DUI test, I feel certain that the machine would have exploded.

Uncle Bill appeared to be in the most serious condition. He was setting down with his back and shoulders propped against the tree and appeared to be paralyzed. He demonstrated some shenanigans that I cannot explain here, since my children and grandchildren will be reading this.

Sometime in the late afternoon, a fellow from the other side of Welch's Creek came by. He didn't tarry too long, just said howdy, and sort of circled around the group under the tree. As he walked away our dog, Speed, barked at the man. So the man picked up a rock and threw it at our dog and continued on his way.

Shortly thereafter, someone mentioned that it wasn't very nice for that man to throw a rock at our dog. Just who does this guy think he is, trying to hurt our dog? Someone suggested that they should find him and beat the daylights out of him. Another person spoke up and suggested that they should hang him. Everyone roared their approval, and they soon became an angry mob. So they all got up and started walking up the road in the direction the man had went.

On the way past our house, my dad stopped and picked up a rope. I can see him yet, with the rope coiled in his hand as they all walked up the road. Thank goodness, the man didn't stop. After walking about one half mile, someone become rational enough to suggest that they give up the search and return back to the oak tree location.

It's an example of what can happen when you mix alcohol, fate, and unusual circumstances together. The people involved were all good people, who under normal circumstances would rather help than to hurt. It's frightening to think how many lives could have been destroyed had this tragedy actually happened. It all begin so innocent, the sale of a giant oak tree, for which my dad received seventy five cents.

107

THE SLINGSHOT

Homemade slingshots were a very popular toy for boys in the early part of the 20th century. They were considered safe because of the low velocity of the projectile. As boys growing up in the Long Branch School District and other parts of the county, we made a substantial amount of them. There were at least two reasons for this. Number one: Slingshots provided a toy for boys, ages six to sixteen, when there was no money available for non-essentials. Number two: The materials to make them were readily available around our house. To build a slingshot, only five pieces of material were needed: a small forked branch cut from a tree, two strips of rubber from a blown out inner tube, a small piece of leather from the tongue of a discarded shoe, and a piece of string twelve inches long. The tools needed would be a pocket knife and a pair of scissors.

In those days, automobile tires were made in two pieces: the inner tube, which held the air, went inside the tire, and protected it. This system didn't work very well. Friction between the inner tube and the tire generated heat, which caused the tire to blow out, that was why obtaining rubber was no problem. There were plenty of old inner tubes available. In 1947, B. F. Goodrich developed the tubeless tire. After extensive testing, the tubeless tire proved to be a great step forward in automobile safety and dependability. By 1954, tubeless tires were standard equipment on all cars.

If I wanted to make a slingshot today, I wouldn't know where to start looking for the necessary material—the two rubber strips that provide the power to hurl the projectile and all the other components one would need. However, slingshots are now available in many retail stores. While the principal is the same, the design is much different than the little ones we made when I was a small boy. The Trumark Company in Nebraska is about the only company still producing slingshots in America today. Most are highly engineered, with wrist braces, self-centering ammo pockets, sighting devices, and other improvements.

Even though our slingshots were rudimentary, I can still remember the thrill of having one, and the satisfaction of having made it myself. Unfortunately our slingshots would not last very long. The first thing that would wear out was the rubber pulls. They were made from natural rubber, which has a low resistance to aging, and how old the inner tube was that we cut them from was anyone's guess. Finding the right ammunition for these weapons was also a chore. Small steel balls, half inch in diameter, were the ideal projectile. Of course, nothing like that was available in those days so we used small stones which were readily available but the search was always on to find some that were reasonably round. Round ones improved the accuracy of the shot.

There was always some competition about who was the better marksman. Using flat, half round, and stones with jagged edges was a disaster. They would get caught in the air and spin off on all directions, the same principal that makes a golf ball hook or slice.

I have always fostered the opinion that it was good for young boys to have a slingshot. Having one at a young age helps builds self-confidence, character, and responsibility. It will cause them to have more respect for guns when they become old enough to handle one.

108

THE MORGANTOWN FERRY

The beautiful and historic Green River divides Butler County into two sections, with approximately the same amount of land on either side. These sections have always been referred to as the north and south side of the river. For many years, it was the Morgantown ferry that linked the north and south sides together. The fact that Morgantown was the only town nearby, and was also the county seat, made the ferry vitally important to the people that lived on the north side. I have no information as to when the ferry first began operations. History indicates that most of the ferries in Butler County and the surrounding area started operating in the early part of the 19th century, in the years 1800 through 1825.

There could have been some method of getting across the river as early as 1811 when Morgantown was founded. From 1790 to 1815, pioneers heading west through St Louis crossed the Mississippi River on boats that were called Dugouts. They were made by hollowing out a large log and were similar to a canoe. These boats were capable of carrying only two or three people. To get horses and other heavy items across the river, they would lash two Dugout boats together and make a platform for the horses to stand on. After 1815, the Keel boat was introduced, which was a great improvement. It could transport horses and wagons and other large items.

I recall the Morgantown ferry boat as being rather small compared to the general run of ferry boats. It had space for one wagon and mule team, or two automobiles, which were small in those days. The ferry boat was held in place by a steel cable that was anchored on both sides of the river, the cable was in the vicinity of one half inch in diameter and traveled through two pulleys secured to the post rails on the upstream side of the boat. Power to move it across the river was provided by the ferryman, with a piece of wood two by two inches, and eighteen inches long, with one end shaved down to make a handle for gripping. On the other end was a notch that fit over the cable. By hooking the notched handle over the cable and pulling backward, the boat was propelled across the river. There was usually some extra pull handles on the boat, and passengers could lend a hand if they had a desire to do so. At times, when the river was running very swift, it could be used to move the boat across the river. This was achieved by extending the rear pulley on a rope so the rear end of the boat was at a slight angle to the river. The power of the current would carry the boat to the other side.

Exiting the ferry boat was considered to be the most hazardous part of the crossing, especially on the north landing. The bank on that side was very steep, and if the river was receding from high water, the road at the end of the ferry would be soft and muddy, causing problems for the mules to get the wagon off the boat and up the hill. Also, if the front wheels of a car got stuck in a mud hole, the power from the rear wheels would spin on the boat, causing the anchoring chain to pull up the iron stake, sending the boat backward, and the rear end of the car would drop into the water. I'm not sure that this ever happened, but I can remember everyone was concerned about that possibility.

The ferry house was on the south side of the river, and was located on a narrow ledge that over looked the river. The back side of the house was very close to the bluff, which is something like forty feet high. One day, the young sons of Jack Bratcher, a well-known lawyer in Butler County, were climbing the trees along the edge of the bluff. They were no doubt enjoying the great view from that vantage point, when one of them fell from the tree. The story is a little hard to believe, but I am sure that it was true, as it was talked about for months. When the boy fell from the tree, he glanced off the sloping edge of the bluff, that prevented his fall from being straight down, which resulted in a forward angle. When he reached the bottom, he crashed into the screen door of the ferry house, which cushioned his fall. I don't remember if he walked away from the scene, but as I recall, his injuries were not life threatening. A lucky break, or being looked after by an angel, we all have our opinion.

There were times when the ferry created lots of excitement as the revenue agents would use it to capture some of our Butler County boys that were dabbling in the moonshine business. I recall on one occasion when the agents got on the ferry with a fellow who had his car loaded with moonshine. Being in the middle of the river made it very difficult to try and escape, and I'm sure that the man must have felt very helpless. The reason I remember this incident so well, was because a very close friend of mine happened to be on the boat at the same time. My friend had his pockets full of moonshine, nicely bottled up in pint and half pint bottles. His intent was to do a little bootlegging in Morgantown. However, watching the events unfold, as the driver was forced to open up his car exposing the many jugs of illegal moonshine, then he was arrested and handcuffed, put some fear into my friend. He thought he might be next, so he moved to the opposite end of the boat and gently disposed of his bottles by slipping them into the river. My advice to him was, if you are going to be a bootlegger, you have to expect this type of thing to happen.

Have you ever wondered how the word bootlegger originated? Well recently I discovered the answer. In 1790, just after the Revolutionary War, our country was hard pressed for money. Alexander Hamilton was secretary of the treasury. He proposed a tax on whisky, and got it approved by Congress. It was a very unpopular tax and created what was known as the whiskey tax rebellion. There was such a large uprising that President Washington had to send troops to Philadelphia to control the violence. In the years that followed, and in an attempt to evade the tax, people that were in the business of selling whiskey would hide it in their boots. That is how the name bootlegger originated.

As best I can remember the ferry belonged to the county, and people that were interested in becoming the operator would bid for the job. Hubert Hudson, and my Aunt Kate, were successful bidders. I was very small at that time, but I seem to remember that his bid was $35 dollars, and he would get to keep the money collected from the ferry fees, which I believe was five cents per person walking, and ten cents for horses, wagons, and cars.

I still think that the Green River is the most beautiful river there is. In the early days, Morgantown must have felt that way. History indicates that Morgantown was a child of the river, and may have stayed tied to its mother's apron strings too long. But don't give up on that quaint and beautiful little town. As we all know, cream always rises to the top.

109

THE NORTHERN MOCKINGBIRD

There are many birds that imitate other birds, but the Northern Mockingbird, as they are known in North America, are considered the best. They not only imitate other birds but other sounds as well including animals, mechanical noises, and car alarms to name a few. Some feel that the mimic serves as a tool to increase their vocabulary in an effort to attract females. In addition to being great mimics, they are the loudest and most vocal of our song birds, especially the bachelors, when trying to attract a mate.

For the most part, they sing their songs year around, even at night, especially when there is a full moon. In addition to their beautiful songs which they prefer to deliver from high roof lines, utility poles, and other high perches, they are loved and respected by most everyone. They are the state bird of five states: Arkansas, Florida, Mississippi, Tennessee, and Texas.

One other noticeable thing about their personality is that they are aggressive defenders of their territory. They have been known to attack dogs, cats, and even people, when defending their young. In my lifelong association with these birds, 1 have found only one that appeared to harbor a real imbedded mean streak. Once, we lived in Hendersonville, North Carolina, and as usual we wanted to feed the birds. Our location was ideal for feeding and watching birds as there were open fields, lots of trees, and a beautiful stream that bordered the property. As it appeared to be a great habitat for birds, we build a larger than average bird feeder down by the stream. For a while everything went well, we had lots of birds and took some great pictures. After a while we noticed that the bird population was disappearing. Upon a closer survey, we found that a mockingbird was chasing away all birds that tried to feed there. She had a perch in the top of a high tree about a hundred yards from the feeder, and when other birds would visit the feeder, she would sweep in like a dive bomber and frighten them away. I must admit that I was almost angry enough to commit murder, but I was unable to follow through on such harsh punishment. Instead, we decided to call her Leona. Perhaps you remember Leona Helmsley, she was the multi billionaire that owned many hotels and other properties in New York, including the Empire State Building. Of course she had thousands of people working for her. She was nicknamed the "Queen of Mean" for her tyrannical behavior and the harsh manner in which she treated her employees. There appeared to be some similarities between Leona, and our mockingbird.

In our world, it is difficult to find something that is perfect. There is some bad in the best us, and some good in the worst of us. Perhaps, this applies to our feathered friends, as well. One way to resolve this problem is to add up all the positive features, place them on one end of a balance scale. Do the same with liabilities. If the positive outweighs the liabilities, you have a winner. That's the way I feel about Leona and her mockingbird family.

I find one of the best locations to listen to the songs of the mockingbird is along the Long Branch School Road in Butler County, Kentucky. When we think of all the pleasures they provide with their beautiful songs, we have no other choice but to embrace them.

110

THE PERSIMMON TREE

I understand that there is a book written by Brice Courtenay called "The Persimmon Tree." I've heard that it's a great book but has nothing to do with persimmon tree. It is based on the struggle of two young people trying to survive in a country torn by war. I believe the author's reason to title the book the way he did was to compliment the toughness of the persimmon tree.

The heartwood of this tree is very resistant to wear. It has been used to make high quality golf club heads, longbows, and spindles for the textile industries, and in many other places where tough wood is required. The genus name for the American persimmon is "the Fruit of the god's." This is in reference to the delicious golden-orange fruit that usually hang on the tree after the leaves drop in autumn. When fully ripe, these fruits are very sweet and delicious. If you try to eat them before they are totally ripe, your mouth is most likely to pucker from the bitter taste of tannic acid.

Persimmons were a very popular food for Native Americans and other wild life that was abundant in the early days. This fruit has been used to make persimmon bread, pudding, perseveres, beer, brandy, and can be dried for winter use.

The American persimmon is found in the southeastern states, south of the great lakes, and west as far as east Texas. I've had a life long association with persimmon trees and the fruit that they produce. In fact, there is a straggly one that grows on the vacant lot in back of my house. Each fall, I gather in some of the fruit and share it with the family, most of whom have never seen or tasted them.

There were several trees on or near our farm where I grew up on Long Branch School Road. The tree I remember most vividly was located on the road just a short distance beyond the Sylvester Burden Spring, and a short distance before reaching my grandmother's place. It stood near some large oak trees and the fork in the road that leads up the hill to the James Childers farm. It was a beautiful tree that was ten to twelve inches in diameter, and perhaps thirty to forty feet tall, and produced an abundance of fruit. It was located on a nice level spot of land that may have been the homestead of some early settlers. I often thought that if people did live there at one time, they were very lucky. They could run down to the creek and catch some yellow bellied catfish and have them for breakfast.

We have all heard the story about the brave and patriotic Captain John Smith, who sailed to America on the Mayflower and established the first permanent settlement of Jamestown, located there on the James River in Virginia. It been said that without the leadership of Captain Smith, Jamestown could have suffered the same fate as the lost colony on Roanoke Island. History tells us the stories about how the pilgrims suffered due to the unusually cold winters and the shortage of food and shelter. Some historians believe that they were able to survive because they had dried persimmons and used them to make persimmon pudding. It's been reported that Captain Smith was very fond of persimmon pudding. We Americans should be grateful for the persimmon fruit that helped sustain life for these brave people, and give thanks to the Indian girl, Pocahontas, who pleaded with her father, who was the chief of the Algonquian tribe, to spare the life of Captain Smith.

It's been said, and it could be true, that come November, mountain people turn their thoughts to persimmons, possums, and politics.

111

THE RIPPLES OF LIFE

You may have not done it lately, but most of us have at some time in our lives tossed a stone into the waters of a placid lake, or pond, and watched the little waves head off in all directions until they lose their momentum or crash onto the shore line. These ripples come about because we made a decision to toss the stone, and it disturbed the normal condition of the water. Watching these little ripples caused me to wonder if the decisions we make in our lives and these little ripples may have a lot in common.

In our lives we find it necessary to make millions of decisions. In fact, we make a vast number of small ones each day. Such as, what clothes will I wear today? What will I have for breakfast? Will I shave today or put it off until tomorrow? The list goes on forever. They are the ones that make such a small ripple in our lives, that in a short time we have forgotten that we made them.

However, within every life we are also faced with many major decisions. Some of these lifelong decisions start early in our lives, and at a time when we may not be fully equipped to make such major decisions. Whether made early or late in life, it doesn't matter how old we get, or how rich we get, the ripples of these major decisions will play a very important role in our lives. These big ripples have a tendency to either improve our lives, or create unintended and unrepairable consequences.

One of the major decisions that must be made early in life is about obtaining a good education. As a rule, education paves the road to more opportunities and a more productive and satisfied way of life. However, we see some people that do well with a minimum amount of education, which is generally an exception to the rule. There is something to be said about college: Not everyone is college material. Some people do well by working with their hands.

Other major decisions, such as, what profession will I follow? Will that profession be in demand several years down the road? Will it be necessary to move to another location where more opportunities that fit my training are available? Will I find the right person to swim with me in the stream of life? Will I be able to segregate the good people from the evil ones?

The above decisions, and many more similar ones have to be addressed in each lifetime, and along the way there will be no shortage of advice about what is the right course of action. Advice is a very beneficial commodity in our lives. We should listen to it very intently, and be careful not to interrupt the friend or person that is offering this help. The good thing about advice is that it's not a binding contract; we all have the option to accept it or reject it after careful consideration.

As we grow older, we all look back at the path that we have followed in our lifetime. Some parts of our path are not very bright, and are shaded by the misty veil of time. However, if you are like me, the major decisions you have made, both good and bad, are always fresh in our mind. Most of us have made both good and bad decisions, and hoped for the best. Even though some of mine looked unattainable at the time, and contrary to the advice that I received, I'm reasonably pleased with the tough decisions I have made. Some have been beneficial and rewarding. I'm not opposed to listening to advice. I just have a tendency to listen closely to my guardian angel for guidance.

112

THE SANDS OF TIME

There is no shortage of sand on the planet that we inhabit. Sand is a hard, granular comminuted rock material, finer than gravel but coarser than dust. It's produced by wind and water, which has eroded rocks, mountains, and many other materials over the past millions of year. It comes in many different colors, due to the color of the rocks in certain parts of the Earth that are being eroded. The blessing we receive from sand is the work of Mother Nature. It's difficult to believe, but scientists tell us that there many more stars in the sky than there are grains of sand on Earth.

Due to its biblical linkage, the sands of the Sinai Desert in Egypt are probably the most recognized and discussed sands on Earth. According to the Old Testament, it is where Moses and the children of Israel wandered for forty years in an effort to find the promise land that they had been told about, and to escape the bondage imposed on them by the ruthless Egyptian Pharaoh. Many other events that affect the Christian faith today happened in the sand and in the mountains of the Sinai Desert. It's where the Israelites built a tabernacle, and God presented Moses with the Ten Commandments. The stories can be found in Exodus, the second book of the Old Testament, which took place approximately 1400 BC.

There is an island in the Pacific Ocean called Iwo Jima. Many Americans have forgotten or have never heard of the battle of Iwo Jima which happened in World War II. It's where we suffered 26,000 casualties, and 6,800 brave Americans lost their lives in that black volcanic sand that covered most of the island.

Sand, as we know it today, is a very useful product. It's used as a base for making mortar and cement, and in manufacturing it is used to produce sand molds that make brass and other metal castings. With a few additives, glass is made from sand. It's my thought that we appreciate sand most when we are walking barefoot along the beach in nice warm weather, and get to view a beautiful sunset as a bonus. I can still recall how pleasant it was to walk barefoot in the white sands of Long Branch School Road.

The sand hourglass is a device used for measuring time. History indicates this time measuring device is not old, as time is measured. Relics found indicate that it was first used around the middle of the 14th century. This timing device was used extensively on ocean going ships, and went through a number of changes. The hourglass is made up of two connected glass bulbs allowing a trickle of sand to flow from top to bottom. Once the top bulb is empty, it can be inverted to start the timing process all over again. Unlike most other methods of measuring time, the hourglass appears to represent the present as being between the past and the future, and this has made it an enduring symbol of time itself.

The hourglass is often depicted as a symbol that human existence is fleeting, and the sands of time will someday run out. Recognition of the hourglass as a symbol of time has survived its obsolescence as a timekeeper. Since their first soap opera broadcast, the show Days of Our Lives has displayed an hourglass in their opening, with the narrative, "Like sand through the hourglass, so are the days of our lives."

113

THE SORGHUM MILL

As I look back on my family and my childhood years in Butler County, I am convinced that we were a part of the pioneer movement. If you review the way of life at that time, it is easy to come up with that assessment. The land and Mother Nature provided us with almost everything we needed for survival. Yes, we had moved beyond the spinning wheel, but not very far. The land produced many things, including one of my favorites – sorghum.

My dad's Aunt Laura and her husband Will were farmers and owned 100 acres or more of land. They also owned and operated the sorghum mill that produced sorghum molasses. The making of molasses happened every year around the middle of October. Uncle Will grew the cane in the bottom land down near the creek and we would always see him working in the field while we were fishing. Sugarcane is a tall, strong, jointed plant with a large seedy top, and is grown mostly in tropical regions. It is used as a source for sugar and molasses. When the cane matures in the fall, it is cut and transported to the sorghum processing site, which for us was just down the hill from where Uncle Will and Aunt Laura lived, on the bank of the Long Branch which flowed through their land. Sometimes the long leafy branches were stripped from the stalks before it was harvested, and sometimes they were stripped at the processing site.

The method of extracting the juice was with a machine with two steel up right rollers that meshed together. The cane stalks were fed in between the two rollers, and when they turned they would pull the cane through and squeeze out the juice. The power to operate the squeezer was provided by one of Uncle Will's mules. The squeezer had a boom pole about twenty feet long. When the boom moved the squeezer rollers would turn. The mule would walk in a forty foot circle, and every time the boom came around, the person feeding the squeezer would have to duck his head to keep from being bumped.

Then there was the evaporator used to boil the juice down to sorghum consistency. It was a large pan, six feet wide and ten feet long, with baffles about eight inches apart with an opening on every other end. As the juice flowed from the squeezer, it would travel down through the baffle arrangement. As it got closer to the end, it would have cooked and become thicker. The people doing the work had something similar to a broom handle with an eight inch flat board attached to one end that fit between the baffles, this way they could control the flow of the juice. Once it was in the last baffle area, they could decide if it was the proper viscosity for molasses. If not, they could push it back to be cooked some more, before turning the spigot to let it drain into the container.

Our family visited the mill at least once each year, usually in the early evening around twilight time. I can still remember how beautiful it was, the balmy weather, the big Harvest Moon hanging out there in the sky, the fire and the sweet smell of the cooking molasses. The grownups would talk about how the summer had been, how much their farms had produced, the depression and politics. There was also a treat for the children as well. In the cooking process, a certain amount of foam would rise to the top. In order for the molasses to be of high quality it was necessary to skim this foam off, using a screen type skimmer. Using a makeshift spoon made from a 6-inch piece of cane, the children could help themselves to the foam which was very tasty. Our parents would always warn us that if we ate too much we would be sick.

We would always buy a few gallons to carry us through the winter. As a child, I had a difficult time learning to drink coffee. Since there were many times we had no sugar, I would use sorghum as a substitute for sugar. Besides making the coffee taste better, sorghum is a very nutritious food. It has no fat, is high in protein and potassium and many other vitamins and minerals with practically no sodium. It is very tasty on pancakes, waffles and biscuits.

Now days pure sorghum is somewhat difficult to find. But do yourself and your family a favor and purchase some the next time you find it available.

114

THE STORM CELLAR

Kentucky had its share of tornadoes and when I was a child growing up in Butler County, they were of some concern to everyone in our neighborhood. At that time, most everyone I knew called them cyclones. Regardless of what we called them, they were very destructive, and a threat to life and property. When I was twelve or fourteen years old, one of those twisters visited Butler County, and passed through near our home. As I recall, several homes were destroyed, and a number of people were injured.

It would be easy to image how concerned the people on the north side were, especially those of us that lived near the storm's path. I was no exception. There was a nice incline in the land about seventy five feet in back of our house. It was an ideal spot to build a storm cellar. The next day found me with my long handle shovel out there digging in the dirt, must have neglected to tell the rest of the family what I was doing. When they asked, I explained that I was building a storm cellar. They must have felt that it was a worthwhile cause, because before long the rest of the family joined in to give me a hand. We decided that it should be a room ten by ten, and the ceiling should be approximately six feet high, give or take a few inches.

Once the excavating was finished, it was time for the framework. And what did we use for framing? Chestnut logs of course, the wood that played a very important part in building America. My brother and I carried the logs from the Possum Hollow, and with the crosscut saw cut them to the length needed. In order to keep the logs in place and to make a sound structure, each end of the logs needed to be notched so they would fit together more snuggly, and not leave to large a gap between them. I believe that the correct terminology for this is mortise, and since we were not experts, gaps between the logs were the rule rather than the exception.

The structure of the roof was made of logs laid as close together as possible, then covered with tar paper to prevent leaks. Then to cover the logs and paper we piled on about two feet of soil. The storm cellar turned out to be a valuable asset to our family. In addition to providing peace of mind in stormy weather, the even temperature it provided made it an ideal place for my dad to incubate chickens. The cellar was also a great place for storing fruit and vegetables, and since I was the one who initiated building it in the beginning, I received all the praise for my efforts.

For the first few years everything worked beautifully, until my dad developed a phobia about thunderstorms. I believe astraphobia is the correct phobia for that. Dad got to the point where he believed every thunderstorm was likely to contain a tornado. It became routine, especially at night, when the rain and wind started beating on the house, that he would yell for everyone to run for the cellar. Even though it was just a short distance from the house, one would become drenched from the blowing rain. There were times when storms were quite frequent and we would make the journey to the cellar two or three times in one night.

By that time the cellar was getting old, it had started to leak, and the log structure was beginning to decay, and it became infested with chicken snakes. The family finally got fed up with this exercise and informed Dad not to wake them up the next time a rainstorm was approaching. They also informed him that they would rather take their chances in the house than face the rain and those big chicken snakes.

115

THE STORY OF THE CHESTNUT TREES

At one time this area was covered with chestnut trees. Beautiful trees that produce big burry pods full of chestnuts. The wood and fruit from these trees was very beneficial to the first pioneers that settled in Kentucky and other nearby states. At some time in the early part of the 20th century, a blight destroyed every last one of them. I can remember gathering chestnuts with my parents, and filling a paper bag, but that has been some time ago, and I cannot recall where that location was.

However, I can still remember the last and lone survivor in this area. It was a huge tree in size, and it stood in a clearing just north of the Johnson place, near the road. The fact that it was alone with no other trees near is no doubt the reason it was one of the last survivors. The number of dead chestnut trees that lay on the ground in the Possum Hollow was a testament to how many had grown there. The forest floor was covered with white logs. For some reason unknown to me, these trees, when dead, shed their bark and turned white. They must have had some special resistance to rot, because they were around for most of my childhood life. Besides being white they were much lighter in weight than other types of trees that grew there.

There is a special place in my heart for this wood because it kept the Martin family from freezing to death. Some winters were severe and I can recall temperatures below zero for 30 day periods. It was so cold the Green

River would freeze over, and people would go ice skating there. In the beginning, our house was heated by a potbellied stove, and the fuel was coal. However, the potbellied stove burned out and as usual this happened when the depression was in full swing. With no money to buy a new heating stove we were in trouble. A friend of my dad's had made a stove from a 55 gallon steel drum. So my dad had his friend make one for us. The cost for cutting a door in one end and an opening for the pipe to carry out the smoke, and welding on four legs, cost my dad $1.50.

My brother and I had the job of providing wood for the barrel stove. Since we had to carry the wood from up in the hollow, and since the chestnut wood was plentiful and light, it became our major wood source. The problem was that this wood was light and dry, and would burn up in a very short time. So my brother and I spent our winters trying to keep enough wood available for that hungry monster.

When everyone went to bed the fire would burn out and it needed to be rebuilt again in the early morning requiring more wood. My brother and I would alternate who would gather the wood, one morning for him and one morning for me. I can tell you this was a difficult chore. Jumping out of bed in your long johns in very cold weather was not something young boys like to do. After the fire warmed up the room, the rest of the family would get up to start their day. It was just one of the many hardships pioneer families had to face in Butler County.

116

THE SUNFLOWER

The sunflower is no stranger to Butler County. As I recall, most everyone living along Long Branch School Road had a few sunflowers growing in their garden. My grandmother Lillie Oller always had a large group of them in the lower section of her garden, so did my dad's Aunt Laura Childers and her husband Will. The seeds they produced were used to feed the poultry, and in those days, most everyone had a flock that ranged from chickens to ducks, geese, and guinea hens. Of course, wild birds love sunflower seeds, and when the seeds were developing it was necessary to cover the heads with some type of netting to protect the seeds from the birds.

There are several reasons that this plant is called the sunflower. If we look at the head closely, we find that its round face and yellow colored petals emulates the sun very much. The sunflower is a native of North America, but the commercialization of the plant took place in Russia.

It was only recently that the sunflower become a cultivated crop in America. In the beginning, all sunflowers were multiple heads, and history indicates that it was the American Indians who first domesticated the plant into a single head, with several different seed colors. It was a common crop with the Indians. Evidence suggests that it was grown in present day Arizona and New Mexico sometime around 3000 BC. Some archeologists believe that the sunflower may have been domesticated before corn. The Indians used the sunflower in many ways. The seeds were pounded with stones to make flower for bread, cake, or mush. The seeds were also cracked and the kernels eaten as snacks.

Today, we can purchase sunflower kernels from most food stores. Research shows that they provide a powerhouse of benefits that protect against many diseases, including cardiovascular disease. The kernel has grown to the point where it is now considered to be a functional food, and adds a nutritional wallop to a wide array of products, such as bread, muffins, and crackers. Manufactures of these products are pleased because it gives them the opportunity to add nutrition to their products, which is in demand by their customers. Restaurants and food processers are beginning to become aware of the health benefits of sunflower oil. It is high in vitamin E and has a low level of trans fat. It performs better at high temperatures and has a smoother taste than other oils. Most of the potato chips we eat today are cooked in sunflower oil. At the Lays Potato Chip Company, the recipe calls for using sunflower oil only. Currently, much research is being done to improve on what is already a great product.

Yes, the sunflower head does follow the sun across the sky from east to west. However, they stop and keep their faces tuned to the east when the blossoms and seed start to form. This appears to be a defensive action to prevent the hot evening sun from scalding the seeds. At this point, no one in the world has been able to understand what causes this miracle to happen.

117

A VOICE WITHIN

To most of us, life is so precious that there is no way to explain how valuable it is. Today we may be happy and carefree, however, come tomorrow, we may find ourselves all battered and bruised with a heart that is filled with pain and sorrow. Because these sad and troubling conditions are sure to happen in every life, we should make sure that we don't lose our faith and courage. It's important that we leave no stone unturned, and look for all the help that's available.

Most everyone is familiar with, or has heard about the small inner voice that speaks from deep inside of us. This voice speaks very softly and we must be relaxed in some very quiet location and listen very closely in order to hear the message. The purpose of this message is to provide guidance in our lives and to give us the ability to understand what is good or bad, and the difference between right and wrong.

My cousin Rollie Childers and I both listened to this small voice when we were young. The Childers family lived on the Morgantown Road near the Buzzard Bluff. It was up the Long Branch School Road about a mile from our place. Since we were cousins, and about the same age, we were close friends and spent a great deal of time together. One day we were enjoying the view from the bluff. It's very high above the Green River, and the view of the river and the land beyond is breathtaking. At that time, there was a very steep trail on one side of the bluff that went down to the river. Rollie told me that one day he had been down to the river and was on his way back home, and while walking on this trail his inner voice became audible to him. As Rollie explained this to me, there was no doubt in his mind that it was the Lord asking him to become a Christian and to follow in His footsteps. It must have been a strong message as Rollie never wavered from his belief that working to promote Christianity was his calling for the rest of his life. I feel certain that his family, his friends, and all the people that he helped in his lifetime regard him as a living example of God's love and kindness.

My first experience with this little voice inside me happened when I was eight or nine years old. I estimate the age because I was big enough to carry a gallon pail of water from the Sylvester Burden spring to our house, a distance of approximately three quarters of a mile. One hot day in late summer, July, or August, I was walking up the little incline about halfway between the spring and Aunt Laura's place. This little inner voice surprised me by saying, "You are now a person. You should live your life by being kind and helpful to everyone. Don't lie, steal or harm anyone."

Listening to this made me think that I was being told to follow the Ten Commandments. Something I have always tried to do. However, being human, we all stumble on occasions. It was a pivotal point in my life, and I firmly believe that this little voice was the key that opened the door to my life.

The world we live in is not evil. Just some of the people who inhabit it are. Makes one wonder what small voice these people are listening to. One thing for certain, it's not the same voice that Rollie and I listened to.

118

TIME IN ITS FLIGHT

Backward, turn backward O' time in your flight, make me a child again just for tonight. This this is a very beautiful poem that appears to have been written by a person near, or approaching, the twilight years in their life. And as most of us do, he or she was missing their mother, and longed to go back to the time when they were a child. But as we all know, that is not possible in this life. However, that doesn't keep us from remembering the times when our mother rocked us to sleep. Those of us who have a vivid memory of our childhood are very fortunate indeed.

The flight of time, how swiftly it flows, from the days of our youth, till we are aged and old. That last sentence is not part of the poem. Just something I inserted to see if I had any poetic talent. But let's not complain. Our generation has lived in the greatest of times. All the convenience and amenities that make for a very enjoyable life have been ours. They were the changes we were all searching for when I was growing up there in Butler County. However, the flight in time has brought some changes that are somewhat painful.

I am reminded of these painful changes when I visit the food market to purchase a few steaks for grilling. The price for a good ribeye steak is approximately $10.50 cents per pound. When this happens, it causes me to remember a purchase my father made when we lived on Long Branch School Road.

Our neighbor, Mr. Will Coleman and his family lived on top of the hill just above the Possum Hollow. Mr. Coleman was a very ambitious and hardworking man. He operated the grist mill, where we took our corn to have it ground into meal, a saw mill, and a small factory, where he made chairs. The chairs were the upright type with the hickory bark bottoms. He was also a farmer and raised hogs for market. My father contracted to purchase two porkers from him. The agreement was that Mr. Coleman would dress them out and deliver them to our house. I was small, but I can remember the transaction very well.

Mr. Coleman brought the two porkers in his wagon, dressed as agreed. They were estimated to weigh approximately 150 pounds each. He helped my father hang them in our smoke house, and my father paid him the agreed on price of three cents per pound. My father gave him a ten dollar bill and said no change was necessary. That was less than one pound of steak today.

I am not sure how long Mr. Coleman ran the chair factory. The original site for the factory was over on the Green River, and was operated by Mr. Lon Burchfield and his son Noble. I believe that Mr. Coleman purchased it when the elder Mr. Burchfield passed away, and it became more than the son Noble could handle by himself. Some of these chairs could still be in use in the county. To my knowledge, it was the only manufacturing plant to ever operate on the north side of the Green River.

One nice Saturday morning, my brother and I carried our corn up to Mr. Coleman's place to have it ground into meal. It so happened that Mr. Coleman had to go back to the farm for some reason, and left his son Clyde there with my brother and me, with instructions to build a fire in the big steam boiler to build up enough steam to power the mill. We were advised to toot the steam whistle when the steam pressure gage reached one hundred pounds or so, and he would come back and start grinding the corn. I don't know what happened, but we got carried away with the sound of the steam whistle. We keep blowing it until we used up all the steam, and in all the excitement, we forgot to stoke the boiler with more wood. As you can imagine, Mr. Coleman was very unhappy about the fact that there was no power to start grinding the corn. I can still remember his comments. "It sounded as if you boys had all the steam in the world, the way you were blowing the whistle," and some other words that I don't dare print. It took about forty-five minutes to get the steam back up and start the mill operating.

I was in the building with him when the meal started coming from the grinder, and Mr. Coleman would catch some in his hand and check to see if it was of the proper consistency. It is said that a good miller knows if the meal will make good bread by the way it feels. He must have done a good job, I don't recall anyone complaining. The process to grind the corn was done by millstones. Many people think that a millstone is a hand held stone used to pound the grain into meal or flour, however, the millstone is a much more complicated process. I recall seeing some of the millstones that were there in the building, they were large round stones, perhaps twenty-four or thirty inches in diameter, and six or eight inches thick, and they must have weighed several hundred pounds. The face, or grinding surface had furrows and lands cut in them, deeper in the center and almost disappearing as they reached the outer edge. This design allows coarse grinding in the center and very fine material as it reached the outer edge of the millstones. It takes two millstones to do the job. The bottom one is stationary, the top one rotates on top of the stationary one. However, they never touch each other, if they did they would destroy the furrows and lands.

Over the years, millstones have killed and injured many people, mostly by being dropped or by breaking loose from the spindle and flying through the building walls. Because of that, a superstition has surrounded them. If the stone had ever hurt anyone, they were considered evil. You may have heard the old adage about keeping your nose close to the grindstone. There's a good possibility that it originated with the early millers of the world. Burning of the material that was being ground has always been a problem, therefore it was very important for the miller to keep his nose close to grinding stones, so he would be able to smell it if the material started to burn. In addition, he would be able to detect any other problems, such as pieces of foreign material entering the grinder, or running out of material, which would cause the top stone to spin out of control.

Taking this short ride on the history train of the gristmill may help us understand why Mr. Coleman was more than a little annoyed when he returned to the mill that day and found no steam in the boiler. But it probably won't do anything to slow down "time in its flight."

119

THE TOPMILLER COAL TRAIN

Ben Topmiller was the Casey Jones of Butler County: they both lost their lives when they wrecked the trains they were driving. Legend has it that Casey lost his life on April 30, 1900, when he slammed into a parked train down near the small town of Vaughn, Mississippi. It has been reported that Casey was a nickname that he earned while working with a railroad crew because he lived in Casey, Kentucky. This story could be stretching the truth a little bit, because there is no town by the name of Casey in Kentucky. There is a city named Caseyville, up the Ohio River north of Paducah. There is also a Casey County up near the middle of the state in the area where the Green River rises. Since the legend has been handed down through several generations, his nickname could have come from either of these locations, but his real name was John Luther Jones.

The Topmiller coal train was, and is, the only railroad to ever operate in the County of Butler. My research indicates that Mr. Topmiller was a native of Bowling Green and Warren County. In the early part of the twentieth century he had a dream about building a railroad that would transfer coal from the mines in the upper reaches of Bull Creek to the Green River, a distance of approximately two miles, where it could be loaded on river barges and shipped to most any place in the country.

In the year of 1907, his dream became a reality when he built the trestles and laid the rails for his little steam engine to pull the small gondola cars loaded with coal. It is believed that the train became operational sometime in the year of 1908. My dad was born there on Bull Creek in the year of 1896 and would have been twelve or thirteen years old when the railroad was in operation. When I was a boy my dad told me how he would hook a ride on the rear car and ride down to the river, or Martin Lake, to go fishing. He indicated that Mr. Topmiller would give him a tongue lashing when he found him riding on the train. Of course, being a kid at that time, he didn't know that that the track and trestles were unsafe. However, after he grew up, he said that he was not surprised that the trestles collapsed; they were supported with timbers a little larger than a tooth pick.

Looking backward over the past 100 years, details and facts become very fuzzy. It is believed that the train operated for one or two years. Sometime around 1909, a trestle did collapse and caused the death of Mr. Topmiller. There is a photo of the train wreck taken by Ally Childers in which it appears that the engine is turned upside down and is lying on the ground, and three of the gondola cars have crashed and dumped their coal, leaving only one car upright on the track. Unfortunately this photo is faded and unable to be reproduced due to the ravages of time.

The collapse of the trestle, and the death of Mr. Topmiller, did not stop the delivery of coal to the Green River. It's been said that one of Mr. Topmiller's sons repaired the tracks and damaged equipment. He made a floor between the rails with rough sawed lumber so it could be walked on, and he used mules to pull the coal cars down the tracks. This method of delivery continued for some time.

It's my hope that my stories will help keep the history of the Topmiller coal train alive for at least the next hundred years.

120

TWINE THAT BINDS THE HAY

Our southern states are prone to hot dry weather. If we look back in history, we will find that they have a drought every few years. Some are small and manageable. Others are very severe and devastating. The one that I remember well happened sometime in the late '90s... in 1995 through 1997. The state of Georgia and the surrounding states suffered severally. There were times when the area received only a smidgen of rain in a six month period, which resulted in a shortage of water causing all the crops to burn up in the fields and farm animals were dying from the shortage of food. Of course the news of this disaster was widespread. This prompted some of the northern states to take notice and become concerned. They decided to help their neighbors to the south by sending hay to feed their livestock.

Railroad cars were loaded with hay and shipped south. They were called hay trains. I was impressed by this very kind gesture. And while it was fresh in my mind, I wrote a poem about this humanitarian effort and wanted to share it.

> A southern gentleman with hair snow white,
> Watched the hay train roll through the night.
> A gift of kindness from friends whose names
> he did not know, although their ancestors

Once met long ago at Gettysburg, and Shiloh.

How strong the twine that binds the hay.
Can it mend the torn and tattered gray?
Will it erase the scars and wounds
That have lingered for so long?

The twine is strong that binds the hay.
And holds it in a caring way.
It stands up strong for those that give,
And help for those in need.

These helping hands, and special twine
Could hold a heart in time,
And mend its strings with bailing twine.

As far back as we can remember, Butler County has had its share of drought. Most of us can remember some summers when corn would dry up in the fields due to lack of moisture. The spring of 2013 was exactly the opposite. It rained so much, and the bottom land was so wet, that farmers experienced difficulties in getting their corn planted, and in some instances were compelled to plant other crops. As most farmers love to grow corn I'm sure they would have been much happier had they had the opportunity to plant their corn early in the spring.

The poet John Greenleaf Whittier expressed his love for corn in one of his poems. The following is a few words of what he had to say about that wonder crop. *"Heap high the farmer's winter hoard. Heap high the golden corn. No richer gift has autumn poured from out her lavish horn. But let the good crop adorn, the hills our fathers trod. Still let us for his golden corn. Send up our thanks to God."*

121

WE MISS YOU

Our dog was named Mundy. He was Cocker Spaniel with long floppy ears and furry paws. He shed enough hair every day to stop up the vacuum cleaner. Even though he could be naughty at times, our family loved him very much, and it would appear that his love for us was unlimited.

After our children were no longer at home, if either my wife Ruth or I was out of the house, he would lie by the door with his paws out front, and his chin on the floor between them, waiting patiently for our return. Now that he is no longer with us, we still love and miss him.

Perhaps your family has lost a pet that left you broken hearted. I'm sure you miss them. As our lives move forward we are faced with losing the ones that we dearly love, which leaves an empty spot in our hearts that seems impossible to fill. The passing of time appears to help some. However, it's a long way from being a cure, and when we speak about our loss, about all we can say is what is in our hearts, and how much we miss them.

Have you ever thought about families where their loved ones were lost in battle and buried in some far away land, never to return to their home and loved ones again? There are many of them. Perhaps you have personally experienced this very difficult situation. How painful it must be for the ones left behind. I am sure that words cannot explain how much they are missed.

I read a few words recently about our lost military people and wanted to share them. *"They shall grow not old as we that are left grow old. Age shall not weary them, nor the years condemn. At the going down of the sun, and in the morning, we will remember them."*

It's been some time now since World War II ended. However, I still miss members of my family and friends that lost their lives in that very difficult struggle to save the world from terror and intimidation. My sister Irene lost her husband, Johnnie Elmore. Johnnie was a Butler County boy who at one time was a teacher at the Long Branch School. He gave his life defending our country in the snow covered Ardennes Forest of Belgium. Johnnie left behind his wife and their baby daughter Velda, who was nine months old at the time. My very dear friend, Robert Lee Fields, from Louisville, Kentucky, lost his life in Belgium as well. Robert left behind his wife and two daughters, ages six and eight years old. My friend and buddy, Jack Kesterson, a small, likeable, tough as steel boy from Dyersburg, Tennessee, died, too. Jack died when his company was trying to make some progress in the rugged mountain war in Italy.

Wars are terrible, incredibly inhumane and I so wish there was a way to eliminate them forever. However, at this time in history it appears that there is no end in sight. As long as some dictators and terrorists try to impose their will and ideology on other people, wars are sure to continue.

In the scheme of things that God has designed for all living creatures, most of us humans feel that life is short and complicated, filled with happiness today and sorrow tomorrow. For the most of us, our greatest sorrow comes when we lose our loved ones. We feel devastated and helpless. It may help if we remember that old saying, "No one is gone as long as they are missed and remembered."

122

WELCH'S CREEK

In some of my stories I have mentioned Welch's Creek. It was the closest stream of any size near the farm where I grew up. There is also a small village near the creek's headwaters called Welch's Creek. I never knew if the village was named after the creek, or the creek was named after the village.

Welch's Creek rises in northeast Butler County and flows southeast across the county until it empties into the Green River near Morgantown. As the crow flies, it is approximately 15 miles long. In actuality, it is probably close to 25 miles long. It twists and turns like a serpent's tail on its way across the county. When it passes through our area, it is 25 to 30 feet wide in its normal state.

Due to the fact that it was only about three quarters of a mile from our house, it was our favorite place to fish. It is home to several types of fish. Yellow belly catfish were the most plentiful and easiest to catch. They would range in size from approximately three quarters of a pound to around two pounds. You could catch a few of them in the daylight hours, but for the most part they were night feeders. One of the best times to go fishing for them was after a rain. As the water would rise and become muddy, this would excite them and they would start searching for food that had been washed in by the rain. For some reason it didn't take much rain to make the creek rise and start flowing rapidly. Some people expressed the thought that if a frog urinated upstream it would cause the creek to overflow its banks downstream.

It was probably the easiest place on Earth to go fishing. All you needed was a fishing line, hook and sinker. When you got to the spot where you wanted to fish, you could cut a pole from one of the many trees that grew along the bank. Then with a sharp stick you could dig up some earthworms that were plentiful and use them for bait. Most of the time you could go home with a nice string of fish. The large fish that came up from the Green River would only bite at night. The best method to catch these big guys was to set out several lines up and down the creek late in the evening, and bait them with cut bait. Small fish would not bother the cut bait, so it would just stay there until the big guys came along late at night. Some of them were so large they would pull the fishing pole out of the bank, but it was usually nearby, hung up on some drift wood. When we had hooks set out at night, I would get up early and run to the creek and gather in the fish. Then run back to the house, clean the fish and we would have them for breakfast. It would be difficult to find fish more fresh than that.

One day my brother asked me to give him some help on a project that he had dreamed up. He wanted to construct a net to use in the creek. We used some heavy wire to make the round hoops, then we used some small mesh poultry netting to make the funnels and the net itself. Since the net was round, it would roll down the creek bank into the center of the creek. With some of mom's cornbread for bait, we were in business. In a day or so we went back and pulled the net up on shore. To our surprise, the net was full of fish. Many of them we did not know were in the creek such as bass and trout, as we had never been able to catch them with a hook and line. Our dad considered himself to be quiet a fisherman, but you should have seen his eyes when we showed him our catch. Of course, we did not tell him until a good many years later how we had managed to catch so many fish.

Even though the law was quiet lax in those years, we didn't use the net for long. We were afraid that we might get caught, and that would have caused many problems. A word to parents. "If you have boys, keep a close watch on them, for you never know what they will do next."

123

WHERE THE DOGWOOD BLOSSOMS BLOW

A good indicator that spring has arrived is when the dogwoods start to bloom. I believe that we will all agree, that it would be difficult to find a flower more beautiful than the dogwood when it's in full bloom. They do a great job decorating our lawns, highways, and forest. About the only negative thing I can find about this beautiful flowering tree is when we have suffered through a long winter season and think that spring is here, it brings us a cold snap, commonly known as dogwood winter. Most of us are familiar with dogwood winter, we have heard about it all our lives. You won't find it on the calendar, but it is as real as the other seasons. It happens every year when the dogwoods bloom.

Dogwood trees are of rare elegance and beauty, and are loved by most everyone. It is the state tree of Missouri, and the state flower of North Carolina. Virginia loves the dogwood so much that they have decreed it both the state tree and the state flower. The Tulip popular is the state tree of Kentucky, and the Goldenrod is the state flower. Today, most towns and cities celebrate their blooming by providing parks and trails to show their splendor and beauty. The lighted trail in the City of Paducah, Kentucky, is considered to be one of the most beautiful. It's about twelve miles long and can be viewed by walking, driving, or by trolley. It has been in operation since 1964.

The quaint little city of Madison, Georgia, has a population of about 4,000 and is located approximately forty miles east of Atlanta on the north side of Interstate 20, with Highway 441 running through the center of the city north to south. In past years on our trips to and from Florida in the spring, we always made an effort, or found some excuse, to go through Madison. Both sides of Main Street are lined with dogwood trees placed very close together, and when they are in bloom it's such a beautiful sight to behold. In addition to its beautiful dogwood trees, Madison is famous for other things. In the early days before automobiles, it was considered to be the luxurious stopping place for the stagecoach that traveled between Charleston, South Carolina, and New Orleans, Louisiana. Legend has it that during the Civil War, when General Sherman made his destructive and burning march across Georgia, Madison was spared from destruction because it was the hometown of pro-union Senator Joshua Hill.

History doesn't tell us much about how the dogwood got its name. One thought is that over the years it evolved from the Celtic word Dagwood. The dag was a small pointed wooden tool. The tight grained wood contained no silica, and was used to clean small pieces that were easy to scratch, such as watches and jewelry. Our present dogwood trees have a reputation of being a very hard wood. Legend has it that at one time the dogwood grew tall and straight like other trees. The wood from the dogwood was said to have been used to construct the cross that Jesus was crucified upon. The dogwood was distraught over this particular use, and Jesus took pity upon it, promising that never again would it be used for crucifixion. Since then the dogwood tree has grown bent and twisted, unable to reach any significant height. And since that time the petals of its flowers have grown in the shape of the cross, each bearing the reddish mark of a rusty nail.

Butler County is blessed with many of these beautiful trees. I have pleasant memories of them growing in the woods and fields, and along the Long Branch School Road.

124

WHITE CHRISTMAS

I believe everyone was as excited as I was about the beautiful White Christmas we had in 2010. For us who live here in the south, snow at Christmas time is rather unusual, it's something we don't experience very often. For me, it brought back memories of past Christmases when I was growing up on Long Branch School Road. Like children of today, we loved to play in the snow. As I recall, we would manage to put together some boards that resembled a sled, and slide down the hills.

As a child I loved Christmas, and it would appear that I haven't changed much over the years. I still get sad and sentimental when it comes time to put it behind me. The wreaths are gathered up and put back in their boxes. The beautiful multi-colored Christmas lights that we all enjoy so much must be bundled up and stored for the next eleven months, and if you use a fresh green tree it can always be placed out back for the birds to shelter in. After that, only one more task remains, that is to check the refrigerator, you may need to pour the sour eggnog down the drain, and put the left over fruitcake in the freezer.

Of course, we Christians celebrate Christmas because it is the birthday of Christ, the son of God, who was sent here to lead His children out of darkness. There are twenty-two different faiths or religions throughout the world. There are a few more small ones with memberships less than 500,000, and Christianity being the leader with an estimated 2.1 billion members. Although Christianity is under attack here in America, it is growing at an astounding rate throughout the world.

Of course, after Christmas comes the New Year. It comes so fast that I was just beginning to get accustomed to writing one year and the next year shows up. The first few days of 2011 were very eventful. Birds all over the world were falling out of the sky. It was very sad and heart breaking to see this happen to our bird population. Whatever was causing it, I hope someone found an answer and a cure. Besides providing us with their beauty and musical songs, birds are necessary to keep our ecological balance in order.

Another event around the New Year, is that every two years the American voters send a new group of people to Washington to serve in the United States Congress. I'm sure that it is the hope of all Americans that each of them are blessed with wisdom, common sense, and a burning desire to do the right thing under the most trying circumstances. If they possess these qualities, they will be noted in history as leaders.

History tells us many stories about the great leaders of the world. In the early centuries, kings, queens, and other leaders would arrive in gold trimmed carriages. Today, most arrive in private jet planes. This draws a sharp contrast between how the greatest leader of all times arrived. He arrived in a manger. He has made the greatest impact on the world of any leader, with His ability to change people's hearts and minds. That's why we celebrate His birthday.

125

YOU CAN'T GO HOME AGAIN

It's a fact that many of us spend the first half of our life running away from the homestead where we grew up, and the last half running back. *You can't go home again* has become part of our current everyday speech. It's the title of one of Thomas Wolf's bestselling books, along with "Look Homeward Angel." Mr. Wolf was a native of Asheville, North Carolina. The novel tells the story of George Webber, a beginning author who writes a book about his hometown, Libya Hill. When the residents of Libya Hill read the book and noticed all the egregious distortions about their town, they were very angry and threatened George's life if he ever showed his face in Libya Hill again. That's right, George; you will never be able to go home again— back to your family, back to where you can recapture your childhood memories.

Of course, there are many forces that prevent us from going home again. Pride prevents some people from going back to the family home because they haven't been successful out in the world. Changes in the American landscape is the one thing that presents the greatest problem. My friend Bill Mastin grew up in Chattanooga, Tennessee, and tells me his old home place was located in the pathway of US Interstate-24, which was built in the mid '60s. My friend Kelly Helgren, who grew up in New Jersey, tells me that where his childhood home once stood, there is a 500 car parking lot.

It's easy to see that my friends, and others like them, are deprived of going back to their childhood, back to their dreams, back to the old systems of things that once seemed everlasting, which is sometimes referred to as our roots. Being able to visit where we grew up is a very important part of our lives, and in some instances tends to guide our footsteps and makes the rocky road of life much easier to navigate.

I'm fortunate and very grateful that I can visit my old home place there on Long Branch School Road any time I become homesick. Although the buildings are gone, and the fields that we use to plow have become a forest, the land remains the same. The big Sycamore, where I spent many of my childhood hours under its shady branches, is still growing, and appears to be doing well. The branch that runs down from the Possum Hollow still makes the same babbling sound as it runs over the roots of the Sycamore. The spring where my mom washed our clothing has not changed, just the inhabitants. It is now used by the deer and other wildlife as a watering place.

It's my opinion that this land will remain about the same for many years. It's a little difficult to envision a four lane highway running through there, or a supermarket with parking space for several hundred cars.

It been said, and I agree, that it doesn't really matter how far we have roamed around the world, or how many states or countries we have lived in, we always think of home as the place where we grew up. It's true that my parents are not here to share memories with me, but those of us who live long enough will become orphans, and we miss our parents very much. However, if we live by the creed of the great Indian Chief Tecumseh, who was the chief of the Shawnee nation, when being pressured to give up more of his land to the white man, he stated that God in Heaven is his father, and the Earth is his mother.

If we agree with the Chief there is no reason we should remain orphans.

126

THE BRASS RING

Most of us are familiar with the legendary saying "grab the brass ring." History indicates that this phrase got its start in the heydays of the big circus and was used to promote riders on the carousal, better known to most of us as the merry-go-round. The owners of the carousals were aware that the American male population was inclined to be big showoffs. Men do these things to demonstrate strength or dexterity as a way to impress the ladies or a girlfriend. Knowing that men were prone to this weakness, the owners thought that they might collect a few more nickels and dimes by setting up a group of rings beside the carousal, which under certain conditions could be grabbed as the riders passed by. The owners made it somewhat difficult by placing only one brass ring among a group of black iron rings. If you were lucky enough to grab the brass ring, it provide you with a free ride on the carousal. This program began somewhere around the turn of the 19th century which makes it more than a hundred years old. Over the years the brass ring has been transformed into an expression of good luck and success.

Many people believe that some time in their lives a brass ring of opportunity will present itself and if they are able to grab this imaginary ring their lives will change for the better and success and happiness will find its way into their lives.

Grabbing the brass ring depends on the decision we make when promising opportunities present themselves and will not happen unless we make the decision to grab it, both mentally and physically.

If we look back in our lives we can recall the decisions we make and ponder if the decisions we make at the time were the correct ones. Like everyone else, I have faced my share of these tough decisions. My first real job was working in the plant that produced automobile parts. After I had been there a few years the company approached me with an offer to join the management team. The title of my new job was Marketing Engineer. My customers were the automobile and appliance manufacturing companies in America. It was a great job and when I decided to open my own company, it was this previous experience that made it successful. It has always been my thought that when I took the management offer, I grabbed the brass ring.

However, there have been times when I was too timid to gab the brass ring. While working in Detroit, the owner of a company that produced motor oil dip sticks asked me if I would be interested in buying his company. It was a nice company that had always made a profit and the price was very attractive. After wrestling with it for several days I decided not to buy it. The reason being that cars were in the process of being computerized, and everyone believed that in a short time dip sticks would be replaced by pushing the oil button. Much to everyone's surprise, and after 25 years, the dip stick is very much alive and as far as I know is used in all cars and other motor vehicles.

As time moves along each of us will be confronted with many important decision and when we are forced to make these decisions we should give considerable thought to each of them. One of them could contain that lucky brass ring that would change our lives forever.

127

REVIEW THE PAST

Morgantown and Butler County have always had a special place in my heart. It is where I spent the first eighteen years of my life growing up with my family and friends, even though life could be difficult at that time in history. I have always been proud of the land that produced me and grateful for the memories that have lingered over the years.

I am of the opinion that the mid thirties and early forties were the heyday for Morgantown and Butler County. It was a time when Morgantown was a booming city. All building were occupied with some type of business. On Saturday the courthouse yard was filled with people taking advantage of the big shade trees. The streets were so crowed they were difficult to walk down. This was about the time that Girlie Smith built the new Smith Hotel on what was at that time known as "Dog Walk Street." It was a very modern building with a very nice restaurant, juke box for music, and pool rooms on the first floor and hotel rooms were on the upper level.

I once had the opportunity to spend a night in one of those rooms. This all came about because when I was young I worked for Girlie down on his Eden farm. He usually drove me down near the farm, where there was a boat I could use to cross the river. This particular evening he was tied up and could not drive me down there, instead he said, "Use one of the rooms upstairs and we will drive down early tomorrow." Sleeping in a hotel room was certainly a new experience for me. It was my introduction to inside plumbing. I am not going to try and explain how awkward and strange those plumbing fixtures were. I always looked forward to my trips with Girlie. He was easy to talk to and he was usually well dressed with a white shirt and three piece suit. He drove a new Chrysler car that had the smell of expensive cigars. At that time in history, being able to smoke these cigars was considered to be an indication of wealth, and being a boy of very limited means, this kind of wealthy atmosphere had a profound effect on my dreams for the future. Like me, Girlie had started from the bottom of the social ladder. I convinced myself that if Girlie could be successful, perhaps I would be able to accomplish some degree of success in my lifetime.

Up "Dog Walk Street" a few doors from the new hotel was a small restaurant. It had been there for a good many years, and had been operated by a number of people. The one person I remember was a gentleman by the name of Jake Odom. The reason I remember Jake so well was the big sign that he hung out over the sidewalk to advertise the quality of his restaurant. The sign read "Down on Dog Walk 49, you will always see Jake Odom's sign, the cooking is done before your eyes there is no chance you will get any flies." In the days before insecticide, screen doors, and air conditioning, flies were a major problem.

When I visit Morgantown I always expect it to look the way it did in the early years. However, we know that is wishful thinking. Everything changes. Cities and towns are prone to changes as a rule they never stay the same for a long period of time. They either grow or they decline. Like many other cities in our county Morgantown and Butler County is finding it a struggle to survive. Declining feeds on itself. Businesses close due to lake of customers. Tax revenue is lost because people spend their money elsewhere. Young people go where there are jobs and opportunity. I am sure that everyone is anxious for the city and the surrounding county to grow and prosper. It's my hope that this historical little city that sits on a bluff overlooking the majestic Green River will have a new birth and become a center of activity once again.

128

THE THREAD THAT BINDS

Most families have a sewing basket in their home. In these baskets we find many spools of thread. Thread comes in many different colors, strength, and size. This is necessary because it is used to mend many different colors and types of material. This type of thread is made from different colors and types of material and becomes thread when two or more filaments, such as flax, cotton, silk, and others are twisted together. In the early part of the last century the needle and thread was necessary in order to keep the family clothing mended. This type of thread is visible and is much different from the invisible thread that binds the human race together.

We are all related in some way, and face many of the same problems each day that everyone else on earth does. While this common thread that binds us is invisible, it is structured in much the same way as the visible thread. However there are many more strands in this moral and spiritual thread than in the visible ones, like love, friendship, charity, inclusion, harmony, wisdom, and a caring heart. With all these strands twisted together you have a very strong thread and it is considered to be one of the cornerstones of civilization. While it is impossible to see or to hold this thread in your hands, we can see in our everyday life that the benefits it provides for the human race. When tragedy strikes it is this thread that causes so many of our friends, neighbors, and even strangers to make a sacrifice by giving of themselves with love, kindness, and inspiration. It is this thread that provides the unconditional love that holds families together in times of misfortune and adversity. It has been said that the most beautiful things in the world cannot be seen or touched, rather they must be felt with the heart.

All humanity is saddled with this relentless clock of time that continues to run unstopped forever and the only good thing it leaves behind is memories. You may have noticed that as this clock continues to run, many changes are taking place in our world. There are wide spread differences of opinion about what effect these changes will have on the human race. Some think it is a great step forward. Progress they call it. Other are not so sure. Their concern is about the current attack on Christianity. Is the value of life becoming less valuable? In some parts of the world life has no value at all. They are also concerned about greed. Greed has been one of mankind's greatest sins from the beginning of time and at this time it appears to be on the increase.

With all these problems facing the human race, what will happen to this thread that binds us together? Will the weight of the problems in the world be so strong that this thread will fracture and fall apart and cause the world to slide back into the dark ages? Or will the good people of the world stand up and fight to preserve the better way of life that they have always enjoyed? Especially we Americans who have, over the years paid such a heavy price to defend freedom. It is my opinion that when the going gets tough the regular and hardworking people of the world will be the winners. I hope the above statement is not wishful thinking on my part.

129

THE BEST THINGS IN LIFE

Most of us are familiar with the old adage that the best things in life are free. It's a fact that on this earth we are blessed with many things of natural beauty. Mountains, oceans, rivers, and waterfalls. Beautiful flowers in the spring, green forest in the summer, and autumn leaves of red and gold in the fall, and our feathered friends that lift our spirits with their songs. These are just a few of the many things that the universe provides us with that are free, and all of us should be thankful that we were lucky enough to live in America where we have the freedom to enjoy them.

However, if we want to live a meaningful life, there are a multitude of things we must do to accomplish that task. Life is a journey that resembles a ship on the ocean, some days are smooth sailing, and other days are filled with problems. Storm clouds gather, and trouble winds try to uproot the anchor we have planted in life's ocean. The best things in life are not material things. They are the things that money cannot buy, such as love of family, friends, courage and kindness. If we don't have faith and courage to go forward our lives could become a wrecked ship on the ocean of life. There are many things that we can do to repair our wrecked ship of life. First we should make love with the universe. The vastness of the sky should be the amount of love we hold in our hearts. We should remember that the flame from one candle can light a thousand candles and its life won't be shortened.

I was inspired to write about this topic because of what my granddaughter Noelia did for me. Noelia, better known as Lina, and her husband Richard live in South Dakota. Sometime ago I had a health problem. As soon as she heard about it she was on the plane to Tennessee so she could care for me. She sacrificed thirty days of her life to make sure that I had the best care possible. And since she is a highly trained nurse with a heart full of love, I feel that she contributed substantially to my early recovery. Love is very strong. It is the foundation of the best things in life. It is the closest we will ever come to knowing God. It is the gateway to gratitude and inner peace and the bridge from this life to the next.

All humanity is saddled with this relentless clock of time that continues to run unstopped forever and the only good thing it leaves behind is memories. You may have noticed that as this clock continues to run, many changes are taking place in our world. There are wide spread differences of opinion about what effect these changes will have on the human race. Some think it is a great step forward. Progress they call it. Other are not so sure. Their concern is about the current attack on Christianity. Is the value of life becoming less valuable? In some parts of the world life has no value at all. They are also concerned about greed. Greed has been one of mankind's greatest sins from the beginning of time and at this time it appears to be on the increase.

130

THE PAGES OF TIME

Turn back the pages of time, and keep my old memories alive. I don't feel like that's asking too much, and I believe that you will agree. However, this imaginary journey that we are about to embark upon has somewhat of a delicate history, and must be handled with the utmost of care.

These pages have been in existence for a very long time, and in order to review these pages, we must first understand that they are not tangible pages that we can touch or physically turn. They are all securely locked in our memory, and have been for our entire life. To review them we must use our mind and memory to penetrate the misty veil of time that surrounds them. Most everyone looking to turn back these pages would most likely want to start at on the first page, and of course that page would be what you can remember about our childhood.

These pages are old, and the bindings that cover them are dark and heavy with age. Sometimes, we find it difficult to strip away this darkness so the real pages of our early life can be seen. When this happens, we should be able to develop a mental picture of our life as a child. The home or homes where we lived. The bedroom we occupied. The kitchen table where we had our meals, and complained about having to eat your vegetables. The yard or fields where we played. Most of us feel that our childhood years are among the happiest times of our lives, growing up with brothers and sisters. Free from worry, because we knew that mom and dad would take care of us. That same feeling is what makes us want to turn back that page in time.

As we become a little older, school becomes a very important time in our life. We start learning about life, the world we live in, it's where we come in contact with other young people our age. We make some very close friends, some that last through the years. Some bullies that become enemies, and we find it necessary to defend ourselves in order to maintain respectability. Somewhere along the way, most of us will fall in love with the teacher, or one of our friends that we think is beautiful or handsome. Each school year represents a separate page in our lives. That's why we would like to turn back these pages in time.

The responsibility of becoming an adult is a very difficult time in our lives. We struggle with all the many serious decisions that we are un-accustomed to making, but as an adult we have other choices. Many of these decisions will affect our families, as well as our lives in the future. Questions like, what profession will I choose? Will I be capable of providing for a family? Will I find the right person to swim with me in the stream of life? All are major decisions that we must wrestle with at that stage in our lives. As we turn back this page of time, we hope that the decisions we made were the correct ones, and we will be comfortable with what this page displays.

If one is fortunate enough to become a senior citizen, this decision making process usually continues and may even increase in volume, which will provide additional pages to review. Turning back the pages of time is a condition that effects mature people. Young people have not had enough time to write many pages. Besides, they are too busy looking to the future to be concerned about the past. Fortunately, most of us are able to turn back these pages of time and watch these indelible memories as they pass in review. They are without a doubt, a blessing to the human race.

131

PHOTOS FROM THE PAST

Vander Wright Martin, Mary Ellen West Martin, and Leora Martin, Butler County, KY 1890

Kate Oller, George Oller, Pernie Oller, Mattie Oller and Lillie Napier Oller, Butler County, KY 1898

Pernie Oller Martin, and James Otis Martin, Long Branch, KY circa 1940

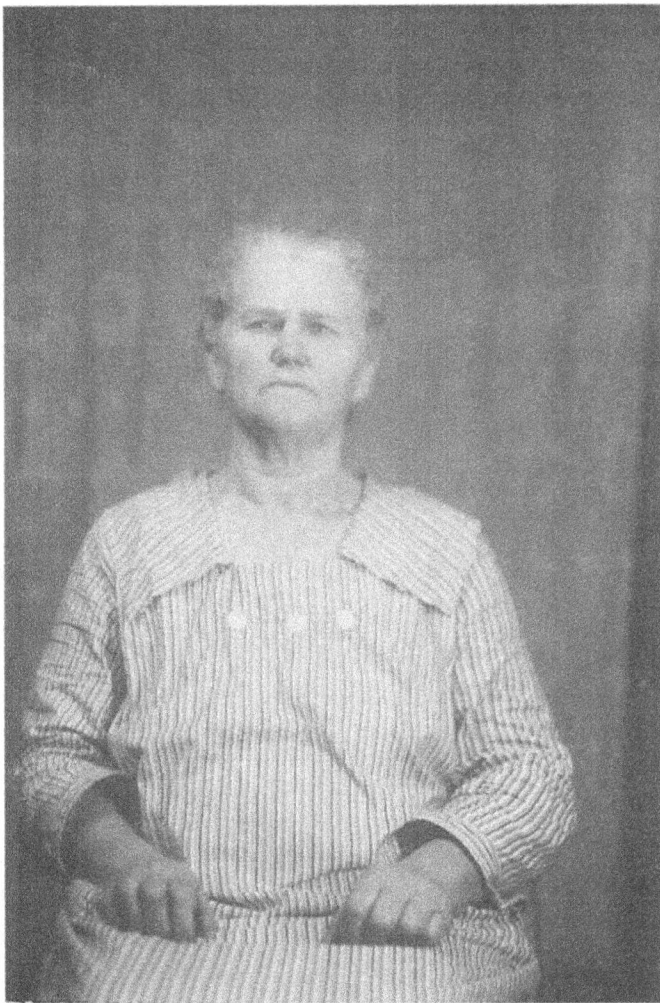

Lillie Napier Oller, Butler County, KY circa 1940

James Otis Martin, Butler County, KY 1920

James Otis Martin Jr., Elmo Lincoln Martin, Bonnie Martin, Irene Martin, Long Branch, KY 1926

James Otis Martin Family Farm Long Branch, KY circa 1920

Long Branch School
Long Branch, KY circa 1950

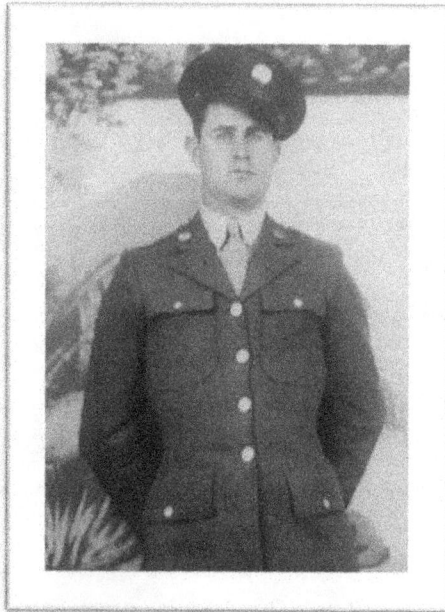

James Otis "Tommy" Martin Jr.
Butler County, KY 1941

Bonnie Martin Flener
Bowling Green, KY 1944

Irene Martin Constant
Bowling Green, KY 1942

Ruth Benson Martin and Elmo Lincoln Martin
Butler County, KY circa 1941

ABOUT THE AUTHOR

Elmo Lincoln Martin grew up in the foothills of Kentucky just outside of Morgantown. After finishing school he served in the 99th Infantry Division in World War II, and upon his return he began a successful career in the automotive industry.

Elmo is now retired and makes his home outside of Knoxville, TN where he regularly works on his golf game and is a contributing writer to the Banner Republican News.

ACKNOWLEDGMENTS

This book would not have been possible without the support of my family and friends who encouraged me to write down my memories. A special thank you to my daughter Linda Sue, grandchildren Lina, Richard, Jack, and Dee Dee, who each had a part in making the dream of compiling these memories into a book a reality.

A note of gratitude to Dana of Dana Martin Writing for her work in editing these stories while carefully keeping the voice and heart in which they were written.

www.ingramcontent.com/pod-product-compliance
Lightning Source LLC
LaVergne TN
LVHW011321080426
835513LV00006B/143